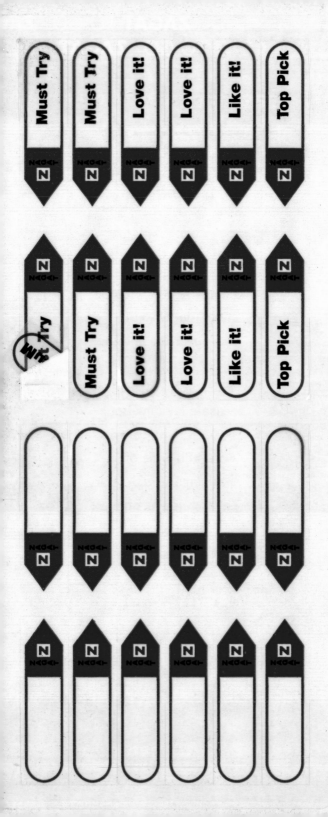

ZAGAT®

San Francisco
Nightlife
2008/09

LOCAL EDITOR
Sharron Wood
STAFF EDITOR
Randi Gollin

Published and distributed by
Zagat Survey, LLC
4 Columbus Circle
New York, NY 10019
T: 212.977.6000
E: sfnightlife@zagat.com
www.zagat.com

ACKNOWLEDGMENTS

We thank Ron Carmel, Tara Duggan, David Huffman, Julie Jares, Bob Jesse, Michael Lazar, Denise Leto, Kristina Malsberger, Steven Shukow and Kurt Wolff, as well as the following members of our staff: Caitlin Eichelberger (assistant editor), Sean Beachell, Maryanne Bertollo, Sandy Cheng, Reni Chin, Larry Cohn, Bill Corsello, Deirdre Donovan, Alison Flick, Jeff Freier, Shelley Gallagher, Roy Jacob, Natalie Lebert, Mike Liao, Dave Makulec, Andre Pilette, Kimberly Rosado, Becky Ruthenburg, Liz Borod Wright, Sharon Yates, Anna Zappia and Kyle Zolner.

Contents

Ratings & Symbols

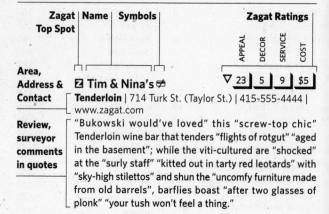

Ratings **Appeal**, **Decor** and **Service** are rated on the Zagat 0 to 30 scale.

0	–	9	poor to fair
10	–	15	fair to good
16	–	19	good to very good
20	–	25	very good to excellent
26	–	30	extraordinary to perfection
∇			low response	less reliable

Cost reflects our surveyors' estimated price of a typical single drink.

For **newcomers** or survey **write-ins** listed without ratings, the price range is indicated as follows:

I	below $5
M	$5 to $10
E	$11 to $14
VE	$15 or more

Symbols Ⓩ Zagat Top Spot (highest ratings, popularity and importance)

⇗ no credit cards accepted

About This Survey

This **2008/09 San Francisco Nightlife Survey** is an update reflecting significant developments since our last Survey was published. It covers 651 bars, clubs and lounges in San Francisco and the surrounding areas, including 50 important additions. We've also indicated new addresses, phone numbers and other major alterations to bring this guide up to the minute.

WHO PARTICIPATED: Input from 2,827 avid local nightlife denizens forms the basis for the ratings and reviews in this guide (their comments are shown in quotation marks within the reviews). Since our surveyors go out an average of 2.0 nights per week, they collectively bring an annual total of roughly 298,000 nights worth of experience to this Survey. We sincerely thank each of these participants – this book is really "theirs."

HELPFUL LISTS: Whether you're seeking sophisticated cocktails, an after-work scene or drinks plus entertainment, our top lists and indexes can help you find exactly the right place. See Most Popular (page 7), Key Newcomers (page 9) and Top Ratings (pages 10–16). We've also provided 70 handy indexes.

OUR EDITOR: Special thanks go to our local editor, Sharron Wood, who writes about the California Wine Country as well as entertaining, edits cookbooks and who is said to shake up simply smashing sidecars for her friends.

ABOUT ZAGAT: This marks our 29th year reporting on the shared experiences of consumers like you. What started in 1979 as a hobby involving 200 of our friends has come a long way. Today we have well over 300,000 surveyors and now cover dining, entertaining, golf, hotels, movies, music, nightlife, resorts, shopping, spas, theater and tourist attractions worldwide.

SHARE YOUR OPINION: We invite you to join any of our upcoming surveys – just register at **ZAGAT.com,** where you can rate and review establishments year-round. Each participant will receive a free copy of the resulting guide when published.

AVAILABILITY: Zagat guides are available in all major bookstores, by subscription at **ZAGAT.com** and for use on web-enabled mobile devices via **ZAGAT TO GO** or **ZAGAT.mobi.** The latter two products allow you to contact your choice among many thousands of establishments by phone with just one click.

FEEDBACK: There is always room for improvement, thus we invite your comments and suggestions about any aspect of our performance. Is there something more you would like us to include in our guides? We really need your input! Just contact us at **sfnightlife@zagat.com**.

New York, NY
June 4, 2008

Nina and Tim Zagat

What's New

The economy is dicey and prices continue to climb skyward – but that doesn't stop night owls from prowling the town, wetting their beaks at the Bay Area's spanking-new hot spots (and beloved watering holes) about twice a week and downing about 3.1 drinks an outing, at around $9.01 a pop.

GRAPE NUTS: Last year's explosion of wine bars shows no sign of fizzing out. Vino lovers squeeze into the snug Wine Jar for a pre-dinner sip and pour into the splashier Bin 38, Local Kitchen & Wine Merchant and Uva Enoteca, the latest kid on the block, pairing selections with full food menus, while those who prefer their wines au naturel opt for organic and biodynamic choices at Terroir Natural Wine Merchant. Given that 56% of our surveyors prefer to frequent nightspots close to home, it's no surprise that Oakland oenophiles turn to local finds like Franklin Square Wine Bar to raise a glass.

SOMETHING'S BREWING: About 27% of surveyors say they typically drink beer on weeknights, and a new spate of suds specialists are widening the options. Draft fans soak up a view of the vats at Wunder Brewing Co., which crafts its own brews on the premises, while other hops worshipers file into La Trappe and Monk's Kettle to down pints and bottles from far and wide, with an emphasis on hard-to-find selections like Dubbel, Flanders red ale, Lambic and Witbier from Belgium. And those who think raw oysters are the perfect accompaniment to beer take a seat at the bar of Anchor & Hope, the latest restaurant from the Salt House/Town Hall crew.

CULT OF THE COCKTAIL: Vodka tonics are so passé. Lately it's all about creative cocktails concocted with fresh-squeezed juices and obscure imported liqueurs. Beretta is at the front of the pack, luring sophisticates with unusual drinks dreamt up by star bartender Thad Vogler, while the posh Le Club keeps pace with classic libations. Bar 888 goes out on a limb, mixing grappa into many of its offerings; Bossa Nova specializes in Brazilian caipirinhas made with cachaça; and happy-hour hangout 83 Proof shakes and stirs a fine collection of the hard stuff.

ON THE WATERFRONT: The area along the Embarcadero just south of Market Street got a big boost this year with the near-simultaneous openings of EPIC Roasthouse and Waterbar, two extravagant Pat Kuleto–designed restaurant/bars with knockout views of the Bay Bridge. Even the more modest Hi-Dive is getting in on the action, with plans to add a deck that's practically in the shade of the bridge. And a block away, Perry's Downtown is readying its new space on Steuart Street near margarita maven Mexico DF.

San Francisco, CA
June 4, 2008

Sharron Wood

Most Popular

Places outside of San Francisco are marked as follows: E=East of SF; N=North; and S=South.

1	Medjool	**21**	Balboa Cafe
2	Bubble Lounge	**22**	Badlands
3	Redwood Room	**23**	Tamarine/S
4	BIX	**24**	Blowfish Sushi/S/SF
5	Slanted Door	**25**	Americano
6	Aqua	**26**	Absinthe
7	Top of the Mark	**27**	Evvia/S
8	Zeitgeist	**28**	Le Colonial
9	Nectar Wine/S/SF	**29**	Gordon Biersch/S/SF
10	bacar	**30**	Bimbo's 365 Club
11	MatrixFillmore	**31**	Harry's*
12	Boulevard	**32**	Lion Pub
13	Gary Danko*	**33**	Vesuvio*
14	César/E	**34**	Zuni Café*
15	Left Bank/E/N/S	**35**	Tonga Room
16	111 Minna	**36**	Ace Wasabi's
17	Lime	**37**	Buckeye Roadhouse*
18	Betelnut Pejiu Wu	**38**	Auberge du Soleil/N
19	Yoshi's/E/SF*	**39**	Harry Denton Starlight*
20	Buena Vista	**40**	Michael Mina

* Indicates a tie with place above

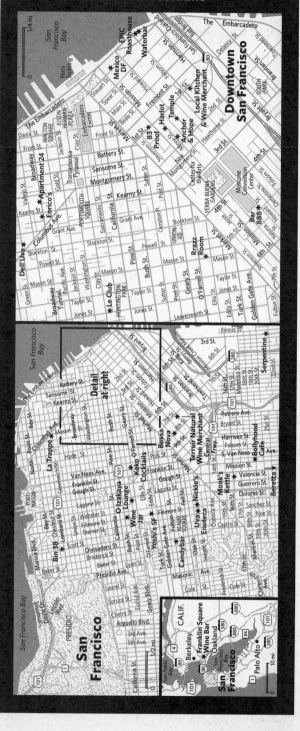

Key Newcomers

Our editors' take on some of the year's main arrivals. For a full list, see page 146.

Anchor & Hope	La Trappe
Apartment 24	Le Club
Bar 888	Local Kitchen & Wine
Beretta	Mexico DF
Bin 38	Monk's Kettle
Bollyhood Cafe	Nickie's
Bossa Nova	O Izakaya
Candybar	Rrazz Room
Dell'Uva	Serpentine
83 Proof	Temple
Enrico's	Terroir Natural Wine
EPIC Roasthouse	Uva Enoteca
Franklin Sq. Wine/E	Waterbar
Harlot	Wine Jar
Koko Cocktails	Yoshi's San Francisco

There's always something new and exciting to look forward to on the San Francisco nightlife scene, and this year should be no exception. Self-proclaimed 'spirits gypsy' Dominic Venegas will be bar director at **Gitane,** which is taking over the old Blupointe space Downtown. In the works for over a year, upscale dance club **Infusion,** boasting an East-meets-West look by Hong Kong–based designer Kinney Chan, is slated to finally open underneath the Hotel Fusion. The **Long Bar and Bistro** will fill the former Fillmore Grill space with a 30-ft.-long mahogany bar while its antonym, **Mini Bar,** will inhabit a sliver of space in the Western Addition. And the posh indoor-outdoor restaurant and nightspot **Om Lounge,** located next door to the Tenderloin's Gaylord Hotel, is certain to make a splash.

Top Appeal Ratings

Excludes places with low votes.

28	Highlands Inn/S	Top of the Mark
	Sweetwater Saloon/N	Aqua
	Auberge du Soleil/N	Sushi Ran/N
27	Gary Danko	Sam's Anchor Café/N
	Fillmore, The	Bouchon/N
	Pelican Inn/N	Lobby/Ritz-Carlton
	Mandarin Lounge	Oliveto Cafe/E
26	Paramount Theater/E	Specs Bar*
	Seasons Bar	César/E
	BIX	Big 4
	View Lounge	Little Shamrock
	Pied Piper Bar	Kokkari Estiatorio
	Boulevard	Albatross Pub/E
	Lark Creek Inn/N*	Martini House/N
	Parkway Theater/E*	Ana Mandara
	Jardinère	Brazen Head
	Bourbon & Branch	Toronado*
	Tra Vigne/N	
	Millennium	**24** Cityscape
25	Lobby/St. Regis	Yoshi's/E/SF
		Vesuvio

BY CATEGORY

AFTER WORK

26	Pied Piper Bar
25	Lobby/St. Regis
24	Slanted Door
23	Americano
22	111 Minna

BARS

28	Highlands Inn/S
	Auberge du Soleil/N
26	View Lounge
25	Albatross Pub/E
	Brazen Head
	Toronado*

BEAUTIFUL PEOPLE

26	BIX
25	Aqua
	César
24	Betelnut Pejiu Wu
	Redwood Room

BEER SPECIALISTS

25	Albatross Pub/E
	Toronado
24	Lucky 13
23	Luka's Taproom/E
	Magnolia Pub

BLUES CLUBS

28	Sweetwater Saloon/N
23	Boom Boom Rm
	Rancho Nicasio/N*
22	Lou's Pier 47
21	Saloon, The

COCKTAIL EXPERTS

26	BIX
	Bourbon & Branch
24	Orbit Room Cafe
	Alembic, The
23	Rye

COFFEEHOUSES

23	Mario's Bohemian
21	Café Royale
	Cafe Flore
	Grove, The
20	Caffe Trieste/E/N/SF

DANCE CLUBS

24	Shine
23	El Rio
22	Mr. Smith's
21	Mezzanine
	Pink

subscribe to ZAGAT.com

DIVES

23 Club Mallard/E
Uptown
22 Li Po
500 Club
Alley, The/E

FINE FOOD TOO

28 Highlands Inn/S
Auberge du Soleil/N
27 Gary Danko
26 BIX
Boulevard

FRAT HOUSE

24 Raleigh's/E
22 Ireland's 32
21 Jupiter/E
19 Savoy Tivoli
Irish Bank

GAY

22 Mecca
21 Eagle Tavern
Lush Lounge
Cafe Flore
eight

HOTEL BARS

28 Highlands Inn/S
Auberge du Soleil/N
27 Pelican Inn/N
Mandarin Lounge
(Mandarin Oriental)
26 Seasons Bar
(Four Seasons)

IRISH

25 Little Shamrock
22 Beckett's Irish Pub/E
Ireland's 32
O'Reilly's Holy Grail
21 Kennedy's Irish

JAZZ CLUBS

26 BIX
24 Yoshi's/E/SF
Jazz at Pearl's
23 Shanghai 1930
21 Savanna Jazz

JUKEBOXES

25 Toronado
24 Lucky 13
23 Club Mallard/E
15 Romolo
Tosca Cafe

LATIN

22 Tommy's Mexican
Café Valparaiso/E
21 Puerto Alegre
20 Impala
Maya

LESBIAN

23 El Rio
22 Wild Side West
19 Aunt Charlie's
White Horse/E
Lexington Club

LIVE MUSIC CLUBS

27 Fillmore, The
26 Paramount Theater/E
24 Great American
Bimbo's 365 Club
23 Knockout, The

LOUNGES

27 Mandarin Lounge
26 Seasons Bar
View Lounge
25 Lobby/St. Regis
Lobby/Ritz-Carlton

MATURE CROWDS

28 Highlands Inn/S
Auberge du Soleil/N
27 Gary Danko
26 Pied Piper Bar
25 Top of the Mark

MEAT MARKETS

24 Harry Denton Starlight
Betelnut Pejiu Wu
Redwood Room
23 Medjool
21 MatrixFillmore

QUIET CONVERSATION

28 Highlands Inn/S
27 Mandarin Lounge
26 Seasons Bar
25 Lobby/Ritz-Carlton
Big 4

ROADHOUSES

28 Sweetwater Saloon/N
25 Toronado
23 Rancho Nicasio/N
Zeitgeist
21 Eagle Tavern

THEME BARS

24 Farallon
23 Conga Lounge/E
   Bissap Baobab
22 Tonga Room
   supperclub

WINE BARS

26 Tra Vigne/N
24 Hôtel Biron

23 Bacchus Wine
   Ottimista Enoteca
   Nectar Wine

WINES BY THE GLASS

27 Gary Danko
26 Boulevard
   Lark Creek Inn/N*
   Jardinère
   Millennium

BY LOCATION

CASTRO/NOE VALLEY

24 Orbit Room Cafe
   Lucky 13
   Noe Valley Ministry
23 Café du Nord
22 Mecca

COW HOLLOW/ MARINA

25 Brazen Head
24 Betelnut Pejiu Wu
23 Ottimista Enoteca
   Nectar Wine
21 Liverpool Lil's

DOWNTOWN/ EMBARCADERO

27 Mandarin Lounge
26 Seasons Bar
   BIX
   Pied Piper Bar
   Boulevard

FISHERMAN'S WHARF

27 Gary Danko
25 Ana Mandara
23 Buena Vista
22 Lou's Pier 47
20 McCormick & Kuleto's

HAIGHT-ASHBURY/ COLE VALLEY

24 Alembic, The
23 Zam Zam
   Magnolia Pub
22 Kan Zaman
   Eos

HAYES VALLEY/ CIVIC CENTER

26 Jardinère
24 Hôtel Biron
   Zuni Café
23 Absinthe
22 Martuni's

LOWER HAIGHT

25 Toronado
20 Noc Noc
18 Mad Dog in Fog
   Underground SF
17 Molotov

MISSION DISTRICT

24 Foreign Cinema
23 Knockout, The
   El Rio
   Medjool
   Nihon Whisky

NOB HILL

25 Top of the Mark
   Lobby/Ritz-Carlton
   Big 4
22 Tonga Room

NORTH BEACH

25 Specs Bar
24 Vesuvio
   Jazz at Pearl's
   Bimbo's 365 Club
23 15 Romolo

PACIFIC HEIGHTS/ UPPER FILLMORE

23 Florio
21 Lion Pub
   Elite Cafe
   Grove, The
19 Harry's

POLK GULCH

22 O'Reilly's Holy Grail
21 Lush Lounge
   Harris'
20 Hemlock Tavern
19 Element Lounge

RICHMOND/ INNER RICHMOND

- 24 540 Club
- 23 Pig & Whistle
  Cliff House
- 22 Tommy's Mexican
  Ireland's 32

SOMA

- 26 View Lounge
- 25 Lobby/St. Regis
- 24 bacar
  Roy's
  AsiaSF

TENDERLOIN

- 26 Bourbon & Branch
- 24 Great American
- 23 Rye
  Whiskey Thieves
- 22 Edinburgh Castle

WESTERN ADDITION

- 27 Fillmore, The
- 24 Yoshi's
  nopa
- 23 Boom Boom Rm.
- 22 Independent

EAST OF SF/BERKELEY

- 25 César
  Albatross Pub
- 24 Raleigh's
- 22 Beckett's Irish Pub
  Café Valparaíso

EAST OF SF/OAKLAND

- 26 Paramount Theater
  Parkway Theater
- 25 Oliveto Cafe
  César
- 24 Yoshi's

NORTH OF SF

- 28 Sweetwater Saloon
  Auberge du Soleil
- 27 Pelican Inn
- 26 Lark Creek Inn
  Tra Vigne

SOUTH OF SF

- 28 Highlands Inn
- 24 Tamarine
  Evvia
  Hog's Breath Inn
  Roy's*

Most Visited

FEMALE
1. Slanted Door
2. Medjool
3. Nectar Wine
4. Americano
5. Trader Vic's/E/S

MALE
1. Slanted Door
2. Trader Vic's/E/S
3. Medjool
4. Lime
5. Gordon Biersch/S/SF

BY AGE

TWENTIES
1. Medjool
2. Slanted Door
3. Bar None
4. Nectar Wine
5. Suede

THIRTIES
1. Slanted Door
2. Medjool
3. Nectar Wine
4. Americano
5. Trader Vic's/E/S

FORTIES
1. Slanted Door
2. Trader Vic's/E/S
3. Michael Mina
4. Town Hall
5. Americano

FIFTIES
1. Slanted Door
2. Boulevard
3. Buena Vista
4. Top of the Mark
5. Aqua

Top Decor Ratings

<u>29</u> Paramount Theater/E

<u>28</u> Farallon
Redwood Room

<u>27</u> Auberge du Soleil/N
Jardinère
Lobby/St. Regis
Highlands Inn/S
Mandarin Lounge

<u>26</u> Ana Mandara
Pied Piper Bar
Bourbon & Branch
Tra Vigne/N
Seasons Bar
Gary Danko
BIX
Aqua
Lobby/Ritz-Carlton
Boulevard

<u>25</u> Kokkari Estiatorio
Lark Creek Inn/N

Big 4
Martini House/N*
Cafe Van Kleef/E
Campton Place
Pelican Inn/N
Rye
Le Colonial

<u>24</u> supperclub
Tamarine/S
MatrixFillmore
bacar
Ozumo
Mecca
Foreign Cinema
Nihon Whisky
nopa
Lime
Evvia/S
downtown/E
Insalata's/N

OLD BAY AREA AMBIANCE

Buena Vista
Great American
Heinold's Saloon/E
House of Shields
John's Grill

Little Shamrock
Saloon, The
San Fran. Brewing
Tadich Grill
Vesuvio

OUTDOORS

Bambuddha Lounge
Cafe Flore
Calistoga Inn/N
El Rio
Jupiter/E

Kelly's Mission Rock
Pier 23 Cafe
Sam's Anchor Cafe/N
Waterbar
Zeitgeist

ROMANCE

Ana Mandara
Auberge du Soleil/N
BIX
Bourbon & Branch
Highlands Inn/S

Hôtel Biron
Lark Creek Inn/N
Le Colonial
Le Club
Tosca Cafe

VIEWS

Auberge du Soleil/N
Carnelian Room
Cityscape
Cliff House
EPIC Roasthouse

Harry Denton Starlight
Highlands Inn/S
Medjool
Pres a Vi
Top of the Mark

Top Service Ratings

28 Seasons Bar

27 Gary Danko

26 Highlands Inn/S
Mandarin Lounge
Auberge du Soleil/N
Lobby/Ritz-Carlton

25 Campton Place
Boulevard
Big 4
Lobby/St. Regis*
Michael Mina
Whiskey Thieves
Aqua

24 Lark Creek Inn/N
Jardinère
Sushi Ran/N
Club Mallard/E
Millennium
Rubicon
Little Shamrock

Tra Vigne/N
Bouchon/N
John Colins
Alembic, The

23 Pelican Inn/N
BIX
nopa*
Roy's/S/SF
Evvia/S
Farallon
Oliveto Cafe/E
Bacchus Wine
Martini House/N
Pied Piper Bar*
César/E
Postrio
Fireside Bar
Pig & Whistle
Kokkari Estiatorio
Town Hall

NIGHTLIFE
DIRECTORY

City of San Francisco

Abbey Tavern ⇗ | 15 | 10 | 17 | $7 |

Outer Richmond | 4100 Geary Blvd. (5th Ave.) | 415-221-7767 |
www.abbeytavern-sf.com

USF students and "homesick Arsenal and Hotspur fans" yearning for
"a slice of ye olde countrie in the Richmond" congregate at this "classic tavern" dive with "friendly" barkeeps; "kick back" and "chug pints"
of Guinness in between playing pool, darts, video arcade games,
watching sports on TV and listening to "some amazing bands" and DJs
several nights a week.

Ⓩ Absinthe | 23 | 23 | 21 | $12 |

Hayes Valley | 398 Hayes St. (Gough St.) | 415-551-1590 |
www.absinthe.com

The "delicious drinks", "great Parisian-style bar scene" and Thursday
flight nights make this "very swank" Hayes Valley brasserie a "wonderful" "place to impress a date"; the "classy clientele", "cozy cama-
raderie", Euro "character" and "attentive 'tenders" with a flair for
"showmanship" make you "feel like you're in another world"; *oui*, it can
be "a touch too noisy before and after the symphony and opera", but
it's "perfect" once the performance "crowd has thinned."

Ace Wasabi's | 20 | 17 | 19 | $12 |

Marina | 3339 Steiner St. (bet. Chestnut & Lombard Sts.) | 415-567-4903

"Like your old party friend from college, it's always a pleasure" to hang
at this "lively" sushi-and-Sapporo spot in the Marina where the "foxy"
bartenders are aces at mixing "sake bombs" and the music "makes
you want to get your groove on"; "survey the crowd" for "hot" singles –
there's plenty of "young meat market activity" – just "don't expect to
wow your date with witty repartee" since it's "deafeningly loud."

Acme Chophouse | 20 | 18 | 19 | $11 |

South Beach | AT&T Park | 24 Willie Mays Plaza (bet. King & 3rd Sts.) |
415-644-0240 | www.acmechophouse.com

"Noisy and packed when the Giants are playing", this "jumping"
chophouse practically "grafted onto" AT&T Park serves up "bathtub-
sized martinis", "great oysters" and "hearty appetizers" "to nibble on
while you drink"; sure, the libations "aren't cheap" and sometimes
it's crowded with "touristas galore", "but you can guzzle while
watching the game with other baseball-minded" meat lovers, which
"makes visiting worthwhile."

Alembic, The | 24 | 24 | 24 | $9 |

Haight-Ashbury | 1725 Haight St. (bet. Cole & Shrader Sts.) | 415-666-0822 |
www.alembicbar.com

"Just what the Haight needed" – a no-reservations "temple to whiskey", with an "excellent" selection of "single-malt scotches and other
hard-to-find spirits"; "boy, do they know their stuff", whether you're
talking "old-school" cocktails "that remind me of what my grandpa
used to drink" or "unusual, delicious beers" in bottles; add in "interesting, tasty" bar bites made from mostly local ingredients and an
"intimate, cozy" ambiance and you've got the "perfect respite from
a stormy night."

	APPEAL	DECOR	SERVICE	COST

Ambassador, The
| - | - | - | E |

Tenderloin | 673 Geary St. (bet. Jones & Leavenworth Sts.) | 415-563-8192 | www.ambassador415.com

You'll find the ghosts of Frank, Sammy and Dean at this swank spot in the Tenderloin, where just past the velvet rope is a Vegas-centric space fitted out with logo wallpaper, chandeliers and phones at the tables for dialing other patrons; employ diplomatic conduct and wade through the crowds if you want to get your groove on to contemporary DJ beats.

Amber ⊅
| 19 | 19 | 20 | $7 |

Castro | 718 14th St. (bet. Belcher & Church Sts.) | 415-626-7827

"One of SF's few places where you can shamelessly indulge in a sinful cigarette" while downing "dangerously-easy-to-drink mojitos", this "glam" Castro "favorite" feels right out of a "'70s gangster movie", or a scene from *Miami Vice*; "get there early to snag a couch" and everything's golden; otherwise light up and enjoy the "boozy atmosphere" as you hang with the "hipster crowd" (including "good-looking women").

Amelie
| - | - | - | E |

Russian Hill | 1754 Polk St. (bet. Clay & Washington Sts.) | 415-292-6916 | www.ameliesf.com

With high ceilings, moody lighting and a glowing red wall, this Francophilic wine bar makes for a dazzling entry on Russian Hill's *terroir*; the vino selection is as rich as the decor: mostly France, and a few other locales, including California and Spain, are featured by the glass (with over 36 choices), in flights (check out the weekday happy hour offering three glasses for $10) or on an affordable list of bottles.

☑ Americano Restaurant & Bar
| 23 | 24 | 17 | $11 |

Embarcadero | Hotel Vitale | 8 Mission St. (The Embarcadero) | 415-278-3777 | www.americanorestaurant.com

"Holy meat market, Batman" – "talk about an after-work scene!" – "everybody's eyes seem to be scanning" the "cast of beautiful" "young professionals" while they sip "appealing cocktails" at the Hotel Vitale's "buzzy, hip, immensely popular" restaurant/bar on the Embarcadero; the outdoor patio "can't be beat on a warm night", but Friday happy hour is "sardine time" ("trying to get a drink makes you feel like the ugly girl in a beauty contest") so go earlier in the week and "watch evening settle over the Bay Bridge."

Amnesia ⊅
| 19 | 14 | 19 | $6 |

Mission | 853 Valencia St. (bet. 19th & 20th Sts.) | 415-970-0012 | www.amnesiathebar.com

"Forget your troubles at this oh-so-red velvet underground" Mission bar boasting an "eclectically delicious" array of "offbeat" – even "oddball" – live music acts ranging from jazz and indie rock to bluegrass and gypsy; "while it's nothing fancy and a bit dingy", the vibe is "unpretentious", plus "Tuesday karaoke is a blast" and the "young staffers" steeped in "old-school charm" serve up "scads of brews on tap"; N.B. no hard liquor.

☑ Ana Mandara
| 25 | 26 | 21 | $12 |

Fisherman's Wharf | Ghirardelli Sq. | 891 Beach St. (Polk St.) | 415-771-6800 | www.anamandara.com

"You feel like you've stepped into a palatial Vietnamese estate" at this "sexy . . . very sexy" lounge upstairs from this "romantic" Fisherman's

Wharf restaurant blessed with a "standout view" of Alcatraz; order exotic cocktails from the "awesome bartender", then "relax and enjoy the trip" advise "wanderlust junkies" who "sink into the deep couches" and canoodle to "low-playing" live jazz Thursday–Saturday; natch, the bill is "eye-bulge inducing", but the "captivating atmosphere" is "well worth" it.

NEW Anchor & Hope

| - | - | - | M |

SoMa | 83 Minna St. (bet. 1st & 2nd Sts.) | 415-501-9100 |
www.anchorandhopesf.com

Brothers Steve and Mitch Rosenthal and biz partner Doug Washington, the folks behind Salt House and Town Hall, vie for a trifecta with their third SoMa venture, a New England–inspired fish shack set in a barn-like 1911 brick building; nautical is the byword, from the ropes hanging from the rafters and the lobster cages to the mariner's seafood menu; though no hard liquor is served, the 35-ft.-long zinc bar begs for a pint of beer from the unusual selection or a glass of wine from the all-coastal list, ordered with oysters, of course.

Andalu

| 20 | 20 | 19 | $10 |

Mission | 3198 16th St. (Guerrero St.) | 415-621-2211 |
www.andalusf.com

"Meet your people, meet new people, have a little fun and move on your way" but not before you've sampled "the best white wine sangria this side of Spain" and "spot-on tapas" at this "sleek" Mission "favorite"; an "interesting wine list" further boosts its cred as the "perfect" place for a "large group", and if a few counter it's "really loud" with "snooty service", well, even they admit it's "hopelessly cool."

Annie's Social Club ⊘

| 20 | 13 | 19 | $7 |

SoMa | 917 Folsom St. (5th St.) | 415-974-1585 |
www.anniessocialclub.com

"It takes all kinds . . . and they're all here", "from bikers to bankers", at nightclub owner Annie's SoMa spot set in a "strange area" "in the middle of bail bonds row"; head to the back parlor boasting a "Chinese-boudoir-meets-pinup-heaven" ambiance for "wheee!" "punk rock karaoke!", sip "fabulous Cosmos" as you admire the "tattooed" barflies – and don't forget to mark your calendar for the "great DJ nights" or open-mike comedy.

Anú

| 18 | 15 | 17 | $7 |

SoMa | 43 Sixth St. (bet. Market & Mission Sts.) | 415-543-3505 |
www.anu-bar.com

"Don't be intimidated" by the "dicey" location on one of SoMa's grittiest blocks, because there's a "great vibe inside" this "popular hangout spot for dance music enthusiasts"; though the floor is "small", "they do get the talent on the turntables", and "on any given night, the music is always sure to bump your clothes off", plus the "very friendly and funny" bartenders sling a "good selection" of infused vodkas.

NEW Apartment 24

| - | - | - | E |

North Beach | 440 Broadway (bet. Kearny & Montgomery Sts.) |
415-989-3434 | www.apartment24sf.com

The brains behind Bin 38, Circa, Harlot and Slide have put their stamp on this North Beach nightclub featuring a faux San Francisco cityscape that changes colors and VIP areas that are marked off by a curtain of gold chains; look for a younger crowd that appreciates the DJs' lineup of rock, house and hip-hop; N.B. open Thursday–Saturday.

☑ Aqua
25 | 26 | 25 | $15

Downtown | 252 California St. (bet. Battery & Front Sts.) | 415-956-9662 | www.aqua-sf.com

If you "can't make it here for dinner", then "hang out with the big boys and girls" for a "sophisticated" after-work cocktail at this "upscale, chic" Downtown seafooder with "old-world class"; whether you "sit and watch the chicks come in looking for high rollers" or take an "important client", the "really terrific vibe" and "truly attentive", "skilled" staff makes it "quite the place to see and be seen" – "though it's hard to imagine not staying for the fabulous food."

Argus Lounge ⊘
19 | 15 | 21 | $6

Mission | 3187 Mission St. (Valencia St.) | 415-824-1447 | www.arguslounge.com

Join the mix of Outer Mission-aries – "young, old and middle-aged" – playing pool and jamming to the jukebox at this "low-key" "neighborhood haunt"; but while lounge lizards suggest ordering a "good cocktail" like the "creepy but delicious drink special, the JonBenet Ramsay" from the 'tender with the "super personality", the befuddled fail to see the humor, carping "there's just something weird about the vibe."

AsiaSF
24 | 19 | 20 | $12

SoMa | 201 Ninth St. (Howard St.) | 415-255-2742 | www.asiasf.com

"Are they or aren't they? is the buzz around" this SoMa "party place" where the "beautiful ladies" (er, "tranny waitresses") "can fool any guy" and the "shock value is high"; in between delivering "exotic tropical drinks" and "food fit for the queens that serve it to you", the "gender illusionists" put on a "great floor show" that "starts your night out right"; whether you're taking "outta towners" or hosting a "bachelorette party", you'll "spend a bundle."

Attic Club ⊘
20 | 16 | 19 | $5

Mission | 3336 24th St. (Mission St.) | 415-643-3376

Offering a "relatively relaxing respite" from the "lively Mission District", this "small", "mellow yet fun" "hole-in-the-wall" is a "great" spot to "drown your sorrows"; DJs spin almost nightly, but there's no dance floor – perhaps that's for the best, considering the "bad feng shui" and "low" lighting (it's "quite possibly the darkest bar" around), so the bartenders "may not see you begging for a drink."

Aunt Charlie's ⊘
19 | 11 | 18 | $11

Tenderloin | 133 Turk St. (bet. Jones & Taylor Sts.) | 415-441-2922 | www.auntcharlieslounge.com

"Prissy folks" steer clear of this "awesome drag bar" in the "seedy" Tenderloin – that's how it "keeps its great edge" insist insiders who relate to its "chill" feel; adoptees vie for "cheap drinks" in the "small, small, small" space, particularly on "packed" Friday and Saturday nights, when it "transforms into a cabaret", and "queens who really know how to lip synch and entertain the crowd" take center stage.

	APPEAL	DECOR	SERVICE	COST

Azie

22	23	22	$12

SoMa | 826 Folsom St. (bet. 4th & 5th Sts.) | 415-538-0918 |
www.azierestaurant.com

"Still a good place to hang before a movie", this "hip, urban and sexy"
SoMa sibling to neighboring Restaurant Lulu seduces with a "fusion
menu of eats and drinks", including "martinis galore"; a "great staff"
and a "rich, exotic" East-meets-West setting with "funky booths" and
high ceilings complete the "friendly, not stuffy" picture; still, a wistful
few sigh it's "not as busy as it should be."

Azul Bar and Lounge

-	-	-	E

Downtown | 1 Tillman Pl. (Grant Ave.) | 415-362-9750 | www.azul-sf.com
Glowing blue lights illuminate the navy walls of this aptly named, multilevel Downtown lounge in a sort of 'secret' location tucked down an
alley near Union Square; the high-backed white couches and matching
ottomans are usually most crowded during happy hour, when young
working stiffs sample a small menu of cocktail fare, but DJs spinning
hip-hop, salsa, electronica and downtempo grooves Tuesday-
Saturday keep the hard-core here until closing.

⊿ bacar

24	24	21	$13

SoMa | 448 Brannan St. (bet. 3rd & 4th Sts.) | 415-904-4100 |
www.bacarsf.com

This "eclectically elegant", "sought-after" "SoMa spot has it all for those
who enjoy live jazz", "fine food" and a "fantastic wine" list, including an
"extensive by-the-glass selection"; join the "beautiful people" in the
"open, loftlike space" with an "upmarket vibe" and linger over "creative
flights" sure to "open your palate" or "handcrafted seasonal cocktails"
served by a "passionate staff"; sure, the "expensive" elixirs are a
"throwback to the dot-com days", but for most, it's "worth the visit."

Bacchus Kirk

17	17	19	$9

Downtown | 925 Bush St. (bet. Jones & Taylor Sts.) | 415-474-4056
"Lively local regulars" rendezvous at this "go-to neighborhood bar"
Downtown with a "mellow", "dark" "retro ski-cabin feel" and "friendly
bartenders" who add that "personal touch"; "even if you're not with
the 'in' crowd" mix of "hipsters" and "collared shirts" it's a "great after-
work social club" given that the "happy hour goes to 9 PM" and you
"can hear yourself think, not to mention talk."

Bacchus Wine & Sake Bar

23	21	23	$11

Russian Hill | 1954 Hyde St. (bet. Union & Warner Sts.) | 415-928-2633
"The upside and downside is the size" of this "local favorite" "on a
quaint Russian Hill block" observe oenophiles who compare the
"intimate-as-you-can-get" dimensions to a "Manhattan studio" apartment; but while diehards back up the bartender who's "tops for his
knowledge of wine and his always-on witty humor", disbelievers toss
it off as a "tiny waiting spot for your table at Sushi Groove" nearby.

⊿ Badlands ⊘

17	16	16	$9

Castro | 4121 18th St. (bet. Castro & Collingwood Sts.) | 415-626-9320 |
www.sfbadlands.com

"All the pretty boys" come to "play" at one of the "busiest gay bars in the
Castro", which is "just sleazy enough to guarantee a good time"; expect

"long lines" on weekends, when it's crowded with "young 'uns" "getting their groove on" to "extremely danceable" music videos; but naughty naysayers nix the "I'm-too-sexy" bunch, adding look "in the dictionary under S&M – 'Stand & Model' – there's a picture" of this place.

⚡ Balboa Cafe | 20 | 18 | 18 | $9

Cow Hollow | 3199 Fillmore St. (Greenwich St.) | 415-921-3944 | www.plumpjack.com

"Totally timeless because it doesn't try to be trendy", this circa-1913 Cow Hollow "meet market" (er, "cougar den") with an "old SF ambiance" is always "hopping" with "politicos, blue bloods, frat boys and single women"; sure, "everyone's crammed in, waiting for a glimpse of Gavin", but it's also "famous" for its "mean burger" and "reasonable" wine list; P.S. "if you leave here alone, it was by choice, or you were wearing repellent."

Bamboo Hut | 19 | 18 | 20 | $8

North Beach | 479 Broadway (bet. Kearny & Montgomery Sts.) | 415-989-8555 | www.maximumproductions.com

"A taste of the tacky tropics right on Broadway", this "freaky tiki bar" in North Beach tricked out with a waterfall, a "faux thatched roof" and a huge Polynesian idol is a "cheesy" "fun place all around"; "go with friends if you want to let loose and dance" to rock, funk and hip-hop in between sips of "enormous" "fruity" "girlie drinks with little umbrellas and flowers."

Bambuddha Lounge | 21 | 22 | 15 | $9

Tenderloin | Phoenix Hotel | 601 Eddy St. (Larkin St.) | 415-885-5088 | www.bambuddhalounge.com

"In the middle of the mayhem" of the Tenderloin lies this "sexy", "surreal" "little oasis" where you can "park" your bum and peruse the "trendy" crowd or spend happy hour by the Phoenix Hotel pool nibbling on "tropical food galore" (if you "close your eyes you can pretend to be in LA – not that there's anything wrong with that"); but Buddha-bashers bemoan "distracted" servers "too busy looking in the mirrors at themselves" to serve you "pricey" drinks.

Bar Bambino | - | - | - | M

Mission | 2931 16th St. (Mission St.) | 415-701-8466 | www.barbambino.com

Head to The Boot by way of the Mission at this spanking-new, glass-fronted wine bar/cafe kitted out with communal tables, wood floors, a back patio and, most important, a marble-topped bar; no trip to Italy is complete, of course, without a full assortment of vinos, so get to it and explore the moderately priced selection while grazing on small bites, including cheese, bruschetta, salumi and other artisanal meats or full-size entrees.

NEW Bar Drake | - | - | - | E

Downtown | Sir Francis Drake Hotel | 450 Powell St. (Sutter St.) | 415-392-7755 | www.bardrake.com

Set in the Sir Francis Drake Hotel, this lobby bar transports tipplers to the Roaring '20s with its over-the-top chandeliers and its old-school martinis and Manhattans; purists may prefer one of the many scotch and American whiskey offerings (all lined up in front of an antique mirror), but everyone will want to get here early as there are only 36 seats and it closes down at midnight Sunday–Thursday and 1 AM on weekends.

NEW Bar 888
- | - | - | E

SoMa | InterContinental San Francisco | 888 Howard St. (5th St.) | 415-616-6566 | www.intercontinentalsanfrancisco.com
Located on the ground floor of the new InterContinental San Francisco, this sleek SoMa bar banks on an extensive selection of grappas (and wines) that is served straight or in innovative cocktails dreamt up by winemaker/mixologist Francesco Lafranconi who, along with Michael Mondavi, also co-owns the restaurant Luce next door; the square bar is vaguely futuristic in keeping with the translucent, 32-story building, but you can expect to rub elbows with down-to-earth business travelers.

Bar 821 ⊘
20 | 21 | 20 | $8

Western Addition | 821 Divisadero St. (Fulton St.) | unlisted phone | www.bar821.com
"Shhh, don't tell anyone" about this "neighborhood bar" implores the sign outside, and secretive sorts comply, cozying up to this "small" "chill" Western Addition "speakeasy" with a "good vibe" and a "kick-ass happy hour"; but the less discreet stage-whisper that it's a "wonderful spot to enjoy a glass of great, affordable Pinot, your favorite micro-brew" or "creative", "delicious champagne" and soju cocktails poured by "attentive, friendly" bartenders; N.B. no entry after 11 PM.

NEW Bar Johnny
- | - | - | M

Russian Hill | 2209 Polk St. (Vallejo St.) | 415-268-0140 | www.barjohnny.com
Despite the name, this narrow nook in Russian Hill is equal parts restaurant and bar; oversize cylindrical lamps, a dramatic mural and polished concrete floors create a midcentury-modern-meets-industrial feel, a just-right setting for well-dressed Russian Hill regulars who dine on burgers and garlic truffle fries at the elevated banquettes, or gather in the corner for seasonal-theme cocktails and wine (mostly from California producers) and small plates; N.B. the kitchen is open until 1 AM.

Bar None
14 | 11 | 15 | $6

Cow Hollow | 1980 Union St. (Buchanan St.) | 415-409-4469 | www.barnonesf.com
"If you miss your fraternity" head to this "dark", "overcrowded" basement brat-skeller, a "straight-up college bar" with "sticky" floors that's also Cow Hollow's "best place to get hammered while playing beer pong" or darts, bar none; join the "twentysomething barflies" "scoping the cuties", downing "super-cheap" brewskis, "grinding to house beats" – and "prepping for that inevitable morning walk of shame."

Bazaar Café
20 | 16 | 22 | $6

Outer Richmond | 5927 California St. (bet. 21st & 22nd Aves.) | 415-831-5620 | www.bazaarcafe.com
"Drop in" to this "unique mom-and-pop-style" morning-into-night coffeehouse in the Richmond and "enjoy" the "very nice schedule of live entertainment: original singer-songwriters, comedy, political commentary, academic conversations", even open-mike nights, in "intimate" surroundings; "fun board games" add to the "extension of your living room" feel – and so does the sound of laptop toters using the "free WiFi"; P.S. the backyard patio is "very sweet."

	APPEAL	DECOR	SERVICE	COST

Beach Chalet Brewery
21 | 19 | 16 | $9

Outer Richmond | 1000 Great Hwy. (bet. Fulton St. & Lincoln Way) | 415-386-8439 | www.beachchalet.com

"Does it get much better, locationwise?" wonder wags who wander to this "delightful" brewpub, a "shining lighthouse of activity along an otherwise quiet nightlife shoreline" on the Richmond's west edge to enjoy the "fantastic view" of the Pacific Ocean; walk through the Golden Gate Park Visitor's Center below and peek at the "lovely" WPA murals, then join the "boisterous crowd" jamming to jazz and "drinking in the sunset" – what a "treat."

Beale Street Bar & Grill
∇ 18 | 11 | 19 | $8

Embarcadero | 133 Beale St. (Mission St.) | 415-543-1961 | www.bealestreetsf.com

At this "appealing old-school dive" near the Embarcadero, "you can't beat drinking and sharing stories with truckers and techies alike"; while it's open on Saturdays and closed on Sundays, it's mostly a "good after-work" spot, when "sweet happy-hour deals" make it "super for unwinding", but snarky sorts snicker it's simply "a great place to work on your alcoholism out of sight of the beautiful people."

Beauty Bar
18 | 19 | 17 | $7

Mission | 2299 Mission St. (19th St.) | 415-285-0323 | www.beautybar.com

"It's hip to be a beauty school dropout" at this "cheeky, kitschy, crowded" Mission "throwback" to a *Grease*-era curlers-and-comb-out shop, with a "pink, sparkly interior" and a "great-looking staff"; sure, "some serious dancing can be had", but you can still "get your nails done while rocking out to your local mashup DJs"; but claustrophobes claim the "space feels as big as a bathroom stall", adding it "sounds more glamorous than it really is."

Bell Tower, The
16 | 15 | 18 | $8

Polk Gulch | 1900 Polk St. (Jackson St.) | 415-567-9596

"Score an outdoor table on a sunny day and watch the world go by" at "one of the few bars in the area" with sidewalk seating; otherwise, this "nondescript corner spot" on Polk Street is merely a "good place to get a decent drink and quick snack", though a "very dog-friendly" policy means people with pooches are partial.

NEW Beretta
- | - | - | M

Mission | 1199 Valencia St. (23rd St.) | 415-695-1199 | www.berettasf.com

A pizza place might not seem the most likely location to sip couture cocktails created by 'tender extraordinaire Thad Vogler (formerly of Bourbon & Branch, Jardinière, The Slanted Door), but that's exactly what you'll find on this Mission corner; dimly lit by chandeliers and candles, it's a sexy spot for sharing antipasti at one of the communal tables, or ordering a late-night pancetta pizza with Rangoon gin punch on the side; *naturalmente*, the wine list is heavy on the Italian varietals.

☒ Betelnut Pejiu Wu
24 | 23 | 19 | $12

Cow Hollow | 2030 Union St. (Buchanan St.) | 415-929-8855 | www.betelnutrestaurant.com

The "fun tropical cocktails kick your butt" at Cow Hollow's "sexy", "colorful" Asian "haunt" with an "awesome atmosphere" and "always lively, always packed" lounge area; enjoy the "pretty people scene" at the bar where the "friendly bartenders remember you" or head to the heated outdoor tables, "a great place to sit in the sun"; but others aren't easily Wu-ed on weekends when it's a "sardine can" – "chances are you'll get jostled and spill your saketini."

B44

20	17	19	$12

Downtown | 44 Belden Pl. (bet. Bush & Pine Sts.) | 415-986-6287 | www.b44sf.com

You "feel like you're on vacation in Spain" at this Catalan eatery set on Belden Place, "one of the best alleys in town for people-watching"; skip the "darkish" "cramped" bar area indoors – instead, "sit outside on a summer's eve", "mix with the chic" crowd and soak up the Euro vibe, along with sangria or one of the "good" Iberian wines, and some tapas "for a treat."

Bigfoot Lodge

19	19	19	$6

Polk Gulch | 1750 Polk St. (Washington St.) | 415-440-2355 | www.bigfootlodge.com

What a "hoot" confirm Sasquatch seekers who stake out a spot by the "kinda scary giant Bigfoot" standing watch by the "really fake fireplace" at this "quirky" Polk Street haunt with a "kitschy hunting lodge motif" and "lots of character"; "newcomers get excited" when they bear witness to the "nightly set-the-bar-on-fire" "shtick" to the "sounds of Axl Rose", but thanks to the "potent" drinks, "many don't even remember the pyrotechnic tricks" by morning.

Z Big 4

25	25	25	$14

Nob Hill | Huntington Hotel | 1075 California St. (Taylor St.) | 415-771-1140 | www.huntingtonhotel.com

"Step back to the 1920s at this ultradark", "swank", "clubby" "speakeasy" "named for the 'Big Four' railroad tycoons" tucked into "tony Nob Hill's" Huntington Hotel; the "white-shirted bartenders serve up classic cocktails", while the "roaring fire" and piano player "take you back years" – you feel like a "captain of industry", or at the very least, a "grown-up"; add in a "kind, knowledgeable staff", and you've got the "perfect establishment for the establishment."

Z Bimbo's 365 Club ⊘

24	21	17	$10

North Beach | 1025 Columbus Ave. (Chestnut St.) | 415-474-0365 | www.bimbos365club.com

"Red velvet, chandeliers and mirrors transport you to the 1950s", when Sinatra and "supper clubs were in vogue", or even the 1930s, when Rita Hayworth danced at this "glamorous, old-school", "acoustically sound" live music venue in North Beach; modern-day Dean Martins can't decide "whether to sit in a swanky banquette with a martini" and watch the "exceptional talent" from "top indie acts" to "retro-cool bands" or "boogaloo on the dance floor."

NEW Bin 38

-	-	-	M

Marina | 3232 Scott St. (bet. Chestnut & Lombard Sts.) | 415-567-3838 | www.bin38.com

The number 38 refers to SF's latitude and the nibbles are locally sourced, but the vinos (and unusual beers) are from all over the map at this Marina hot spot with a heated back patio; order by the taste, glass, flight or bottle – the selection of small production New World wines (especially Australia and New Zealand) is so tempting, and the menu descriptions so cheeky, you may be tempted to go on a bin-der.

Biscuits & Blues

21 | 15 | 16 | $12

Downtown | 401 Mason St. (Geary St.) | 415-292-2583 | www.biscuitsandblues.com

"Biscuits and drinks? hell, biscuits and anything is a winner with me!" quip carboloaders who get their fill of "killer crooners" and "fine blues musicians" with a side of "solid Southern cooking" at this "affordable" live music venue Downtown; head to the Down Beat Lounge upstairs to catch smaller-name acts, DJs and some "late-night fun"; still, nostalgists sigh it doesn't have the "same vibe" as it did pre-renovation.

Bissap Baobab

23 | 18 | 21 | $8

Mission | 2323 Mission St. (19th St.) | 415-826-9287

Little Baobab ⊅

Mission | 3388 19th St. (Mission St.) | 415-643-3558
www.bissapbaobab.com

"Senegal meets scenester" at this "funky spot" in the Mission and its Little Baobab offshoot where "zesty cocktails" (like the "best hibiscus margarita this side of the Sahara") and foreign beers are delivered by a "friendly" staff along with "exotic" West African dishes; the vibe is "intoxicating", especially once you join "world music-loving" folks on the "small", "hot" dance floor and "shake your booty to ethnic grooves."

Bitter End

21 | 17 | 21 | $6

Inner Richmond | 441 Clement St. (bet. 5th & 6th Aves.) | 415-221-9538

This "cozy" two-floor "neighborhood joint pretty much typifies what a great pub should be" – whether you're a "homesick" expat or a Richmond local, "you just want to hang here all night" drinking pints and noshing on "surprisingly good grub", including a "mean shepherd's pie"; barflies play darts and angle for pool tables but what really packs 'em in is Tuesday's "rip-roaring trivia night."

⊠ BIX

26 | 26 | 23 | $12

Downtown | 56 Gold St. (bet. Montgomery & Sansome Sts.) | 415-433-6300 | www.bixrestaurant.com

"Slink down" a Downtown alley, duck into this "hidden" doorway and, egads, "swank! glamour! booze!" – a "lively", "tastefully enticing speakeasy" with a "low-lit" "1930s supper club look and feel"; "step back in time" – and "bring your top hat" – you're in for a "magic night" of "smooth jazz" and "purrfect martinis" served up by an "impeccable" staff that "fits the role to a tee"; it's a "classy" place to "impress a date, though don't expect to hear her thank you."

Black Horse London Pub ⊅

▽ 22 | 17 | 28 | $6

Cow Hollow | 1514 Union St. (bet. Franklin St. & Van Ness Ave.) | 415-928-2414 | www.sfblackhorsepub.com

"Owner James King makes everyone feel welcome" at his "no bigger than a shoebox" Cow Hollow pub (the "smallest in SF") boasting nine barstools, "loads of charm" and a "real dartboard"; you "have no choice but to make friends with the person whose ribs are the temporary home for your elbow" while downing "delicious Chimay" from the "ice-filled bathtub" and "excellent Bavarian" brews – what a "neighborhood gem."

	APPEAL	DECOR	SERVICE	COST

Black Magic Voodoo Lounge ⊄

| | 18 | 12 | 19 | $7 |

Marina | 1400 Lombard St. (Van Ness Ave.) | 415-931-8711

Staffers at this "dark", "grungy" bar do that voodoo they do so well, serving "beer, beer, beer" during "cool open-mike nights" and live music performances; the name alone "adds to the mystique", even if the "small, cramped space" is "pretty nondescript" and though it's in the Marina, "you'd think you were in the Mission", given the "great crowds."

Blackthorn Tavern

| | 16 | 12 | 18 | $6 |

Inner Sunset | 834 Irving St. (bet. 9th & 10th Aves.) | 415-564-6627 | www.blackthornsf.com

Sunset denizens laud this "low-key hangout" for its "reasonably priced drinks", "killer trivia quiz night" and "great live music", agreeing it's a "good spot to start the evening"; tip one back at the bar, manned by "friendly" servers" or slip out to the awning-covered back patio ("don't expect to drink in the sun"); but prickly sorts don't beat around the bush, deeming it "unappealing and dank."

Bliss Bar

| | 19 | 20 | 18 | $8 |

Noe Valley | 4026 24th St. (bet. Castro & Noe Sts.) | 415-826-6200 | www.blissbarsf.com

"Probably the trendiest spot on 24th Street", this "upscale lounge" with DJs spinning nearly every night adds a "little bit of Union Street" to Noe Valley; it "always brings a smile to my face" note "non-neighbors" who hole up in the "cool secluded" Blue Room to the rear – pure "nirvana" when lounging on the "plush couches" with a "fine martini"; but the less blissed-out head here only when "stranded outside the main nightclub thoroughfare."

Blondie's Bar & No Grill ⊄

| | 15 | 11 | 16 | $8 |

Mission | 540 Valencia St. (bet. 16th & 17th Sts.) | 415-864-2419 | www.blondiesbar.com

You'll "catch a buzz on one drink" and "have to crawl home" after two attest Mission martini mavens who meet their shakers at this "minuscule local hot spot"; but while the weekday scene is "quirky and diverse", bashers bristle at the "bulging" weekend crowds of "black-clad Marina residents", teasing it needs "to fix the roots or go brunette – it just ain't workin' like it used to."

⊠ Blowfish Sushi To Die For

| | 22 | 23 | 19 | $11 |

Mission | 2170 Bryant St. (bet. 19th & 20th Sts.) | 415-285-3848 | www.blowfishsushi.com

"If you don't find your date's conversation appealing", the "risqué anime" on the many monitors, the "über-hip decor" with a "sexy Asian flair" and the "young, good-looking" crowd provide plenty of distraction at this "loud", "crazy busy" spot in the Mission (and on San Jose's Santana Row); the "always-fresh", "interesting" sushi selections and sake specialty cocktails are "definitely to-die-for", but "watch out" – it's easy to blow a bundle.

Blue Danube Coffeehouse ⊄

| | 21 | 15 | 18 | $6 |

Inner Richmond | 306 Clement St. (4th Ave.) | 415-221-9041

"Perfect for a first date, studying or a to-go cup of coffee on the way to work", this "mom-and-pop" cafe "on cute Clement Street" im-blued with a "hip local feel" serves up one of the "best lattes"; you can also waltz in

APPEAL | DECOR | SERVICE | COST

at night when occasional live music and spoken-word performances jazz things up, find a "cozy place to lounge on the couches and sip sangria."

Blue Light
16 | 12 | 17 | $6

Cow Hollow | 1979 Union St. (bet. Buchanan & Laguna Sts.) | 415-922-5510 | www.bluelight.ypguides.net

"Jello shots all around!" – "if you want to find the action, look no further" than this Cow Hollow haunt that's "jam-packed" on "popular Taco Tuesdays" with a "sub-25 crowd" that's "perhaps not ready to give up the fraternity"; other nights the vibe is "more chill" – but is the Blue Light "special"? not according to cynics who say it's a "snoozy watering hole."

Blur
17 | 17 | 18 | $9

Polk Gulch | 1121 Polk St. (bet. Larkin St. & Van Ness Ave.) | 415-567-1918 | www.blursf.com

A "great little enclave" in a "perfect area" of Polk Street for barhopping concur acolytes who latch on to this "very laid-back" spot with "low lighting" from the owners of Tonic and Tongue & Groove; local DJs, monthly art shows, "hot 'tenders" and lollipops at the bar clearly add to its appeal for some, but the less-visionary volley back that it can be "very college kid-ish on the weekend."

Bocce Cafe
21 | 21 | 21 | $9

North Beach | 478 Green St. (Grant Ave.) | 415-981-2044 | www.boccecafe.com

The garden patio of this Italian "gem" "off the beaten path" in North Beach is "fabulous for groups who actually want to have a conversation while they sip wine" and slurp "simple pastas" as jazz trios play on weekends; but patrons who score a spot inside shout that the "high ceilings make for noisy" nights so "sitting in the tiny bar isn't a real option."

NEW Bollyhood Cafe
- | - | - | M

Mission | 3372 19th St. (bet. Capp & Mission Sts.) | 415-970-0362 | www.bollyhoodcafe.com

Bhangra beats on the stereo, Indian movie posters on the walls and Bollywood films projected continuously make it easy to pick up on the theme of this warmly lit Mission newcomer; weekends often heat up with DJs, jazz trios and other live music, and while no hard liquor is served, there's Kingfisher and Chimay on tap, plus soju and sake cocktails to go with the tiny tapas menu (e.g. coconut curry and samosas).

Boom Boom Room ⌀
23 | 18 | 20 | $8

Western Addition | 1601 Fillmore St. (Geary Blvd.) | 415-673-8000 | www.boomboomblues.com

"John Lee Hooker may be gone", but the spirit of the club's former owner lives on at this "lively" venue in the Western Addition where nightcrawlers "let loose and dance" to "killer tunes"; you go here to "get your funk" (or blues) on, and the rest – "excellent" service, "alluring black-and-red walls" and a "shady character or two at the bar that add to the appeal" – is "icing on the cake."

NEW Bossa Nova
- | - | - | M

SoMa | 139 Eighth St. (bet. Minna & Mission Sts.) | 415-558-8008 | www.bossanovasf.com

At this cozy SoMa boîte with a Brazilian *futbol* theme, servers score points for their uniforms – yellow soccer T-shirts and tube socks – and

APPEAL | DECOR | SERVICE | COST

for their deft delivery of caipirinhas made with fruit and cachaça and agave-sweetened mojitos; DJs spin samba-inspired beats nightly and occasional live Latin music kicks it up a notch, as do South American small plates like fried plantain chips and salt cod croquettes; N.B. closed Mondays.

Bottom of the Hill

22 | 16 | 19 | $5

Potrero Hill | 1233 17th St. (bet. Missouri & Texas Sts.) | 415-621-4455 | www.bottomofthehill.com

"New talent rolls" through Potrero Hill's "fine indie/underground music spot" "all the time" and no wonder – it's "still the best place" in SF to see "up-and-coming" "punk, emo and alternative" bands "before they become something down the road"; yeah, it can get "hot and crowded", but few mind as the "whimsical" decor, "great outdoor space", pool table and "attentive staff make it easy to enjoy a raucous night of rock."

☑ Boulevard

26 | 26 | 25 | $15

Embarcadero | 1 Mission St. (Steuart St.) | 415-543-6084 | www.boulevardrestaurant.com

"When money is no object", join the "lively" "A-list" cocktail crowd at the Embarcadero's "warm, clubby" "foodies'" spot with a "great wine list", the "best" libations and "on-the-mark service"; "get your space at the bar quick" before it "fills up" – it's the "perfect" perch for "people-watching (not a meat-market scene)" and "conducive to romance"; P.S. if you want to fall under the spell of Nancy Oakes' "magic wand", eat at the marble counter and "watch the chefs create a masterpiece."

☑ Bourbon & Branch

26 | 26 | 21 | $13

Tenderloin | 501 Jones St. (bet. Geary & O'Farrell Sts.) | 415-673-1921 | www.bourbonandbranch.com

"No password, no drink" in the main bar – so call ahead for the "secret" open-sesame code if you want to "step back into the 1920s" with an aught eight twist at this "swanky speakeasy" in the "less-than-savory" Tenderloin; "from the novice drinker to the most elite" "cocktail snob", "all will leave impressed" after sipping "delicious handcrafted" libations made from "hard-to-find spirits" and homemade juices; if a few flap it's "pretentious", most retort "mystery is part" of its "genius" appeal.

Bow Bow Cocktail Lounge

▽ 21 | 14 | 18 | $9

Chinatown | 1155 Grant Ave. (bet. Broadway & Pacific Ave.) | 415-421-6730

Crooners convene at this "hole-in-the-wall karaoke joint" in Chinatown, a "great little" spot to belt out tunes on Friday, Saturday and other nights by request and hang until 2 AM every evening; owner-bartender Candy Wong "serves strong drinks", fortifying bar-flies forced to listen to the "talented and untalented alike"; it's an "entertaining" way to tie one on, even if a handful bark it's a "very random place to end up."

Brainwash

18 | 11 | 14 | $6

SoMa | 1122 Folsom St. (bet. 7th & 8th Sts.) | 415-861-3663 | www.brainwash.com

Where else can you "get your buzz on while you get your suds on" ask clean freaks who cluster at this "neighborhood hideout" in SoMa, a cafe and "one of the coolest laundromats ever" "all rolled into one";

add in WiFi, burgers, "good happy-hour specials" and "nightly entertainment that ranges from annoying to decent", and you've got the "funnest place to fold and dry in SF."

☑ Brazen Head ⊅   25 | 19 | 22 | $8

Cow Hollow | 3166 Buchanan St. (Greenwich St.) | 415-921-7600 | www.brazenheadsf.com

You "feel like you've stumbled onto a secret hiding place", nevertheless you may have to "squeeze in" to this "dark", "civilized", "old-school" Cow Hollow "favorite" that's perfect for a "discreet, romantic" "late-night rendezvous" ("good hearty food" served until 1 AM); "there's no sign outside", which pleases proprietary patrons who pout "quit telling everyone" about the "professional bartenders who know how to make a drink" and the "excellent selection of cocktails and wine."

Brick   - | - | - | M

Tenderloin | 1085 Sutter St. (Larkin St.) | 415-441-4232 | www.brickrestaurant.com

Rotating artwork hangs on the 100-year-old brick wall at this trendy Tenderloin restaurant and gallery combo, where crowds also belly up to the spacious copper-topped bar until 2 AM; the late-night menu varies from the dinner offerings, tending toward simpler fare like herbed fries, meatballs and empanadas, with bottles of wine half price all day Tuesday, and draft beer, vino by the glass and inventive signature cocktails $2 off during the daily happy hour.

Bruno's   - | - | - | E

Mission | 2389 Mission St. (20th St.) | 415-643-5200 | www.brunosolive.com

This Mission favorite swung back into action again late 2006, with new owners and a renovated interior; though old-school regulars may mourn the loss of the vintage booths and the aquarium, you can still catch a jazz show in the music room (dubbed the Cork Club), and come the weekend, DJs rock the house, spinning for a young crowd that's just there to dance; N.B. closed Mondays and Tuesdays.

☑ Bubble Lounge   22 | 23 | 18 | $14

Downtown | 714 Montgomery St. (bet. Jackson & Washington Sts.) | 415-434-4204 | www.bubblelounge.com

The "young", "beautiful" crowd sparkles at Downtown's "ultraluxe" lounge" serving "champagne galore"; upstairs and down are as "different as night and day" – the "sexy" ground level with its "plush velvet decor" is a "classy" "place to seduce a date", while the "cavelike basement" is "tons of fun for dancing and grooving"; but service can span from "spotty" to "snotty", and bubble-bursters whine you'll wake up with a wine "hangover and an empty wallet."

Buckshot Bar & Gameroom   - | - | - | I
(fka Alpha Bar & Lounge)

Inner Richmond | 3848 Geary Blvd. (bet. 2nd & 3rd Aves.) | 415-831-8838

Where can you play skee ball, ham it up in a photo booth and play drunken shuffleboard at a table held together with duct tape? – only at this wacky, tacky '70s-themed dive in the Inner Richmond that resembles a frat house rec room; the selection of liquors is substantial, but

	APPEAL	DECOR	SERVICE	COST

you might want to make like the locals and order a cheap PBR before plopping down on one of the tattered sofas.

Buddha Bar ⊉

| 19 | 18 | 18 | $11 |

Chinatown | 901 Grant Ave. (Washington St.) | 415-362-1792

"Chinese immigrants' offspring mingle with tourists and hipsters" at this "dark" "Chinatown dive" where the bartender may "challenge you to a game of liar's dice" or "flirt like crazy" in between mixing "strong but small drinks"; it's a "friendly" spot to "throw back a few with friends", and "you can actually carry on a conversation", but beware the "scary" "downstairs bathrooms" (it's "a little freaky" – you have to be buzzed in).

☑ Buena Vista Cafe

| 23 | 17 | 20 | $10 |

Fisherman's Wharf | 2765 Hyde St. (Beach St.) | 415-474-5044 | www.thebuenavista.com

Perhaps "the best reason to have whiskey at 11 AM" is the "famous Irish coffee" that "still sets the standard" at this "welcoming" Fisherman's Wharf "institution" "full of history" and tourists; "count your lucky charms if you get a seat" at the bar where you can "make friends" with the "bartenders who've been here forever" or at the communal tables where "good conversation with a diverse clientele is guaranteed."

Bus Stop

| 16 | 12 | 17 | $6 |

Cow Hollow | 1901 Union St. (Laguna St.) | 415-567-6905 | www.busstopbar.com

"Good-looking singles, those who wish they still were" and locals all congregate at this "divey", "most chill of the sports bars" in Cow Hollow that's "always hopping on game days"; "grab a bucket of beers and hang with friends while you watch" flat-screen TVs, "shoot pool or shoot the bull" and when hunger strikes, order from nearby eateries.

Butter

| 18 | 16 | 17 | $8 |

SoMa | 354 11th St. (bet. Folsom & Harrison Sts.) | 415-863-5964 | www.smoothasbutter.com

SoMa's "totally kitschy" "little dive bar" with a "trailer trash" theme butters up its "hip", "urban" "twentysomething" crowd with microwaved Tater Tots, deep-fried "Twinkies and tasty drinks" like bright orange Tangtinis; "wear your wife-beater" top, "head-bang to punk and '80s tunes" and just "go for fun, not to be seen"; but detractors compare it to margarine: "not real, and definitely not cool."

Butterfly

| 21 | 22 | 21 | $12 |

Embarcadero | Pier 33 (Bay St.) | 415-864-8999 | www.butterflysf.com

With a "bar lit up in blue" and an "awesome" Bay view, it's no wonder locals with "out-of-town guests" in tow make a beeline for this "expensive" Embarcadero spot; but while fans are abuzz over "great drinks", jazz and DJs that help your "fun" night take flight, others are bugged by "average food and service" shrugging it's "more restaurant than hangout."

Café ⊉

| 17 | 13 | 15 | $8 |

Castro | 2369 Market St. (Castro St.) | 415-861-3846 | www.cafesf.com

Join the "good-looking crowd" of "young" "gay or straight people socializing" and grooving "away the night" at this Castro hangout; you'll get down with "some hot bodies" and "sweaty" ones – and come Thursday nights you'll "see the male go-go dancers too"; it's a "little tired, a little old" lament the blasé, but even they admit it's "still a great spot to shake your ass when nothing else is hoppin'."

Cafe Abir ⊄

▽ 21 | 14 | 14 | $6

Western Addition | 1300 Fulton St. (Divisadero St.) | 415-567-6503 | www.dajanigroup.net

They roast the beans fresh, but there's more than coffee brewing at this "very cozy", "always lively" recently renovated cafe in the Western Addition where you can also plop down on the couch and "while away some time with a book" and a beer or some wine and pizza or browse in the new wine shop next door; still, a few feel the sometimes "dismissive" staff can be a buzz kill.

Café Bastille

18 | 16 | 16 | $9

Downtown | 22 Belden Pl. (bet. Bush & Pine Sts.) | 415-986-5673 | www.cafebastillesf.com

"Down a glass of Beaujolais" at this "fun", "friendly French" Downtowner with "real cafe atmosphere" "straight out of the Latin Quarter"; but even *amis* confide you'll "be cheek by jowl with everyone", especially "on a warm day", when *tout le monde* wants to sit outdoors in the "cute alley" location and imbibe drinks with those "must-have mussels and fries" or listen to "pleasant" live jazz on Fridays.

Café Claude

21 | 18 | 19 | $11

Downtown | 7 Claude Ln. (Sutter St.) | 415-392-3505 | www.cafeclaude.com

"The Platonic ideal of a French cafe", this "charming" "hideaway in the heart of Downtown" boasts a "teeny-tiny" bar that's "still compelling", drawing soon-to-be-seated Francophiles like "moths to the flame"; the "infused" cocktails and "great jazz" (Thursday–Saturday) are "well worth a little attitude" from the "young" staff, especially when you need a Gallic "fix."

Cafe Cocomo

20 | 16 | 17 | $11

Dogpatch | 650 Indiana St. (bet. Mariposa & 19th Sts.) | 415-824-6910 | www.cafecocomo.com

Twirl to your "heart's content" at Dogpatch's "huge" "salsa hot spot" where "all levels come together" on the "big dance floor"; it may be "a little bit cheesy, but it's a lot of fun", so "find a date or your next partner if you didn't bring your own", take a lesson or "watch the serious *salseros* from the mezzanine", then hang on the "beachy" patio and sip "reasonably priced drinks."

Café du Nord

23 | 18 | 19 | $8

Castro | 2170 Market St. (bet. Church & Sanchez Sts.) | 415-861-5016 | www.cafedunord.com

"Love the underground feel and old-world appeal" of Upper Market's "former speakeasy that's maintained its glamorous", "unexpectedly stylish" "sexy character" coo adoring acolytes; it's a "very relaxed", "intimate" venue to view an "eclectic" roster of performers – and "worth visiting even if you don't know the band" since there's "enough room to have a conversation at the bar without yelling" while sipping "good strong drinks."

	APPEAL	DECOR	SERVICE	COST

Cafe Flore

| | 21 | 18 | 17 | $7 |

Castro | 2298 Market St. (Noe St.) | 415-621-8579 |
www.cafeflore.com

"Grab some coffee or beer with vittles" and people-watch through the "walls of windows" or while seated in the "see-and-be-seen" outdoor area at this "flirty" "Castro classic" that "maintains some funkiness from the *Tales of the City* era"; but while some Flore-frequenters are psyched about the addition of a full bar, the less-floored shrug it's "about as hip as Richard Simmons."

Cafe International ⊉

| | ∇ 21 | 16 | 25 | $6 |

Lower Haight | 508 Haight St. (Fillmore St.) | 415-552-7390

"Everyone seems to be wrapped" up in their "latest creation, be it a novel or knitting" at this "great low-key", "comfortable" Lower Haight coffeehouse offering live jazz on Thursdays and Sundays, open-mike nights on Fridays and a cavalcade of entertainment on Saturdays; the "friendly" owners "make you feel right at home" confides the international set that also globe-trots over for the "nice backyard space" that's "awesome on sunny days."

Café Prague ⊉

| | 17 | 15 | 15 | $11 |

North Beach | 584 Pacific Ave. (Columbus Ave.) | 415-433-3811

A respite from neighboring "noxious tourist haunts", this "North Beach poet's place" exudes an "air that is distinctly SF"; the "relaxing environs" and "diverse wine list" "draw patrons in and make them stay awhile"; but others opt to Czech out, quipping it's "Starbucks in disguise" with "catch-as-catch-can service" to boot.

Café Royale

| | 21 | 20 | 19 | $7 |

Tenderloin | 800 Post St. (Leavenworth St.) | 415-441-4099 |
www.caferoyale-sf.com

"Comfortable, attractive", "neighborhood-y" – it's "my favorite spot" in "da hood" for a glass of wine or beer or a sake or soju cocktail enthuse loyalists; bring friends or a date – whether you want to listen to live jazz and soak up the "cool vibe" or peruse the rotating work of Bay Area artists, it's a "great" Tenderloin "place to relax" – little wonder it's "still going strong, especially with the theater crowd."

Cafe Zoetrope

| | 21 | 22 | 18 | $12 |

North Beach | Sentinel Bldg. | 916 Kearny St. (Columbus Ave.) |
415-291-1700 | www.cafezoetrope.com

When seeking "film director panache in a movie-style setting", fans can't refuse a visit to Francis Ford Coppola's "sleek, stylish" North Beach "find" – or Cafe Rosso & Bianco, its Palo Alto branch; "kick back and sample the wines", and get a pre-paid card and serve yourself from the "fun", "new automated" dispensers – "no more waiting to catch the eye" of the bartender; still, critics "come for the flights, not the food", carping something got "lost in translation."

Caffè Greco ⊉

| | 19 | 15 | 17 | $6 |

North Beach | 423 Columbus Ave. (bet. Green & Vallejo Sts.) |
415-397-6261 | www.caffegreco.com

"They know coffee like no one else" aver java junkies who buzz over to North Beach's "friendly", "upbeat" "neighborhood place where you can hear different languages being spoken"; "grab a cup" of Joe (perhaps the "best espresso" around), "splurge on tiramisu" or sip "bargain"-priced wine while you people-watch; but a few Greco grumps grumble it's just a "generic Italian cafe."

Caffe Puccini ⊅

▽ | 20 | 17 | 18 | $7

North Beach | 411 Columbus Ave. (Vallejo St.) | 415-989-7033
"Sit by the windows" or on the sidewalk, nurse "great coffee and pastries", or possibly a glass of beer or vino and "watch the busy pedestrians" speed by at this "cute" Euro-style coffeehouse in North Beach; true, it's a bit of a "tourist spot", nonetheless insiders sing its praises, citing a "cool, laid-back crowd on weekends" and a "fantastic jukebox."

Caffe Trieste

20 | 15 | 18 | $7

Civic Center | 1667 Market St. (bet. Brady & Gough Sts.) | 415-551-1000
North Beach | 601 Vallejo St. (Grant Ave.) | 415-392-6739 ⊅
SoMa | 199 Montgomery St. (Bush St.) | 415-538-7999
www.caffetrieste.com
"Makes you feel nostalgic for the old days, even if it's your first visit" confide the wistful who join the "Kerouac wannabes, aspiring screenwriters and coffee fanatics" at this Bay Area "stalwart" (and its Sausalito, and Berkeley branches); espresso and pastry is the "perfect way to start a day" – or end it, if you want to be "endlessly entertained" by the "parade of locals and tourists" and the live music on Saturday nights.

Campton Place

23 | 25 | 25 | $13

Downtown | Campton Place Hotel | 340 Stockton St. (bet. Post & Sutter Sts.) | 415-955-5555 | www.camptonplace.com
A "calm" feeling comes over you when you walk into this "subdued hideaway" in one of Downtown's most luxe hotels; when you want to "impress your sedate date" or require a post-shopping "respite from the buzz of Union Square", head to the "perfect little bar" and treat yourself to "refreshing" drinks, "fabulous" wines and a "great bar menu."

NEW Candybar

- | - | - | E

Western Addition | 1335 Fulton St. (bet. Broderick & Divisadero Sts.) | 415-673-7078 | www.candybarsf.com
Indulge your sugar cravings at the Western Addition's new 'dessert lounge', where you don't have to finish your dinner before sampling cake; sure, there are a few savory selections on the menu, but the focus is firmly on the petite treats made by pastry chef Jake Godby, formerly of Fifth Floor and Coi, and even the wine list hits the sweet spot; snag a table in the equally tiny digs and while away the evening with board games and your baked Alaska.

Cantina

- | - | - | E

Downtown | 580 Sutter St. (Mason St.) | 415-398-0195 | www.cantinasf.com
If there were such a thing as a Latino speakeasy, it might look like this dimly lit Downtown art bar, where candelabras, samba music and burnt-orange walls set a sultry tone; cocktail connoisseurs enjoy star mixologist Duggan McDonnell's inventive libations, while everyone else will appreciate drinks served by the pitcher plus a selection of Spanish and South American wines.

	APPEAL	DECOR	SERVICE	COST

Capp's Corner
19 | **14** | **19** | **$6**

North Beach | 1600 Powell St. (Green St.) | 415-989-2589 |
www.cappscorner.com

This "old-time" "family-style Italian restaurant with a small bar" and an "eclectic following" of locals and "wise tourists" has "just the right amount of North Beach flavor", thanks to the SF memorabilia on the walls; while it may not be a "go-to" spot, it's still a "funky" "place to grab a cheap glass of wine" "before going to *Beach Blanket Babylon*" nearby.

Carnelian Room
24 | **22** | **21** | **$13**

Downtown | Bank of America Ctr. | 555 California St., 52nd fl. (bet. Kearny & Montgomery Sts.) | 415-433-7500 | www.carnelianroom.com

You almost feel like "James Bond" as you sip your "smart, exquisitely dry martini at your quiet, romantic little table" with the "city at your feet" quip would-be Daniel Craigs who soak up the "jaw-dropping views" from the 52nd floor of the Bank of America building; still, a few quibble the "drinks are not the reason" to go – "if they were tops, no one would ever get in" – while others wonder whether the "attitude is worth it."

Casanova Lounge ⬆
20 | **18** | **17** | **$6**

Mission | 527 Valencia St. (bet. 16th & 17th Sts.) | 415-863-9328 |
www.casanovasf.com

"Everyone always ends up" at this "hipster nesting ground" in the heart of the Mission, kitted out with a "dim-red", "lit-like-a-darkroom" glow, "cozy" couches, an "awesome jukebox" and "skeezy '70s nude art that's somehow charming"; it's a "good date spot" for the "too-cool-for-school" set and a "great place to chill on a weeknight" with "large, strong drinks" reveal lounge lizards who opt to "avoid the weekend yuppie crowd."

Catalyst Cocktails
- | **-** | **-** | **M**

SoMa | 312 Harriet St. (Bryant St.) | 415-621-1722 |
www.catalystcocktails.com

Hidden in an alleyway near the SF Hall of Justice, and underneath a bail bondsman, is this restaurant/lounge that's more likely to attract SoMa scenesters than parolees; the tattooed barkeeps make crafty cocktails with freshly squeezed juices (the three-page list is longer than the American menu), while the soundtrack is also a throwback, in an early 1990s way, with DJs and live acoustic jazz on tap a few nights a week.

Cat Club ⬆
- | **-** | **-** | **M**

SoMa | 1190 Folsom St. (bet. 7th & 8th Sts.) | 415-703-8965 |
www.catclubsf.com

Live out all of your nine lives at this SoMa dance standby that offers an eclectic crowd a host of events that touch on nearly every genre, from punk, mod and dark electro to industrial and Goth; shake your money-maker on '1984 Thursdays' when DJs spin tunes from Depeche Mode to Duran Duran or, meow, drag out your fiercest look for the occasional lesbian parties – there's always a guilty pleasure in store here.

Cav Wine Bar & Kitchen
22 | **21** | **22** | **$12**

Hayes Valley | 1666 Market St. (bet. Franklin & Gough Sts.) | 415-437-1770 |
www.cavwinebar.com

The staff is "passionate about wine", "steering you toward unusual and tasty" vinos from its "divine", "intriguing" global selection while the "pale wood decor" lends a "mellowness" to the "minimalist" setting – little wonder most consider this "delightful find" a "must-visit" in Hayes Valley; bring a "fat wallet" and order the "gorgeous cheese plate" or other "excellent small plates" along with an "enticing" flight – you're sure to find something to "please an educated palate."

Cellar, The

- | - | - | M

Downtown | 685 Sutter St. (Taylor St.) | 415-441-5678 | www.cellarsf.com
Thanks to an extensive renovation, this Downtown basement bar is rocking a new look that's more futuristic-chic than moody rec room; earthy, pale-colored walls, velvet couches, light installations and six disco balls set the stage for karaoke (Monday) nights and DJ dancing later in the week, when it gets packed with art school students; on weekends a dress code is enforced, meaning no baseball caps and schlumpy jeans.

Centerfolds

∇ 24 | 16 | 18 | $14

North Beach | 391 Broadway (Montgomery St.) | 415-834-0662 | www.centerfoldssf.com
Some of the "best entertainers" are always front and center at this "very posh strip club" in North Beach that's so "friendly and clean" you almost might be tempted to "take your mother"; you'll conserve cash by cutting the cocktails (no alcohol is served), nevertheless, the stickershocked feel as though their pockets have been "vacuumed", huffing "you can rent a lot of videos for the price of one" lap dance.

Cha Cha Cha @ Original McCarthy's

21 | 17 | 18 | $8

Mission | 2327 Mission St. (bet. 19th & 20th Sts.) | 415-824-1502 | www.cha3.com
The "contrast of Carribbean" tapas in an "old Irish bar is inviting" and "immensely popular", so ape the Mission "peeps who drop in midweek to avoid weekend mobs"; whether you join the "loud" crowd at the "great wraparound bar" manned by "knowledgeable 'tenders" or "gather with girlfriends on your night out" be sure to "down pitchers of sangria" – it'll "totally get you in the right mood for a fun time."

Chaya Brasserie

23 | 23 | 21 | $13

Embarcadero | 132 The Embarcadero (bet. Howard & Mission Sts.) | 415-777-8688 | www.thechaya.com
"Soak up the flavor of the city" at this "chic", "lively" Embarcadero "classic", "an ideal spot for apps and signature drinks" boasting an "awesome view" of the Bay Bridge; the "overflowing crowd" of nine-to-fivers can make it a "challenge" to get served and a few crow it's "corporate", but insiders paya no mind, turning up on weekends to listen to the "pretty decent jazz band" when the Downtown suits are home.

Chieftain Irish Pub & Restaurant

21 | 18 | 22 | $10

SoMa | 198 Fifth St. (Howard St.) | 415-615-0916 | www.thechieftain.com
It doesn't take the luck o' the Irish to find a "great pint of Guinness" and "authentic pub food" in SoMa, just a visit to this "extremely friendly" watering hole with dark-wood booths and decor straight from the Emerald Isle; it's "great fun on Tuesday trivia nights", and whenever "Paul, the longtime bartender", is there, unless, perhaps, your pet soccer or rugby team is getting clobbered during the televised games.

Cigar Bar

19 | 17 | 19 | $10

Downtown | 850 Montgomery St. (bet. Jackson St. & Pacific Ave.) | 415-398-0850 | www.cigarbarandgrill.com

Sit on the heated patio with the "great after-work crowd" at this "surprisingly relaxed" Downtowner on a "sunny Friday and kick off" the weekend with a stogie and "hard-core" mojitos; "it's one of the few places in the city that lets you enjoy a cigar with your buddies" "without being arrested", making it a "favorite hangout" for puff-"buffs"; live music, including "amazing local Latin jazz", lights up the "mellow" space Thursday–Saturday.

Circa

- | - | - | M

Marina | 2001 Chestnut St. (Fillmore St.) | 415-351-0175 | www.circasf.com

Doing double duty as a nightclub and restaurant, this Marina multi-tasker is an upscale spot for the former frat and sorority set to hook up over glasses of wine and specialty cocktails and groove to the DJs Thursday–Saturday; come before 11 PM to enjoy the small plates from celebrity chef Eric Hopfinger, otherwise, there might be a line to get into the sexy lounge area, which is typically wall-to-wall with well-dressed drinkers.

Circolo

19 | 22 | 16 | $12

Mission | 500 Florida St. (Mariposa St.) | 415-553-8560 | www.circolosf.com

"Part restaurant, part bar, part nightclub – pick your venue" at this "slick" and "spacious" "ultrachic" boîte reminiscent of a "NYC hot spot"; while it may be "in the middle of nowhere relative to most" Mission bars, the "young", "high-energy" crowd "lured by the scene", "original cocktails" and appetizers asserts it's "worth the trip"; but a circumspect few shape it up differently, pronouncing it "too trendy" and "expensive."

⚡ Cityscape

24 | 23 | 20 | $12

Downtown | Hilton San Francisco | 333 O'Farrell St., 46th fl. (Mason St.) | 415-923-5002 | www.cityscaperestaurant.com

Go for the "beautiful view" from the 46th floor, "stay if you've got an expense account" and enjoy dancing to DJs on Friday and Saturday in a vaguely art deco setting that's an "interesting juxtaposition to the rest" of the Downtown Hilton; whether you're a corporate climber or part of the "tourist set" it's a "relaxing way to end your day"; still, some say that everything is "secondary" to the city vistas, including the "average" cocktails.

City Tavern

15 | 15 | 17 | $8

Cow Hollow | 3200 Fillmore St. (bet. Greenwich & Moulton Sts.) | 415-567-0918

"Bartenders keep the drinks flowing to the twentysomething, I-just-graduated-from-college" bunch that congregates at this Cow Hollow bar for the $2 Tuesday deal (the "best night of the week") and to watch sports on "big screens galore"; it's "crowded to the gills" on weekends too, when it's a "definite meat market", but frat-boy foes who'd rather not "get smushed by overdone sorority girls" scoff it's "nothing special" and "devoid of character."

	APPEAL	DECOR	SERVICE	COST

Cliff House
23 | 22 | 17 | $12

Outer Richmond | 1090 Point Lobos Ave. (Great Hwy.) | 415-386-3330 | www.cliffhouse.com

Talk about a "room with a view" – from Sutro's restaurant's two-story lounge inside this Outer Richmond "landmark" you can see "white waves crashing into the rocks below" – what a "relaxing way to remind yourself of San Francisco's perch on the Pacific's edge"; sure, some sniff it's a "bit touristy" and "slightly stodgy", but most agree it's a "can't-be-beat" destination to watch the "amazing sunset" or "for a romantic late-night drink after a stroll on the beach."

Club Deluxe ⌀
21 | 20 | 19 | $10

Haight-Ashbury | 1509 Haight St. (Ashbury St.) | 415-552-6949

The "friendly, fiery bartenders" "go the extra mile", using ingredients like "fresh mint and hand-squeezed juices" to make some of the "best" cocktails around at this "groovy" Upper Haight bar with a "super-cool" retro vibe; true, it's not as crowded as it was during its swing-dance heyday, but avant-gardists still congregate for "very good free jazz" shows, while open-mike poetry and comedy nights are "just as appealing and fun."

Club EZ5
19 | 16 | 22 | $9

Downtown | 682 Commercial St. (Kearny St.) | 415-362-9321 | www.ez5bar.com

Such a "random spot" it feels like a "Chinatown karaoke bar, but it's not" – it's a "clubby lounge" tucked into a Downtown alley with an "awesome happy hour" and "snacks to nibble on" and it's not "overrun by working stiffs and trendspotters"; whether you play Pac-Man – what a "blast after three lychee martinis!" – or groove to the "upbeat hip-hop tunes", it's a "fun, kitschy place to hang out."

Club 443
- | - | - | E

(fka Forty Four 3)

North Beach | 443 Broadway (bet. Kearny & Montgomery Sts.) | 415-788-0228 | www.club443.com

At the intersection of FiDi, North Beach and Chinatown, what was once the Velvet Lounge has morphed into a nightspot with a dress code and the requisite VIP lounge; DJs get the booty shakers out onto the 1,500-sq.-ft dance space, and once permit issues are ironed out, the owners hope to add live music to the lineup too; N.B. open Thursday-Saturday.

Club Six
18 | 13 | 16 | $7

SoMa | 60 Sixth St. (bet. Market & Mission Sts.) | 415-863-1221 | www.clubsix1.com

"Big enough to avoid someone, but intimate enough to run into everyone", this "delightfully grimy" SoMa club in a "seedy" neighborhood is a "solid spot to listen to good beats"; the "excellent DJs and live shows" are "never boring" so get "ready to sweat like it's Southeast Asia" as you groove in the downstairs area; still, the put-off deep-six it scowling it's like "dancing in a beer dungeon – 'nuff said."

Cobb's Comedy Club
21 | 14 | 16 | $12

North Beach | 915 Columbus Ave. (Lombard St.) | 415-928-4320 | www.cobbscomedy.com

"Why did the human cross the road? to get to Cobb's" in North Beach quip comedy club cultists who arrive "early to get a good seat" for shows by "some of the brightest stars" in stand-up; though the sprawling space "leaves something to be desired" and you sometimes feel "packed in like sardines", the "top-tier performers" are usually good for a "laugh a minute", especially after you've had a couple of "potent" drinks.

Comet Club

| 12 | 8 | 14 | $7 |

Cow Hollow | 3111 Fillmore St. (Filbert St.) | 415-567-5589

"Fun"-seekers who "like hanging out with 21-year-olds" feel right in orbit spinning round the "tough-to-navigate" "small dance floor" to "great" '80s and Top 40 tunes until the wee hours at this "friendly" Cow Hollow club; but not everyone's over the moon - fastidious fuss-budgets bash the "sticky booths", "sweaty" "cheeseball crowd" and "cramped bathrooms", declaring it's definitely "not appealing" unless you're "completely wasted."

Connecticut Yankee

| 17 | 12 | 15 | $8 |

Potrero Hill | 100 Connecticut St. (17th St.) | 415-552-4440 | www.theyankee.com

When you're "looking for something with a neighbah-hood feel", follow Red Sox, Giants, 49ers and Patriots fans to this "homey" Potrero Hill *Cheers* of the West" and "watch Boston or New York sports" on the tube; Yanks also clipper over for "awesome pub food", "delish Bloody Marys" and "up-and-coming musical acts", and sometimes escape to the "cozy" outdoor patio "to get some air or have a smoke."

Cortez

| 22 | 24 | 21 | $12 |

Downtown | Hotel Adagio | 550 Geary St. (bet. Jones & Taylor Sts.) | 415-292-6360 | www.cortezrestaurant.com

A "happening" Downtown pre-theater "spot to start the night" with "creative cocktails" and "carefully crafted", "tasty little treats" - and a "great final stop to chill and say goodnight to friends" confirm fans of the Adagio's "modern", "super-chic" hotel bar; no, it's "not cheap", and the mutinous mutter "less pretense, more substance, please", but most are onboard because it's "very trendy, inviting and romantic at the same time."

Cosmopolitan, The

| 18 | 20 | 19 | $12 |

SoMa | Rincon Ctr. | 121 Spear St. (bet. Howard & Mission Sts.) | 415-543-4001 | www.thecosmopolitancafe.com

Yes, there are "Cosmos to suit every whim" and the "atmosphere is indeed very cosmopolitan" what with the live pianist Wednesday-Saturday, but this SoMa restaurant and bar is also a "swanky" place to "concoct your next merger or acquisition over a martini"; it "gets packed during happy hour", but since "service is excellent" and the crowd "civilized" there's "no need to elbow others" to snag a drink.

DaDa

| - | - | - | M |

SoMa | 86 Second St. (Mission St.) | 415-357-1367 | www.thegallerylounge.net

The modern "art on the walls is always sure to catch your eye" and so will the sculptures and the red-and-white minimalist-meets-old-world decor at this "swanky", "hip" SoMa lounge from the owners of Gallery Lounge; while it feels like a "stealth place" on weekends, expect "big crowds on Friday evenings" when throngs of "young professionals" stop by for happy hour.

	APPEAL	DECOR	SERVICE	COST

Dalva ⇄

| | 20 | 18 | 19 | $6 |

Mission | 3121 16th St. (bet. Albion & Valencia Sts.) | 415-252-7740
"When in doubt", Missionites mosey to their "go-to" bar, a "hipsterish" "standby" with a "certain timeless appeal"; listen to the DJs "spinning some unintrusive beats", sink some change into the "esoteric jukebox" or just enjoy the "interesting art" on the walls ("if you can see in the dark", that is); P.S. though the usually "relaxed vibe" is perfect for a "pre-dinner cocktail", insiders aim to "avoid the late-night crush."

Dave's

| | 13 | 11 | 19 | $6 |

SoMa | 29 Third St. (bet. Market & Mission Sts.) | 415-495-6726
"You wouldn't expect to find" this sort of "gritty local pub" near Market Street in SoMa, surrounded by office buildings and Downtown suits, but this "good old" reliable is popular for "decompressing after work" and hanging out with the "post–Giants game crowd"; just don't expect any atmosphere along with the "cheap drinks" because it's a "real dive."

Delaney's

| | 14 | 12 | 18 | $7 |

Marina | 2241 Chestnut St. (bet. Avila & Pierce Sts.) | 415-931-8529
"Well-pulled pints" (and free popcorn) "take you back" to the Emerald Isle at this "very friendly" pub that "fills a real void" in the "annoying", "sometimes overly trendy Marina"; it "gets packed on the weekends", but "you can always jam in" with the "aging frat-boy" crowd that's a little less "uptight" than at neighboring watering holes and down some "cheap drinks."

Delirium Cocktails ⇄

| | 16 | 15 | 16 | $5 |

Mission | 3139 16th St. (Albion St.) | 415-552-5525
Devotees are delirious for this "cool, dark" Mission dive, a "mecca" for "trendy" "twentysomethings" who "drink and dance the night away to all kinds o' stuff, from electro to doo-wop" in between pool games; though it gets "meat market–like" on weekends, when the back room is "cramped, hot" and "hipster-ish", there's usually "plenty of space for you and your chums" to lounge on the "cold black leather seats" (which "could be more inviting").

NEW Dell'Uva

| | - | - | - | M |

North Beach | 565 Green St. (Columbus Ave.) | 415-393-9930
Though the name is Italian, the wines are from all over the map at this warm, winning North Beach wine bar; belly up to the welcoming mahogany bar, order a glass or flight of vino from Australia, California, Greece and Italy then complement it with well-chosen nibbles like charcuterie, crisp-crusted pizzas and other small plates.

Dirty Martini

| | 19 | 17 | 18 | $12 |

Fisherman's Wharf | 2801 Leavenworth St. (Beach St.) | 415-775-5510 | www.dirtymartinisf.com
"Very friendly" servers, cover bands and DJs draw dirty dancers to this "large warehouse-type" space where a "great time is had by all"; "cocktails are a must" muse martini mavens who imbibe "imaginative drinks", even though purists pout about the "extra-sweet concoctions"; and if it's not the most local crowd ("can you say 'bridge and tunnel'"), "what can you expect in such a touristy neighborhood?"; N.B. club attire is required.

APPEAL | DECOR | SERVICE | COST

District
– | – | – | E

SoMa | 216 Townsend St. (Ritch St.) | 415-896-2120 |
www.districtsf.com

Thanks to its eclectic menu and industrial surroundings, this SoMa wine bar set in a renovated 1918 building near the ballpark makes a stylish stop for sophisticates in search of a decent glass of red, white or bubbly and perhaps an after-work or before-game snack too; accents like a barn-wood bartop and iron chandelier add warmth and balance to the exposed brick and beams in the spacious room.

Divas ⊘
– | – | – | M

Polk Gulch | 1081 Post St. (Polk St.) | 415-474-3482 |
www.divassf.com

"Trannies and the men who love them" – as well as "daring" clubgoers who want to meet them – head to this "gender-bending" three-level bar off of Polk Street with a dance floor, video lounge and stage; transgender weekend drag shows draw the biggest crowds, but Thursday performances by the she-male "'Divas' Darlings' dancers defy description" too.

DNA Lounge ⊘
16 | 12 | 13 | $8

SoMa | 375 11th St. (bet. Folsom & Harrison Sts.) | 415-626-1409 |
www.dnalounge.com

It's "all about moving to the groove" at this "fun, fun, fun" club that has a "superior" sound system in its genes; some SoMa scenesters call it "super-industrial" and "super-cool", saluting "great DJ shows" that inspire even "people-watchers" to "get on that dance floor", but nitpickers note that it's mutated lately, muttering it "doesn't get the acts it once did" – perhaps it's "seen better days."

Doc's Clock ⊘
18 | 13 | 20 | $5

Mission | 2575 Mission St. (bet. 21st & 22nd Sts.) | 415-824-3627 |
www.docsclock.com

"Welcome to the Mission!" exclaim "lots of regulars" who clock a lot of time "shuffleboarding the night away" at this "very retro, very tacky, very nostalgic" dive with "chill bartenders"; whether you hang with the "twentysomethings" and chug "cheap" beer ($1 PBRs during happy hour – "enough said"), clink glasses with "your buddy" or "get your drink on before catching a show" or "heading home", it's such a "fun" "institution."

Dogpatch Saloon ⊘
20 | 15 | 22 | $6

Dogpatch | 2496 Third St. (22nd St.) | 415-643-8592

On the edge of San Francisco in an "odd but up-and-coming" neighborhood is the "coolest little dive bar ever" declare Dogpatch denizens; "it's not a scene", and "there is no one to see", but the "warm and inviting" decor, "friendly" bartenders and an "old-school" crowd ("don't be surprised if you're the youngest" pup there) make it "worth a trip", especially during Sunday afternoon jazz performances.

Double Dutch
23 | 22 | 20 | $7

Mission | 3192 16th St. (Guerrero St.) | 415-503-1670 |
www.thedoubledutch.com

This Mission tenderfoot with the "rockin' '80s decor" from the Magnet camp is a "bit of a scene" ("but in a good way") with "loud music" and

APPEAL DECOR SERVICE COST

a "little dance floor in back" that's "pretty crowded" with a "fun" mix of people; "top-notch" drinks poured by "attentive" servers help make it one of the "best new bars" in the 'hood declare the "pleasantly surprised" who skip on over.

Dragon Bar

| - | - | - | E |

North Beach | 473 Broadway (bet. Kearny & Montgomery Sts.) | 415-834-9383 | www.dragonbarsf.com

The dim crimson lighting makes everyone look sexier at this North Beach club with slick red-and-black Asian-inspired decor replete with paper lanterns, Buddhas and bamboo accents; scantily clad women huddle against the chill, waiting to move beyond the velvet rope, and once inside, don't be surprised to see a few shaking their groove thang on the bar before bopping to pop and hip-hop on the small, crowded dance floor; N.B. club attire required.

Dubliner, The

| 18 | 14 | 20 | $7 |

West Portal | 328 W. Portal Ave. (Vicente Blvd.) | 415-566-9444
Noe Valley | 3838 24th St. (bet. Church & Vicksburg Sts.) | 415-826-2279
www.dublinerbars.com

"A good place to catch a game" ("love those flat-screen TVs") and a "great place to get a Guinness" agrees the green team that fills this "lively", "real Irish" duo in Noe Valley and West Portal; you probably wouldn't head here for a "big night out", but you "gotta give these guys props" because when you want to "chat with locals", including Emerald Isle transplants, shoot pool and listen to the jukebox, it's "everything that a neighborhood bar should be."

Eagle Tavern ⌐

| 21 | 15 | 17 | $6 |

SoMa | 398 12th St. (Harrison St.) | 415-626-0880 | www.sfeagle.com

"If you're into leather-clad men" or just "spectator sports", "you can't miss" this "cruisy" SoMa spot where "mirrored shades are de rigueur" and "anyone in jeans is welcome", provided they're "tight and worn sans underwear"; oftentimes the crowd is "mostly gay", but "quite a mix of types" lands here for the "always-fun" Sunday afternoon beer busts in the courtyard – an "institution" – and the live bands on Thursdays.

E&O Trading Company

| 20 | 21 | 19 | $10 |

Downtown | 314 Sutter St. (bet. Grant Ave. & Stockton St.) | 415-693-0303 | www.eotrading.com

The "seductive" Southeast Asia "vibe is cool, if that's what you're looking for" agree "tourists and professionals" who set sail for this Downtown fusion spot near Union Square (and siblings in San Jose and Larkspur); order "fritters for me!" and to go with, "exotic tropical drinks", then "snuggle with your honey" on the "cozy little sofas"; still, a few renegades carp that it feels like a "formulaic" "theme park."

Eastside West

| 19 | 17 | 17 | $9 |

Cow Hollow | 3154 Fillmore St. (Greenwich St.) | 415-885-4000

On warm days, "few spots beat the outside tables" at this Cow Hollow haunt, where "people lounge all day" eating "sumptuous oysters" from the raw bar; come sundown, it gets "sceney" so "grab a mojito and listen to the DJ spin" or just "chill" by the "crazy fish tank"; still, a few squawk it's a "bit of a meat market" teeming with "typical Marina types"; N.B. music Thursday-Saturday.

	APPEAL	DECOR	SERVICE	COST

Eddie Rickenbacker's

| 15 | 16 | 14 | $8 |

SoMa | 133 Second St. (bet. Howard & Mission Sts.) | 415-543-3498

"Known for its motorcycles and margaritas" ("dozens of very old" bikes "hang from the ceiling"), this "after-work SoMa joint" is still a "hangout for the tech crowd" that works nearby; "maybe it's the antique guns, maybe it's the freshly squeezed grapefruit juice in the greyhounds" – either way, this "eclectic" eatery "does it" for diehards; P.S. you "gotta love the owner, Norm, who is always in the same bar seat."

Edinburgh Castle Pub

| 22 | 17 | 18 | $6 |

Tenderloin | 950 Geary St. (bet. Larkin & Polk Sts.) | 415-885-4074 | www.castlenews.com

"Grab some fish 'n' chips" and a pint from the "wide selection of beers" at this "no-hubbub pub" on an "iffy" Tenderloin block and "life is good", eh laddies?; catch literary readings in the "big open space" downstairs or head upstairs to "kick back and watch the crowd below" or listen to live local rock; P.S. "be prepared to be packed in like sardines and face tough questions" during Tuesday's pub quiz.

eight

| 21 | 17 | 18 | $8 |

SoMa | 1151 Folsom St. (bet. 7th & 8th Sts.) | 415-431-1151 | www.eightsf.com

"A hot gaysian crowd and their admirers" groove to house, hip-hop and mashups at Friday's Club Dragon night at this SoMa "flashback to the '80s" where "friendly" bartenders serve "strong drinks"; other evenings, homosexual and lesbian groups of various sorts pack onto the two dance floors in between smoke breaks on the "darling" patio shaded by "electric faux palm trees."

NEW 800 Larkin

| - | - | - | M |

(fka O'Farrell Street Bar)

Tenderloin | 800 Larkin St. (O'Farrell St.) | 415-567-9326

Formerly the super-divey O'Farrell Street Bar, or OSB, this touched-up Tenderloin watering hole now resembles a Manhattan bachelor pad, replete with leather couches, a spiffy pool table and racy photographs on the walls; though a small menu of specialty cocktails is on offer, chances are the regulars are probably still tipping back bottles of Bud instead of Bloody Marys; N.B. cigarette fiends congregate in the small smoking lounge.

NEW 83 Proof

| - | - | - | E |

SoMa | 83 First St. (Mission St.) | 415-296-8383 | www.83proof.com

Proof positive that Financial District workers are thirsty for happy-hour drinks, this understated addition also attracts its fair share of SoMa scenesters come evening; with around 40 seats total downstairs and on a tiny balcony, it fills up quickly with cocktail cognoscenti, who appreciate the selection of top-shelf liquors; N.B. an upright piano is apt to inspire impromptu performances.

Elbo Room

| 20 | 16 | 17 | $6 |

Mission | 647 Valencia St. (bet. 17th & 18th Sts.) | 415-552-7788 | www.elbo.com

This bi-level bar "works in so many different ways"; head downstairs to linger in "lots of comfortable loungey areas" downing drinks "stron-

	APPEAL	DECOR	SERVICE	COST

ger than Superman on steroids" and indulging in the nightly happy hour, or to the "intimate upstairs" venue to watch "top-notch" local and indie acts with the rest of the "Mission hipster crowd"; but on weekends "you need a freaking shoehorn to find some space" – in other words, "no elbo room here."

Element Lounge

19 | 20 | 17 | $9

Polk Gulch | 1028 Geary Blvd. (bet. Polk St. & Van Ness Ave.) | 415-440-1125 | www.elementlounge.com

"Smaller than a full-blown club, and without a pretentious attitude" too, this "intimate" nightspot off Van Ness Avenue provides "refuge" from the "vagrant"-strewn neighborhood with "modern art hangings" and "really fun" events like the monthly breakdancing night; "young" fans of hip-hop, rock and mashups are in their element, dancing to "every music genre" spun by "some of the best DJs", nonetheless, a few get fired up about the "underventilated", "crowded" conditions.

Elite Cafe

21 | 20 | 20 | $12

Upper Fillmore | 2049 Fillmore St. (bet. California & Pine Sts.) | 415-673-5483 | www.theelitecafe.com

Yup, it "can be tough to find elbow room" since there are only eight stools at this restaurant's "beautiful long bar", but that doesn't deter "sophisticated thirty- to fortysomethings" from "singing the praises" of this "long-standing", "real and original" Upper Fillmore "classic"; grab an "unbelievably good" Sazerac or martini to wash down a New Orleans–style nosh, and if it gets too "crowded", head to the new heated outdoor sidewalk area.

Elixir

19 | 15 | 20 | $8

Mission | 3200 16th St. (Guerrero St.) | 415-552-1633 | www.elixirsf.com

"You feel like you're in your living room" at this "friendly", "no-frills" "neighborhood saloon" that's a "nice reprieve from the craziness of other Mission bars"; a "relatively hip crowd throws back the drinks" during the "great happy hour", and on "mellow" Sundays, "you cannot go wrong with the make your own Bloody Mary bar" – though a few quip "let's leave the bartending to the professionals."

El Rio ⊄

23 | 17 | 20 | $6

Mission | 3158 Mission St. (bet. Cesar Chavez & Valencia St.) | 415-282-3325 | www.elriosf.com

A "diverse, relaxed crowd" (gay, straight and everything in between) gathers at this "fabulously fun" "Mission standby" that "never disappoints" with a lineup of events, from "great salsa" Sundays to live music and DJs to "delicious free oysters" during Friday happy hours; whatever the goings-on, though, "it's all about" the heated patio, "the perfect place to hang out" – even when it's not one of those "rare warm SF nights."

Endup, The ⊄

20 | 13 | 16 | $8

SoMa | 401 Sixth St. (Harrison St.) | 415-357-0827 | www.theendup.com

"The name says it all": "everyone always ends up at The Endup" in SoMa, where a "mixed crowd" of "hard-core" partiers "celebrates the coming of morning" after other clubs close; "go Sunday at 6 AM and dance the morning away" at the weekly 'T-Dance', where the "great house music", "small" floor and "unpretentious" vibe provide the perfect "opportunity to get to know your neighbors", who're too hyped "to go home for a good night's sleep."

NEW Enrico's

| - | - | - | E |

North Beach | 504 Broadway (Kearny St.) | 415-982-6223 | www.enricossf.com

Linking the past and the present, this legendary 50-year-old North Beach institution reopened in 2007 under new ownership with a spruced-up look and feel, including cream-colored ottomans, a black-velvet banquette and radiant-heat flooring on the patio, which also offers a view of the Bay Bridge; while the menu of American bistro fare was also revamped, the live nightly jazz featuring an eclectic array of performers remains a welcome throwback.

Eos Restaurant & Wine Bar

| 22 | 20 | 22 | $11 |

Cole Valley | 901 Cole St. (Carl St.) | 415-566-3063 | www.eossf.com

"Perfect for a romantic interlude" "by candlelight", this "lively" restaurant and adjoining "cool wine bar" in "cute" Cole Valley, now owned by Scott Holley, lures a "fancypants crowd" that likes to linger over a glass of vino or an "interesting flight" from the "genius list"; what a "great getaway" – the staff is "well versed in what they're pouring", so you "always have a good time – even if you spend more – and drink more than intended."

NEW EPIC Roasthouse

| - | - | - | E |

Embarcadero | 369 Embarcadero (bet. Folsom & Harrison Sts.) | 415-369-9955 | www.epicroasthousesf.com

Upstairs from the dramatic Pat Kuleto–designed chophouse on the Embarcadero lies the equally opulent Quiver Bar; hopping from happy hour until closing, it's aquiver with locals and out-of-towners drinking in the positively epic view of the Bay Bridge; though the restaurant's full menu is available, the small (and spendy) bar menu of lamb riblets, house-cured meats and more seems more fitting in the cozy space, where old-school cocktails made with top-drawer ingredients, whiskey and beefy red wines are the drinks of choice.

Esta Noche ⌦

| ▽ 10 | 7 | 14 | $6 |

Mission | 3079 16th St. (bet. Mission & Valencia Sts.) | 415-861-5757

Expect "some nice drag shows" nightly at this "fun, divey" gay bar full of "Latinas", of sorts; but critics of the "cover charge in the evenings" camp it up, calling it "*esta* nightmare" and find the "tragic-looking drag queens" a few notches below expectations; N.B. the Mission location is just slightly sketchy, but at least it's convenient to BART.

Etiquette

| - | - | - | E |

Downtown | Renoir Hotel | 1108 Market St. (7th St.) | 415-863-3929 | www.etiquettelounge.com

At this SoMa spot, masterminded by Neej Gore and Brandon McKee of Element Lounge, etiquette dictates that the suited-up FiDi workers and women in flirty dresses order seductively named cocktails like the 'Adam's Leaf' or the 'Jessica Rabbit' before hitting on one another; the look is minimalist – the high-ceilinged room almost resembles a black box – but witty touches like backlit portraits of chandeliers and white pillars setting off the small VIP area dress up the space.

	APPEAL	DECOR	SERVICE	COST

☑ Farallon

24 | 28 | 23 | $14

Downtown | 450 Post St. (bet. Mason & Powell Sts.) | 415-956-6969 | www.farallonrestaurant.com

"Grab a pre-dinner drink" or slide onto a sea urchin barstool to sip and slurp bivalves in the new oyster bar of this "beautiful" "blue wonderland" Downtown – either way you'll soak up the "first-class" seafooder's "funky" "under-the-sea setting" (think "Jacques Cousteau on acid") replete with "whimsical" jellyfish chandeliers and elaborate mosaics; sure, it's "pricey", but the "extremely attentive" servers make you "feel special the moment you walk in", ensuring you'll "swim away in a good mood."

Ferry Plaza Wine Merchant

22 | 16 | 21 | $12

Embarcadero | Ferry Bldg. | 1 Ferry Plaza (The Embarcadero) | 415-391-9400 | www.fpwm.com

The "knowledgeable staff is always willing to help you find something new" at this Embarcadero wine bar in the middle of the "Ferry Building action"; it's only open till 8 PM on weekdays and till 9 PM on weekends, but few grape groupies mind, suggesting "stop on your way to the ferry", order a "really tasty cheese platter", or just "crack open a bottle", "slip into second gear" and "swill" a few on a Sunday afternoon.

Fiddler's Green

19 | 16 | 19 | $6

Fisherman's Wharf | 1333 Columbus Ave. (Beach St.) | 415-441-9758 | www.fiddlersgreensf.com

Almost "like being in Ireland" cheer "gregarious" cohorts who channel their inner shamrock at this "loud" bar with "affable bartenders" in the "heart of the Wharf"; join the "eclectic crowd" downstairs to watch live musical acts, including Celtic music and rock, or head to the nightclub upstairs (Friday and Saturday only) to experience a "much different vibe" – it's a "dance scene with a lot of room to move around."

15 Romolo

23 | 18 | 18 | $9

North Beach | Basque Hotel | 15 Romolo Pl. (Broadway) | 415-398-1359

"Possibly the only bar on Broadway (off Broadway, actually) that a self-respecting local will be seen at", this "plush", "swanky", "dark" Basque Hotel standby "hidden in an upward sloping alley" is "off the beaten track just enough to keep out most tourists"; "go early to snag a seat" and dig the "cool vibe", "interesting cocktails" (the melon Cosmo is "a must") and "decent jukebox" – it's like "an oasis in a sea of strip clubs."

Fifth Floor

- | - | - | E

Downtown | Hotel Palomar | 12 Fourth St., 5th fl. (Market St.) | 415-348-1555 | www.fifthfloorrestaurant.com

Reopened after a brief remodel, the Hotel Palomar's swank fifth floor restaurant and lounge now has a clubby new look complete with hardwood floors, leather chairs and a low ceiling that gives the bar an intimate feel; the overall vibe is more business than romance, however, with suited-up sorts sipping pricey wines and top-shelf cocktails; N.B. the more casual cafe section features burgers, salads, cheese plates and other light fare.

☑ Fillmore, The
27 | 23 | 19 | $7

Western Addition | 1805 Geary Blvd. (Fillmore St.) | 415-346-6000 | www.thefillmore.com

The "ghosts of rock 'n' roll past" haunt this "iconic", "world-class" Western Addition venue where "you can practically feel the musical history"; "two words: Poster Room" – that "alone is worth the price of admission" confide fans who head upstairs for a cocktail and to drink in the "must-see" visuals commemorating "classic" shows dating back to 1966; even today it "keeps doing it just right" with "stellar acoustics", "great sightlines" and top-notch acts – after all, "dude, it's the Fillmore!"

Final Final
17 | 10 | 20 | $6

Marina | 2990 Baker St. (Lombard St.) | 415-931-7800

"Wear the right color" to cheer your team on at this "quintessential local" Marina sports bar boasting "awesome bartenders", "cheap beer" and free popcorn; it's "not much in terms of decor" and the "pizza is like cardboard", nevertheless, it's the "perfect place" to hang with "low-key", "friendly strangers" and watch a ballgame, especially "if you're under 25, or still think you are."

Finnegans Wake ⇌
20 | 16 | 19 | $6

Cole Valley | 937 Cole St. (bet. Carl St. & Parnassus Ave.) | 415-731-6119

A "ton" of Cole Valley cohorts re-Joyce that "one of the city's truly great neighborhood pubs" is in their own backyard – there's "something about this place that always brings me back"; the "colorful cast of bartenders"-slash–"spiritual advisors" serve a "good selection of brews", and on a "sunny afternoon", you can play Ping-Pong on the outdoor patio – it's almost "like drinking in a friend's backyard" and so "comfortable it's hard to leave."

Fireside Bar ⇌
23 | 20 | 23 | $7

Inner Sunset | 603 Irving St. (7th Ave.) | 415-731-6433

"Cozy up to the fireplace and meet neighborhood folks", including the "UCSF crowd", at this "unpretentious" but "fantastic neighborhood bar" that has its Inner Sunset followers all fired up; with "diverse music in the jukebox", "awesome bartenders" and "everything on tap from PBR to Chimay", this "little hole-in-the-wall" has all the makings of a locals' "favorite."

First Crush
22 | 19 | 20 | $13

Downtown | 101 Cyril Magnin St. (Ellis St.) | 415-982-7874 | www.firstcrush.com

"Tailor-made for the oenophile", this "cozy" Union Square area vin-ue with "rich colored drapes" and "attentive" service is a "good standby" for trying California-only wines "without breaking the bank"; the "charming" confines, "excellent cheese plate" and large tasting menu just right for "sharing with a dining companion" make it a "can't miss for first dates"; still, a crushed few kvetch it's a "tad" "cramped"; N.B. reservations recommended.

Fishbowl
17 | 12 | 18 | $6

Pacific Heights | 1854 Divisadero St. (bet. Bush & Pine Sts.) | 415-775-3630

"Pac Heights socialites meet dive bar" regulars at this "smallish, no-frills" "meat market" on Divisadero that's "crazy crowded" on weekends, with "rowdy" finatics drinking the "strong", "big and fruity" namesake cocktail like, well, fish; little wonder it's most "popular" with the "just out of college" school that can "still tolerate blue beverages in massive quantities" – the "friendly" staff, "great jukebox" and "super-chill" vibe keep reeling them in.

540 Club
24 | 19 | 23 | $5

Inner Richmond | 540 Clement St. (bet. 6th & 7th Aves.) | 415-752-7276 | www.540-club.com

"The staff makes you feel as though you've been friends with them forever" at what may be the "best watering hole in the Richmond" where "DJs spin mod", plus "plenty of rock and punk" and regulars revel in the rotating art shows and "fun theme nights" ('Smartypants Smackdown' trivia quiz, anyone?); "love" the "ridiculously cheap drink specials" too – is it any wonder "it can get a little crowded"?

500 Club, The ∅
22 | 12 | 19 | $5

Mission | 500 Guerrero St. (17th St.) | 415-861-2500

Yup, "yuppies share space with bikers" and a "coterie of hipsters" at this "super-packed", "neighborhoody bar" with that "big martini-glass sign", "one of the last true dive bars left in the Mission District" – and not the kind of place that "takes kindly to girls toting sequined purses"; thanks to the "capable bartenders", "super-cheap beer" and "generous" pours, "everyone is in a good mood, even the dogs" who accompany regulars.

Florio
23 | 21 | 22 | $12

Upper Fillmore | 1915 Fillmore St. (bet. Bush & Pine Sts.) | 415-775-4300 | www.floriosf.com

Amorous Upper Fillmore folks assess the "small" but "lively" bar of this "casual brasserie" as a "wonderful first-date destination", especially when you stay for the "very French" and Italian fare; even if romance isn't in the stars, the "bustling, noisy" space is an "awesome place" to "get to know your neighbor", because the customers are as "friendly" as the staff.

Fluid
20 | 22 | 16 | $11

SoMa | 662 Mission St. (bet. New Montgomery & 3rd Sts.) | 415-615-6888 | www.fluidsf.com

"Sexy and seductive", the scenesters at this "slick", "very Bondish" club may be the "best eye candy in SoMa" reveal revelers who also get juiced up about "celebrity sightings"; fervent fans applaud "top DJ rotations" and "get the fluids moving" on the "small" "lighted dance floor"; but not everyone gets in the flow – a few fume "you can wait an eternity for a drink" and take it to task for "thinking it's cooler than it is."

Fly
20 | 19 | 19 | $7

Western Addition | 762 Divisadero St. (Fulton St.) | 415-931-4359 | www.flybarandrestaurant.com

The "awesome" sake and soju cocktails ("a real party in your mouth") "will make you forget all your worries" – and that no hard alcohol is served – insist barflies abuzz over this "super-chill" Western Addition spot; it's "very hip, without being tragically so", so it "attracts a crowd from beyond the neighborhood", especially "right before or after a show at The Independent" down the street.

	APPEAL	DECOR	SERVICE	COST

Fog City Diner
21 | 20 | 21 | $11

Embarcadero | 1300 Battery St. (Greenwich St.) | 415-982-2000 |
www.fogcitydiner.com

"Sit at the bar and sample something new", head to the outdoor area or just relax at the Embarcadero's "cool art deco diner" with an awfully "good martini" or one of the "best Bloodies"; but "don't just have a drink" insist insiders who haven't the foggiest why you wouldn't order "bar food munchies" or "creative" fare; clearly the Fisherman's Wharf locale increases its "tourist appeal", but it still "beats the heck" out of other spots nearby.

Foreign Cinema
24 | 24 | 20 | $11

Mission | 2534 Mission St. (bet. 21st & 22nd Sts.) | 415-648-7600 |
www.foreigncinema.com

"Taking dinner and a movie to the next level", this "one-of-a-kind" Mission multitasker has a heated outdoor patio where foreign films flicker "right on the wall of the restaurant"; cineastes claim it's "just plain cool" – "dark, loud and trendy" but somehow "not too hipper-than-thou – and "perfect for a celebration", even if a couple of critics pan how "pricey" the "terrific cocktails" are.

440 Castro ⊄
(aka Daddy's)
18 | 11 | 19 | $7

Castro | 440 Castro St. (bet. 18th & Market Sts.) | 415-621-8732 |
www.daddysbar.com

"Cruise central" "for men who like men", this "dark, fun" "welcoming" bar is the "best place in the Castro for Dorothy to find her Levi's- and leather-clad bears" – no wonder regulars still "drop by or drop trou" on "hot" 'Monday Underwear Nights'; but it's no longer "exclusively a daddy hangout" – the "clientele has pleasantly shifted to a younger, hipper crowd", prompting gripers to growl its "former glory" "has faded."

Frankie's Bohemian Cafe
17 | 15 | 22 | $5

Western Addition | 1862 Divisadero St. (Pine St.) | 415-921-4725

When they're in the mood for a "large cold pilsner" (a whopping 22 ounces) and a "delicious turkey burger", an "interesting mix" of suds sippers who prefer not "to go over the hill to the Marina" chooses this "funky but fun" neighborhood spot in the Western Addition; "friendly" bartenders "keep your glass full" – just remember that beer and a few wines by the glass are the drinks on offer.

Fuse
19 | 17 | 16 | $10

North Beach | 493 Broadway (Kearny St.) | 415-788-2706

"A cool spot" in-fused with a "slight rough edge", this "friendly" North Beach nightclub "on the Broadway strip" also sparks attention with its "interesting" "all-blue interior" and art on the walls; DJs spin nightly, nevertheless it's "not too crowded", making it an "excellent place to kill time before heading off to other bars" on the block.

Gallery Lounge
∇ 16 | 17 | 19 | $7

SoMa | 510 Brannan St. (4th St.) | 415-227-0449 | www.thegallerylounge.net

A "mellow", "arty SoMa crowd" of "happy people" head to this "out-of-the-way" space for the "great happy hour", sipping starving-artist-priced martinis, beer and wine while viewing the latest works on the walls from local talent; if the "crowded" digs and "lack of seating" make the evening seem surreal, head to the "nice back patio" where you can also light up.

ⓩ Gary Danko

27 | 26 | 27 | $16

Fisherman's Wharf | 800 N. Point St. (Hyde St.) | 415-749-2060 | www.garydanko.com

It's such a "fabulous" restaurant, "how could you miss having a drink before dining since it's the civilized thing to do, if you can find a spot" at the "small bar" of this "swanky-in-a-Californian-way" "A-list" "favorite" near Fisherman's Wharf where "grown-ups with taste" pop in "for a glass of bubbly and a torchon of foie gras" or order a meal from the full menu; it "costs the earth", but "service is impeccable", the food and spirits "amazing" and it's "worth every penny."

g bar

17 | 19 | 14 | $9

Pacific Heights | Laurel Inn | 488 Presidio Ave. (California St.) | 415-409-4227 | www.gbarsf.com

"Transport yourself to Los Angeles for the night" at this "swanky", "intimate" "real hidden gem" in the Laurel Inn that's quiet enough for an "after-date drink" (you gotta "love the fireplace") and thoughtful enough to grill up $1 burgers and hot dogs on the patio on Sundays; still, some surveyors sulk that "in a city where the greatest appeal of most bars is the lack of pretension" this g spot "has it wrong."

Gestalt Haus ⌐

- | - | - | M

Mission | 3159 16th St. (Valencia St.) | 415-560-0137

Although it caters to cyclists with indoor bike racks, you need not have a two-wheeled fetish to fit in at this Missionite; the joint boasts an indie-rock vibe, from the black walls to the back-to-basics menu of grilled sausages and hearty draft beer; size, however, does matter, as the brew is available by the liter – which may propel a few bike messengers to walk their Schwinns home.

Ginger's Trois ⌐

- | - | - | I

Downtown | 246 Kearny St. (bet. Sutter St. & Hardie Pl.) | 415-989-0282 | www.gingerstrois.com

The barflies are a mite more mixed since Donald Rogers took over this divey little Financial District gay bar, formerly called Reds, in early 2007, but the scene remains as friendly and fun as before; Toulouse-Lautrec–inspired paintings, white tea lights and an eclectic jukebox lend a delightfully campy feel, and the digs are so tiny that you're forced to make conversation with your neighbors and the sociable bartenders, who pour cocktails with a heavy hand.

Gino & Carlo ⌐

18 | 14 | 20 | $7

North Beach | 548 Green St. (east of Columbus Ave.) | 415-421-0896

Think of it as the "Italian *Cheers* – everybody knows your name (and criminal past)" at this "old-time" hangout "filled with local flavor" and serving "cheap beer"; yeah, "it looks dive-ish", and perhaps you "shouldn't play pool here unless you know what you're doing", but the bartenders are "friendly" and the "juke is full of North Beach favorites"; P.S. it "opens at 6 AM for the fishermen, and closes at 2 AM for the rest of us."

APPEAL DECOR SERVICE COST

Glas Kat Supper Club, The
18 | 17 | 16 | $8

SoMa | 520 Fourth St. (bet. Brennan & Bryant Sts.) | 415-495-6620 | www.glaskat.com

"The crowd really depends on the promoter" at this "large" SoMa supper club/bar/event space; on Tuesday it's *the* "salsa hot spot", while at Wednesday's 'Bondage-a-Go-Go', fetish wear is the dress of choice; whatever the goings-on, the "very diverse" patrons, DJs and live music "loud enough to break glas" ensure a "great experience"; P.S. it's "not much for meeting new people – gotta bring your own."

Glen Park Station ⊄
18 | 14 | 22 | $9

Glen Park | 2816 Diamond St. (bet. Bosworth & Chenery Sts.) | 415-333-4633

"Welcome and pull up a barstool" invite gregarious Glen Park regulars who believe "there is no friendlier bar than this"; "if you want decor, go Downtown", but if you just want to "grab a pint", watch sports and hang out with a "mellow crowd" in this "sleepy SF neighborhood", you've found the "perfect" place; P.S. a tournament every Wednesday means it's "right on target for dart lovers."

Gold Cane Cocktail Lounge ⊄
▽ 13 | 6 | 16 | $5

Haight-Ashbury | 1569 Haight St. (bet. Ashbury & Clayton Sts.) | 415-626-1112

With "decor like your parents' basement rec room" and a "somewhat rough crowd" (seems "every night is parolee night"), this "dive of all dives" redeems itself with "good, strong mixed drinks" that may be the "cheapest" in the Upper Haight; yup, the staff can be "obnoxious", but "that's part of its charm" confide locals who just "love" the "unpretentious" atmosphere, pool games and smoking patio.

Gold Club
17 | 17 | 17 | $12

SoMa | 650 Howard St. (bet. New Montgomery & 3rd Sts.) | 415-536-0300 | www.goldclubsf.com

"Good drinks and lots of hot women" are the appeal at this SoMa strip club that the titillated tout as "T&A heaven"; but while solid Gold supporters give the "warm, casual atmosphere" a group hug, it doesn't stack up for the letdown who suggest it's "in desperate need of fresh (and younger) blood", claiming "there are better places on Broadway."

Gold Dust Lounge, The ⊄
22 | 18 | 21 | $6

Downtown | 247 Powell St. (bet. Geary & O'Farrell Sts.) | 415-397-1695

The "oversized red couches and the ceiling mural make for a nostalgic experience" at this "classic SF haunt" beating in the "heart of Union Square" said to have once been owned by Bing Crosby in the 1950s; "very friendly barmen", nightly live music (mostly rock and Dixieland jazz) and even "livelier regulars" ("tourists, shoppers and alcoholics") make it a "must when you want to get away from the glitz."

☒ Gordon Biersch
18 | 16 | 18 | $9

Embarcadero | 2 Harrison St. (The Embarcadero) | 415-243-8246 | www.gordonbiersch.com

"Drink a Marzen and find your mate" at this trio of "cavernous taverns" (with branches in Palo Alto and San Jose), a "prime meat market" where "yuppies" and "scenesters flock" to "grab a microbrew and

APPEAL DECOR SERVICE COST

their deservedly renowned garlic fries"; it's the "ideal place to mingle with a big group", but a few sudsters huff that "happy hour can be a madhouse" and hint at "hit-or-miss" service.

Grand Cafe
21 | 24 | 19 | $12

Downtown | Hotel Monaco | 501 Geary St. (Taylor St.) | 415-292-0101 | www.grandcafe-sf.com
"Love, love, love this bar" at the "wonderful" turn-of-the-century ballroom in the Hotel Monaco – it's an "outstanding place to meet a date for a few" "sit-down classy drinks" and "perfect" pre- and posttheater – "you can actually have a conversation" while cocktailing and devouring "delicious appetizers"; but others say the "worth-thesplurge" dining room is what's "grand indeed", suggesting don't spend "your entire night here" – "check out the beautiful" premises and "move on."

Grandviews Lounge
▽ 24 | 21 | 23 | $13

Downtown | Grand Hyatt Hotel | 345 Stockton St., 36th fl. (bet. Post & Sutter Sts.) | 415-398-1234 | www.grandsanfrancisco.hyatt.com
Thanks to the "picture windows that inspire" its name, "you literally feel like you're on top of the world" seated on the 36th floor of the Grand Hyatt near Union Square assert vista-ficionados wowed by the "wonderful sweeping views of the city"; it's a "good place for a pre-dinner drink" and "light appetizers", and if a few mutter it's "shockingly quiet on a Saturday night" most appreciate that "nobody knows about" it.

Gravity
16 | 15 | 14 | $9

Marina | 3251 Scott St. (bet. Chestnut & Lombard Sts.) | 415-776-1928 | www.gravityroomsf.com
"Despite being unabashedly yuppie", this Marina "hot spot in a wasteland of snoozy Irish bars" is "packed" with a "young, sweaty crowd" shaking it on the "tiny dance floor" or "getting cozy on the couches" and "looking to hook up"; but it's "way too crowded" for claustrophobes, and jaded jet-setters jeer it's "living up to its name and falling at terminal velocity" – "even bridge-crossers are looking elsewhere."

Great American Music Hall
24 | 23 | 19 | $7

Tenderloin | 859 O'Farrell St. (bet. Larkin & Polk Sts.) | 415-885-0750 | www.musichallsf.com
"One of the oldest and most elaborate" live music venues around, this "absolutely beautiful" Tenderloin concert hall set in a former bordello "transports you back" to its Barbary Coast past; "even when the show is sold out, it still feels pretty roomy" – "from looks to acoustics to the music this place has it all" – including a balcony that "provides a great vantage point for shorties."

Greens Sports Bar
18 | 13 | 16 | $7

Russian Hill | 2239 Polk St. (bet. Green & Vallejo Sts.) | 415-775-4287
"Tons of sports memorabilia" and "TVs galore" are "plastered to every inch of the walls" at this "frat boy's dream" in Russian Hill where you can "chill with friends"; "it gets absolutely packed" and even "rambunctious" during games, but otherwise expect your "basic beer hall ambiance"; P.S. no food is served but you can order out "should you need to stave off drunkenness."

APPEAL | DECOR | SERVICE | COST

Grove, The

21 | 17 | 19 | $8

Marina | 2250 Chestnut St. (Avila St.) | 415-474-4843

Grove Fillmore

Pacific Heights | 2016 Fillmore St. (California St.) | 415-474-1419

The "epitome of an urban coffeehouse" complete with a "boho decor" and layabouts "milking one cup of coffee" – it's like the "loungey" *Friends* cafe of the Marina" (and Pac Heights too) cheer cohorts who "curl up with laptops" while "sunning and people-watching" on the sidewalk; sure, it's "more of a daytime, nice-weather kind of place" but "if you're not looking for a scene", "grab a bite" and a drink and "carry on a conversation" till closing time.

Grumpy's Pub

▽ 18 | 15 | 24 | $8

Embarcadero | 125 Vallejo St. (bet. Battery & Front Sts.) | 415-434-3350 | www.grumpys.ypguides.net

"Bikers, media agency types and mid-twentysomethings" who work "near Levi's Plaza" are Happy that this "excellent after-work bar" with a "cozy brick-lined interior" along the Embarcadero is so close to the office; desk jockeys tip back the pints and dig the "awesome burgers" and other "Americana" chow, tended to by "one-of-a-kind" servers; N.B. don't be Dopey and show up on Saturday, because it's closed weekends.

Ha Ra ⊭

19 | 10 | 19 | $5

Tenderloin | 875 Geary Blvd. (bet. Hyde & Larkin Sts.) | 415-673-3148

Blame the "stiff, cheap drinks": "by the end of the night, everyone" at this "true dive" in the Tenderloin "will be your new best friend"; the "feisty" bartender is either "abusive" or "an absolute sweetheart", depending on who you ask, but you don't come here for "friendly service and flashy ambiance", but because it's just a "good old-fashioned watering hole" with a "comfortable air."

Hard Rock Cafe

14 | 18 | 15 | $12

Fisherman's Wharf | Pier 39 (bet. Beach St. & The Embarcadero) | 415-956-2013 | www.hardrock.com

"If you're fighting the tourist crowds at Fisherman's Wharf anyway, you might as well" cruise over to the "most enjoyable tourist trap of them all" agree hardliners; "loud" and "upbeat", it's the "same wherever you go", with "rock 'n' roll memorabilia" taking center stage; but it's a headbanger for bashers who cry "why bother" with this "overpriced", "cheesy" experience when "there are so many other great places in the city?"

NEW Harlot

- | - | - | E

SoMa | 46 Minna St. (bet. 1st & 2nd Sts.) | 415-777-1077 | www.harlotsf.com

Veteran party promoters Martel Toler and Nabiel Musleh have teamed up with Robert Nuñez and designer Jacek Ostoya to tart up a former SoMa printing press space – think dim lighting, racy portraits and servers squeezed into lace-up bustiers; it may look like a den of iniquity, but the sin you're most likely to commit here is drinking one too many cocktails before hitting the dance floor; N.B. there's also a glass-walled smoking lounge.

	APPEAL	DECOR	SERVICE	COST

Harrington's Bar & Grill

| 17 | 14 | 17 | $7 |

Downtown | 245 Front St. (bet. California & Sacramento Sts.) | 415-392-7595
The "longtime waitresses make the regulars feel at home" at this "raucous Irish" "bar in a high-rent district" Downtown – "they don't make pubs like this anymore"; it's especially "popular after work" with "blue-collar workers rubbing elbows with white-collar ones" over a pint and "nothing fancy" fare; if a few harrumph that it's "packed" with "overgrown frat boys", even they allow "if you sit outside, you're golden."

Harris'

| 21 | 19 | 22 | $12 |

Polk Gulch | 2100 Van Ness Ave. (Pacific Ave.) | 415-673-1888 | www.harrisrestaurant.com
"Fantastic martinis" and "good jazz" (Thursday–Saturday) lure thirsty carnivores to this "very upper-crust" steakhouse on Van Ness Avenue that's "older than old-school"; sure, it's "costly", but the "excellent" staff and "very comfortable atmosphere" more than make up for "predictable" decor, though ravenous reviewers recommend "skip the bar and get a table" ("love the leather booths") for the "best steak in SF."

Harry Denton's Starlight Room

| 24 | 22 | 19 | $12 |

Downtown | Sir Francis Drake Hotel | 450 Powell St., 21st fl. (Sutter St.) | 415-395-8595 | www.harrydenton.com
It may be "retro" but there are "plenty of lessons to be learned" from this "classically cool", "sultry red" "special treat" with a "1940s elegance"; the "fantastic views" of the city from the top floor of Downtown's Sir Francis Drake Hotel give it a "great Rainbow Room feel" when live bands play on weekends, while on weeknights a "casual crowd" "dances the night away" to DJs; P.S. make a reservation or "enjoy the wait."

☒ Harry's

| 19 | 17 | 17 | $9 |

Upper Fillmore | 2020 Fillmore St. (bet. California & Pine Sts.) | 415-921-1000 | www.harrysbarsf.com
A "sceney" "standby" every night of the week, this Upper Fillmore chameleon changes its colors constantly: during happy hour, "flirtatious" regulars make eyes at each other over "excellent bar food", on Sundays the "sports rowdies descend" and on weekends, "the music and crowd get pumped up"; still, some sniff about the "yuppie-meets-fraternity" vibe, suggesting there are "too many guys who think they are 'the man.'"

Harvey's

| 18 | 14 | 19 | $8 |

Castro | 500 Castro St. (18th St.) | 415-431-4278 | www.harveyssf.com
This "low-key watering hole" "at the corner of gay ground zero at Castro and 18th Street" may be best known for its brunchtime Bloody Mary Tyler Moore (a "great way to wake up") but it's also a nighttime way station ("meet here and make your evening's plans"); the Tuesday night comedy acts, jazz on Wednesday, piano bar on Thursday and everyday "prime location" for "watching everyone walk by outside" further cements its "classic" appeal.

Hemlock Tavern ⊄

| 20 | 16 | 17 | $6 |

Polk Gulch | 1131 Polk St. (bet. Post & Sutter Sts.) | 415-923-0923 | www.hemlocktavern.com
Polk Gulch's "fine drinking and moshing establishment" is a "big hangout for the artist/hipster crowd" that "catches up-and-coming bands",

from indie rock to punk and beyond, six nights a week; "what it lacks in ambiance" "it makes up for in the mix of people", "cheap", "solid drinks" and the "sweet" enclosed smoking patio, "if that's your bag."

Hidden Vine, The

- | - | - | M

Downtown | Fitzgerald Hotel | ½ Cosmo Pl. (Taylor St.) | 415-674-3567 | www.thehiddenvine.com

Explore new worlds of reds and whites from mostly small producers at this snug nook with cushy seats and low ceilings below street level off the Fitzgerald Hotel's lobby; an enthusiastic, unpretentious staff pours 30 by the glass and, in addition to California-heavy offerings, spotlights flights from different far-flung regions; though not exactly hip, it's just the place for a charcuterie or cheese platter and quiet conversation; N.B. 20% off bottles every Friday.

Hi-Dive

- | - | - | I

Embarcadero | Pier 28½ (Bryant St.) | 415-977-0170

If you opened the window you could leap right into San Francisco Bay from this waterfront watering hole along the Embarcadero; the bare-bones, vaguely nautical decor won't win any prizes, but the view is hi on its list of charms; dive into bar-food favorites (burgers, tacos, fried calamari) if you need a nibble to go with that post- or pregame beer (AT&T Park is a short stroll away) or shots of tequila and bourbon from the tap.

HiFi

16 | 15 | 17 | $7

Marina | 2125 Lombard St. (Fillmore St.) | 415-345-8663 | www.maximumproductions.com

When "fully buzzed", a "young crowd" ("average age: 25") turns to this "nicely remodeled" "bumpin' and grindin'" Marina "oasis for drunken dancing"; the "mood lighting" sets the scene to "get your groove on", and in between moves you can retreat to the "dark corners to smooch"; but while the crowd is "solid neighborhood folks" early in the evening, later on "beware the bridge and tunnel crew."

Hime

- | - | - | E

Marina | 2353 Lombard St. (bet. Pierce & Scott Sts.) | 415-931-7900 | www.himerestaurant.com

Sushi and sake take center stage inside this sleek Marina restaurant, which blends modern touches (curved lines, black lacquered tables) with more traditional Japanese elements like a Buddha behind the bar and striking flowerlike red lamps above; never mind its Lombard location next to an IHOP – those in-the-know find the tucked-away cocktail lounge a cool sanctuary that barely hints at the surrounding hustle-bustle.

Hobson's Choice

18 | 16 | 17 | $7

Haight-Ashbury | 1601 Haight St. (Clayton St.) | 415-621-5859 | www.hobsonschoice.com

At this "crowded", "charming corner bar" in the Upper Haight with the "weird Victorian decor", the signature rum punch is "a must" – "but remember it's called 'punch' for a reason"; if you "like that liquor", you'll be in pirate's paradise – the "excellent selection" here ranges from Bacardi to Bundaberg – and "if you can actually nab a seat" "you might not want to leave"; still, lushes lament it's "too crowded by half."

	APPEAL	DECOR	SERVICE	COST

Hole in the Wall Saloon ⌦

| | 13 | 9 | 17 | $9 |

SoMa | 289 Eighth St. (Folsom St.) | 415-431-4695 |
www.holeinthewallsaloon.com

So perhaps "you're adventuresome, gay and like life a little seedy" – or you want to "scare your relatives from Ohio" – either way, this "aptly named" SoMa dive is for you; among the crowd of "bikers, pool players and druggies" you might even find "businessmen in three-piece suits rubbing elbows (and possibly more) with free spirits wearing nothing."

Homestead

| | ▽ 20 | 18 | 21 | $8 |

Mission | 2301 Folsom St. (19th St.) | 415-282-4663

If you "love that old SF vibe", this neighborhood pub on a quiet block of the Mission is "right up your alley"; the "ornate velvet" decor (which "has a certain coziness", "no matter how tacky it can sometimes look") and eye-catching faux Victorian wallpaper can't mask the fact it's just a "generally unpretentious" saloon with a "nice fire going in the corner."

NEW Horizon Restaurant & Lounge

| | – | – | – | M |

North Beach | 498 Broadway (Kearny St.) | 415-576-1118 |
www.horizonsf.com

Step into this U-shaped haven, distinctly divided into a lounge and a restaurant specializing in custom burgers, and leave North Beach's strip clubs and adult video stores behind; both halves are black from stem to stern, with jet-colored walls, barstools and couches, while a few blue neon lights recessed in the ceiling lend the space a futuristic 1980s-meets-2080 vibe; N.B. reserve a table for dinner to avoid paying cover, usually collected when live DJs spin Fridays and Saturdays.

Horseshoe Tavern

| | 18 | 12 | 21 | $6 |

Marina | 2024 Chestnut St. (bet. Fillmore & Steiner Sts.) | 415-346-1430 |
www.horseshoetavernsf.com

"Grab a couple of pints, play pool, watch the game on the tube and find a new friend to take home with you" recommend regulars who feel "lucky" to have this "small little dive" nearby; "don't show up in your ball gown" and don't worry about jockeying for attention in the "right designer shirt" – there's "less posing" at this "casual" Chestnut spot with "character" than at the "usual Marina haunts."

Hôtel Biron

| | 24 | 21 | 21 | $11 |

Hayes Valley | 45 Rose St. (bet. Gough & Market Sts.) | 415-703-0403 |
www.hotelbiron.com

Proprietary patrons pout "the word has gotten out" about this "sweet little gem" "tucked away in an alley" in Hayes Valley because they'd like to keep the "comfy couches" all to themselves; no wonder, since this "intimate" "brick-walled, candlelit" "wine bar-cum–art gallery" surely "sparks the romance" with its "outstanding" vino list and "friendly, knowledgeable folks" behind the bar.

Hotel Utah

| | 20 | 13 | 18 | $6 |

SoMa | 500 Fourth St. (Bryant St.) | 415-546-6300 |
www.thehotelutahsaloon.com

"You never know what to expect" when you check into this small SoMa saloon set in a circa-1908 building, but "up-and-coming" local "bands that have run out of room in their garage", "offbeat patrons" and "friendly bartenders" are on the list of likely suspects; supporters are psyched "it's still going strong", and suggest "grab a seat upstairs by the rail" for a "bird's-eye view" of the show.

House of Shields

16 | 13 | 17 | $7

Downtown | 39 New Montgomery St. (bet. Market & Mission Sts.) | 415-975-8651 | www.houseofshields.com

"An old-timey classic" since 1908, this "excellent happy-hour spot" Downtown could be "straight out of Philly or Boston", luring an "older crowd" with "charming" leather booths and live music a few days a week; Financial District suits size it up as a "perfect place to start your night on the town" while below-the-radar types whisper "if you're looking for a quiet place for a rendezvous, this is it."

Houston's

20 | 18 | 21 | $12

Embarcadero | 1800 Montgomery St. (The Embarcadero) | 415-392-9280 | www.houstons.com

"The bar is always hopping" at this "comfortably dark restaurant" with "top-notch" drinks, an "impressive" selection of wines by the glass and "must-nosh" "Texas-size appetizers"; "yes, it's a chain", and the "Embarcadero location is flooded with tourists, but you know what you're getting" – namely "excellent service", live jazz Sunday–Thursday and "lovely outdoor patio dining" – so "sit back and enjoy the scene."

Icon Ultra Lounge

- | - | - | E

SoMa | 1192 Folsom St. (8th St.) | 415-626-4800 | www.iconloungesf.com

Replacing the former Luna Lounge in SoMa is this sleek after-dark destination sporting a spiffy design by Charles Doell (Avalon, Red Room); the interior boasts modern lighting, mirrors, neon trim and a dance floor that's large enough to handle the crowds of house and hip-hop fans.

Il Pirata

15 | 10 | 19 | $8

Potrero Hill | 2007 16th St. (Utah St.) | 415-626-2626

Piratical Potrero Hill programmers "rub elbows with UPS drivers from next door" at this "seedy" hangout where "friendly" serving wenches dish out Italian food before tables are cleared for DJs and dancing; some nights "this is the place to be", but other evenings it's "totally dead", so do your homework first – even if the "reasonably priced" grog means you might be three sheets to the wind before the turntables spin anyway.

Impala

20 | 20 | 18 | $10

North Beach | 501 Broadway (Kearny St.) | 415-982-5299 | www.impalasf.com

"Sleek, stylish and a piece of craziness all wrapped into one", this North Beach lounge with a "Goth Mex look" does double duty as a restaurant/dance club; "tourists, bridge-and-tunnel people and locals" dine on "interesting" Nuevo Latino cuisine upstairs, while the "swanky" downstairs is full of "young" dancers in "barely there clothing" moving to "pumping music" (check out Wasted Wednesdays); you can hardly "hear yourself think" – all the "more reason to get your groove on."

Independent, The

22 | 13 | 19 | $7

Western Addition | 628 Divisadero St. (bet. Grove & Hayes Sts.) | 415-771-1420 | www.theindependentsf.com

"Not too big, not too small", this "unpretentious" club in the "sketchy" Western Addition is just right for catching "the best in up-and-coming indie rock bands", plus "killer jam bands, bluegrass/folk music, reggae and more"; no, there's "nothing special about the decor or drinks", but the "interesting crowd" appreciates the "awesome bartenders" who "always chat you up with a smile" and the "cheap and cheerful" vibe.

Ireland's 32 — 22 | 18 | 19 | $6

Inner Richmond | 3920 Geary Blvd. (3rd Ave.) | 415-386-6173 | www.irelands32.com

"Expect a little sass and a thick accent from the bartenders" at this "true Irish experience" in the Inner Richmond, which is now under new management but still a "favorite" "place to drink a beer with a former IRA member"; "put some rebel tunes on the jukebox and order a Guinness", then enjoy "classic diversions (pool table, darts, TVs)" and the "entertaining" near-nightly live music with "space enough to dance."

Irish Bank — 19 | 13 | 18 | $7

Downtown | 10 Mark Ln. (Bush St.) | 415-788-7152 | www.theirishbank.com

You "can't beat sitting in the alley on a Friday after work!" confirm Financial District desk jockeys who bank on this "crowded", "unpretentious", "hidden" bar's outdoor space on "sunny summer evenings"; but even in winter "Downtown dwellers" appreciate the "easy mixing with fellow patrons", gathering around "long wooden tables" to discuss "politics, religion, movies, you name it" over pints and "tasty" pub food.

Jack Falstaff — 20 | 22 | 19 | $13

South Beach | 598 Second St. (Brannan St.) | 415-836-9239 | www.plumpjack.com

"Swank New York meets architecturally cool San Francisco" at this "plush", "clubby" South Beach upstart; the "tiny" but "beautifully adorned bar area" is "crowded with people waiting for tables", which means you might want to "mix and mingle elsewhere", but it's a "civilized" place to "debrief with your date" over "chichi cocktails", or perhaps sip a glass of wine and spot "celebrity attraction Gavin" (Newsom, that is; his company Plumpjack owns the place).

Jade Bar — 20 | 22 | 18 | $8

Hayes Valley | 650 Gough St. (McAllister St.) | 415-869-1900 | www.jadebar.com

With its "indoor waterfall that reminds you to keep the liquor flowing", "stylish" green-tiled interior and two-way mirror in the men's bathroom for that "voyeuristic touch", "the look is Zen, but the noise level is anything but" at this tri-level hot spot; "neo-hipsters" "dig" the "fun finger food" and call the "Jade cocktail a keeper", cooing there are "lots of cozy places to relax"; still, cynics scowl it's "too done up" for Hayes Valley.

⨅ Jardinière — 26 | 27 | 24 | $13

Hayes Valley | 300 Grove St. (Franklin St.) | 415-861-5555 | www.jardiniere.com

When you're "craving champagne and oysters" before or after the show, "venture into the glam" of bygone days at Pat Kuleto's "gorgeous" bi-level Hayes Valley supper club; the recently revamped oval bar "straight out of a Fred Astaire movie" takes center stage, "providing plenty of people-watching opportunities" and the overall feel is "festive" whether you're sipping a "civilized" cocktail or dining on Traci Des Jardins' Cal-French fare; P.S. "prices match the clientele's eveningwear."

Jazz at Pearl's ⊘

24 | 19 | 18 | $17

North Beach | 256 Columbus Ave. (Broadway) | 415-291-8255 | www.jazzatpearls.com

"Jazz is the reason to go" to this "intimate" North Beach "gem" in the "old Beat poet neighborhood" where you'll find "some really big names" performing in an "irresistible" variety of styles; it's an "idyllic" "place to get lost" any night, because the talent is "fabulous", even if it's "pricey"; frugal fans suggest sitting at the bar to "save a few bucks", noting "when the music is on", nothing else matters.

Jelly's

16 | 15 | 16 | $9

China Basin | 295 Terry Francois Blvd. (Pier 50) | 415-495-3099 | www.jellyscafe.com

Open limited hours (typically Fridays–Sundays in summer, Sundays only in winter), this "upbeat" China Basin spot on the water's edge "in the middle of nowhere" gets "busy before Giants games" since it's a "quick walk to the stadium"; enjoy salsa lessons on the "neat dance floor on the pier" or just kick back on the "lovely heated patio" with a margarita.

Jillian's

18 | 18 | 15 | $9

SoMa | Sony Metreon Ctr. | 101 Fourth St. (Howard St.) | 415-369-6100 | www.jilliansbilliards.com

A 50-ft. video wall and "TV screens viewable from everywhere" make this "large", "lively" SoMa spot a "sports bar heaven" "where adults can act like children"; whether you want to "watch the big game", "shoot some pool or just chill after a movie at the Metreon", this "casual" "meeting place" fits the bill; however, chain-bashers carp about the "corporate feel" and clientele of "young" "frat boys and girls in khaki."

John Colins

22 | 21 | 24 | $8

SoMa | 90 Natoma St. (2nd St.) | 415-543-2277 | www.johncolins.com

Catch the scene at this "sophisticated" SoMa spot during happy hour, when working stiffs in "blue shirts and khakis" "hang from the rafters"; later on, "things quiet down" as it "morphs into a hip neighborhood joint" with a "late-night dance crowd"; the "hot" "boys behind the bar are the real stars", though, and their "easygoing manner rubs off on the patrons", who "always have a fantastic cocktail in hand."

Johnny Foley's

19 | 18 | 18 | $7

Downtown | 243 O'Farrell St. (bet. Mason & Powell Sts.) | 415-954-0777 | www.johnnyfoleys.com

This "loud", "cavernous" public house just off Union Square "has all the Irish pub qualities in spades": the "welcoming" 'tenders serve "cold drafts and stiff drinks" (try the "killer Bloody Marys"), and "there's great pub grub" too; join the "convivial" crowd downstairs and "enjoy the music and a draft" – "trust me, you won't be disappointed"; still, killjoys hiss "too many backwards-cap-wearing tourists."

John's Grill

21 | 18 | 19 | $11

Downtown | 63 Ellis St. (bet. Powell & Stockton Sts.) | 415-986-0069 | www.johnsgrill.com

"If you're a Dashiell Hammett fan", make a trip to this "tiny", circa-1908 "SF landmark" where his "memory is enshrined everywhere" – little wonder since the author wrote scenes from his novel *The Maltese Falcon* there; it's "one of the last of the old-time Downtown hangouts", and you may find "*San Francisco Chronicle* reporters drinking and eating" dishes like Sam Spade's lamb chops and listening to live jazz.

jovino

| - | - | - | M |

Cow Hollow | 2184 Union St. (bet. Fillmore & Webster Sts.) | 415-563-1853
The Ace Wasabi's/Tokyo Go Go folks are also behind this Cow Hollow cafe, which with a grown-up focus on wine, sangria, coffee and sandwiches turns the volume down for a softer-rock version of the neighborhood's typically raging nighttime festivities; in other words, read a book, meet your date and dine with conversation in the light-colored wood-trimmed room, but don't expect to dance on anyone's table.

Kan Zaman

| 22 | 19 | 17 | $10 |

Haight-Ashbury | 1793 Haight St. (Shrader St.) | 415-751-9656
A bit of the "Middle East in the middle of San Francisco, complete with live belly dancing" and a hookah bar where you can "pick up a pipe filled with some apricot tobacco", this "unique" Haight-Ashbury hangout has a "chill" "hippie" vibe; there's "always a packed house" of "large parties" sharing meze and drinking mint tea, beer and "spiced wine (lovely on a chilly night)", though a few quibble about the "variable" service.

Kate O'Brien's

| 17 | 12 | 18 | $7 |

SoMa | 579 Howard St. (bet. 1st & 2nd Sts.) | 415-882-7240
"After a long day in the office", SoMa suit monkeys (mostly a "local tech crowd") who want to "get that work colleague drunk" swarm to this "solid" pub with the "super-nice staff"; it's "an Irish bar like it should be", with a "cool wood interior" and "little booth areas" conducive to "good conversation" over pints and "decent grub."

Kelley's Tavern

| 18 | 19 | 17 | $8 |

Marina | 3231 Fillmore St. (bet. Greenwich & Lombard Sts.) | 415-567-7181 | www.kelleystavern.com
You'll see "at least one person you know" at this Marina haunt decked out "like your cool parents' basement" with flat-screen TVs and packed with "friendly" folks "from a six-block radius", playing darts or shuffleboard or listening to live music on Wednesdays; slip into an "armchair next to the fireplace, sip your drink and talk to the hottie" nearby – "what's better?"; still, if you're a thirtysomething, "stay clear" – unless you like hanging with "lots of recent college grads."

Kelly's Mission Rock

| 19 | 15 | 16 | $9 |

China Basin | 817 China Basin Way (Mariposa St.) | 415-626-5355 | www.kellysmissionrock.com
"Couldn't live without" this "funky" "good escape" agree Rock-solid fans who bypass the "loftlike" restaurant to hang outside on the "huge patio overlooking the Bay" in China Basin; it's a "great layout", especially when the DJs kick in, spinning reggae, house and Top 40 during the summer – and you can also stop by for "sunny Sunday morning fun" or afternoon cocktails, but call first, because they often host private parties.

Kennedy's Irish Pub & Curry House

| 21 | 12 | 18 | $5 |

North Beach | 1040 Columbus Ave. (bet. Chestnut & Francisco Sts.) | 415-441-8855 | www.kennedyscurry.com
Aye, a "curry house inside of an Irish bar" may look like a "holodeck error from *Star Trek*" but the reality is "perfection" – "where else can you get

tikka masala with a pitcher of Fat Tire" but this "funky" North Beach pub?; pick from "tons of different beers" and "drink on the cheap" then entertain yourself with "loads of pool tables, darts and arcade games."

Kezar Bar   18 | 14 | 19 | $7

Cole Valley | 900 Cole St. (Carl St.) | 415-681-7678
A "J Crew crowd" congregates at these Cole Valley confines to "catch sports games, hang out and grub on some nachos and wings" ("truly a notch above most bar food"); considering the "cozy atmosphere" and the "super-friendly staff" that "has mastered the art of drink improvisation", it's no wonder that neighbors call it a "good old standby."

Kezar Pub & Restaurant   19 | 13 | 18 | $6

Haight-Ashbury | 770 Stanyan St. (bet. Beulah & Waller Sts.) | 415-386-9292
"If you want game, that is, any sport, any time", no matter how "random" the international soccer or rugby match, you can take 'em all in on the 17 big-screen plasma TVs at this "friendly" "dude hangout" in Haight-Ashbury "filled with kickballers, triathletes" and the "backwards-cap crew"; "breakfast and beer for a morning game can't be beat", but remember, it's also a "fine place for fried nibbles" and "strong drinks."

Kilowatt ⇄   22 | 15 | 18 | $5

Mission | 3160 16th St. (bet. Guerrero & Valencia Sts.) | 415-861-2595 | www.barbell.com/kilowatt
"Rock stars, hipsters and street youth unite" with a "rough-and-tumble crowd" at this "usually loud and raucous" bar; "cheap drinks" (including "tons of beer on tap"), "no hype" and a "great staff (minus one frosty bartendress)" make it the Mission choice for "hanging out with a group of friends and drinking until the pool balls stop dropping."

Knockout, The ⇄   23 | 18 | 21 | $5

Mission | 3223 Mission St. (Valencia St.) | 415-550-6994 | www.theknockoutsf.com
Truly a "super-fun" stop "on a bar hop through the Mission", this hangout lures a "cool crowd (maybe too cool)" with "unique drink specials", DJs and "kickass bands" and "awesome" Thursday night bingo ("you get a card with each beer and can win ghetto-fab prizes"); you "feel more punk just going here", even when just "muggin' in the photo booth."

Knuckles Sports Bar   18 | 16 | 16 | $9

Fisherman's Wharf | Hyatt at Fisherman's Wharf | 555 N. Point St. (Taylor St.) | 415-563-1234 | www.knucklessportsbar.com
Knuckleheads note it's "hard to decide which huge TV to look at" at this "typical sports bar" in the Hyatt at Fisherman's Wharf; given the location, it's no surprise "you'll meet your fair share of out-of-towners", and sure, it's a bit "corporate", but with "all the games on, all the time plus popcorn", fans cheer it as "a great place" to cheer on your team.

❷ Kokkari Estiatorio   25 | 25 | 23 | $13

Downtown | 200 Jackson St. (Front St.) | 415-981-0983 | www.kokkari.com
"Every star in the city eventually passes through" the "welcoming doors" of this "ultrachic Greek" go-to destination that makes you feel "transported to someplace exotic"; though it's a "busy afternoon watering hole for the Downtown crew", it's "better at night with your paramour" when you can slip into the "small" bar area, order "light yet

luscious" "nibbles" and "let the wine flow" – yes, this "taverna has got things figured out"; P.S. "if you can, stay for dinner."

NEW Koko Cocktails ⊘
— | — | — | M

Polk Gulch | 1060 Geary St. (bet. Polk St. & Van Ness Ave.) | 415-885-4788

In early 2008, this longtime Polk Gulch dive got an out-and-out overhaul and new owners, formerly from the Tunnel Top; a neon sign still marks the entrance and the vibe inside is still unpretentious, with dim lighting and low ceilings creating a womblike feel; a DJ often spins in one dark corner, but instead of dancing, the barflies are busy nursing stiff cocktails and canoodling on the refurbished church pews that serve as seating.

Kuleto's
— | — | — | E

Downtown | Villa Florence Hotel | 221 Powell St. (Geary St.) | 415-397-7720 | www.kuletos.com

A wine bar adds legs to this longstanding Downtown Italian favorite, offering some 40 choices by the glass or taste (more by the bottle) in a cozy space tucked between the restaurant's main dining room and the Villa Florence Hotel; sip a Super Tuscan while munching bruschetta, polenta or anything from the full dinner menu.

Larry Flynt's Hustler Club
15 | 15 | 17 | $15

North Beach | 1031 Kearny St. (bet. Broadway & Columbus Ave.) | 415-434-1301 | www.hustlerclubsf.com

"Quick service by an attractive staff" and dancers with a "variety of body types" (some of whom impress with their "acrobatics on the pole") make this "gentleman's bar" a "refreshing change" of pace from others of its ilk note North Beach nabobs who don't mind "pricey drinks" (it's "to be expected"); but taskmasters tut about "tame topless dancing" and suggest this "tacky" club is "trying too hard."

La Scene Café & Bar
▽ 16 | 17 | 19 | $11

Downtown | Warwick Regis Hotel | 490 Geary St. (Taylor St.) | 415-292-6430 | www.warwickhotels.com

The "sedate, quiet" restaurant in Downtown's Warwick Regis Hotel is packed before curtain time with diners indulging in Californian cuisine or perhaps just a pre-performance cocktail; though it's certainly "convenient" to the Tenderloin theater scene, ageists gripe about the crowd of "older theatergoers", sniping "my grandparents would love this place", because it's "slow and tired, just like them."

Laszlo
20 | 21 | 19 | $9

Mission | 2534 Mission St. (bet. 21st & 22nd Sts.) | 415-401-0810 | www.laszlobar.com

Dim lighting gives this "gorgeous nightspot" next to Foreign Cinema a "mysterious atmosphere", attracting "young, hip, upscale" Missionites who want to "meet a date", "chill out with friends" or sway to the DJs every night; "great mixologists, for both the music and the martinis", are pluses, but the hard of hearing shout it's "too loud" and "a disappointment", especially when compared to the "lovely restaurant it sits within."

Latin American Club ⊘
22 | 18 | 20 | $6

Mission | 3286 22nd St. (bet. Mission & Valencia Sts.) | 415-647-2732

"It's not Latin, and it's not a club, but it *is* one of the best bars in town" announce proprietary Missionaries who preach the praises of this "locals' favorite"; the "homey, quirky decor", "friendly bartenders" and "mellow feel" make it "good for late-night relaxation", but watch out for the "super-strong drinks", like the "margaritas made in a pint glass" (just "leave before three" go down the hatch).

🆕 La Trappe

- | - | - | M

North Beach | 800 Greenwich St. (Mason St.) | 415-440-8727

Quietude reigns upstairs where diners nibble on cheese plates and tuck into hearty rabbit stew, but head down the spiral staircase and you'll find all the action at this North Beach newcomer whose pewlike wooden benches, brick walls and faux barrel-vaulted ceiling set a scene that's reminiscent of a Trappist monastery; no hard liquor is served and the wine selection is sparse, but the Belgian brew list is so long that the drinks menu has a table of contents.

🆕 Lava Lounge

- | - | - | M

SoMa | 527 Bryant St. (bet. 4th & Ritch Sts.) | 415-777-1333 | www.lavasf.com

Bearing little resemblance to the space's former occupant (the divey Eagle Drift-In), this SoMa lounge attracts an after-work crowd with its flat-screen TVs, pop music and minimalist aesthetic; comfortable seating abounds, including a long bar as well as tables in back and up front by the window; N.B. a seafood-and-steak menu is in the works.

Le Central Bistro

21 | 18 | 21 | $12

Downtown | 453 Bush St. (bet. Grant Ave. & Kearny St.) | 415-391-2233 | www.lecentralbistro.com

"It feels like Paris" at this Downtown "institution" where you might "catch the city's movers and shakers" sipping wine in the brick-walled bar area or supping on "solid bistro food"; traditionalists tout the "polite staff" and "great value" drinks, but a few wags warn it's "tired" and say the only celebrities you'll see here are "out-of-power politicos."

🆕 Le Club

- | - | - | E

Nob Hill | 1250 Jones St. (Clay St.) | 415-922-2582 | www.leclubsf.com

Once a 1970s nightspot known by the same name, and more recently C&L Steakhouse, this reservations-only lounge/restaurant in an apartment building atop Nob Hill feels like a posh private British club, replete with leather wingback chairs, velvet drapes, mirrors and a purple billiards room; hobnob with the well-dressed crowd clustered around tiny, marble-topped tables or draped over the onyx bar, sip classic cocktails, then drop into the parlor for a civilized game of chess; N.B. Continental fare is served Wednesday-Sunday.

ⓏLe Colonial

24 | 25 | 19 | $12

Downtown | 20 Cosmo Pl. (Taylor St.) | 415-931-3600 | www.lecolonialsf.com

Yes, it's "secluded", but that's what "makes it a cool place to get a drink" declare acolytes of this "beautiful, Indochine-style" bi-level French-Vietnamese restaurant Downtown that's "so sexy, so romantic" it gives you "goosebumps"; "go upstairs, snag a lounging area and pretend you're in Bali" while sipping "fantastic" "fruity drinks" and "sampling crispy hot and cold treats" – or come for the live music and DJs Wednesday–Saturday – there's "some serious grinding going on."

	APPEAL	DECOR	SERVICE	COST

Left at Albuquerque

| | 15 | 14 | 14 | $8 |

Cow Hollow | 2140 Union St. (bet. Fillmore & Webster Sts.) | 415-749-6700 | www.leftatalb.com

The "tequila selection rocks" at this Cow Hollow chain link, with a branch in Campbell (and Santa Barbara too); "nice strong margaritas" and "more chips than you could ever eat" are "perfect after work", but surveyors are split on the restaurant's charms; Left-leaners find the "nice outdoor seating area" a "decent spot to hang and people-watch", but others yap about the "yuppie clientele" and "corporate" feel.

Lefty O'Doul's

| | 17 | 15 | 18 | $7 |

Downtown | 333 Geary St. (bet. Mason & Powell Sts.) | 415-982-8900 | www.leftyodouls.biz

"Half hofbrau, half sports bar", with a smidgen of piano bar thrown in, this "classic" Downtown multitasker near Union Square "has it all"; the folks who "grab a pint" and a "great-big" "corned-beef sandwich" tend to be "older men", and the "servers have been there longer than most people in the Marina have been alive", but once the musician tickles the ivories, even the "rowdy college crowd" "can't help but join in with the singing."

Levende

| | 22 | 23 | 18 | $11 |

Mission | 1710 Mission St. (Duboce Ave.) | 415-864-5585 | www.levendesf.com

"Don't let the blah storefront deter you from checking out" this "sexy", "trendy" Mission mecca; inside is "a perfect mix of all the ingredients that make a lounge worthwhile", including "a long list of drinks", "delectable food that's not too damaging to a budget", "awesome" DJs and "lots of pretty people"; still, the put-off pout about "prima donna bartenders" with "attitude", suggesting it's "begun a slide downhill"; N.B. there's also an Oakland offshoot.

Lexington Club ⚐

| | 19 | 13 | 19 | $6 |

Mission | 3464 19th St. (bet. Mission & Valencia Sts.) | 415-863-2052 | www.lexingtonclub.com

Perhaps the "only real dyke bar in SF", this "low-key hangout" with a "great jukebox" is full of "hip and hot girls of all kinds"; "it can get a little sceney, with every lesbian under 30" in the Mission here on some nights, but if you just want to "catch a drink and play some pool", or maybe "meet someone new for the night", "you'll never be disappointed."

Liberties, The

| | ▽ 17 | 16 | 18 | $6 |

Mission | 998 Guerrero St. (22nd St.) | 415-282-6789 | www.theliberties.com

"Hot waitresses with Irish accents" sling bottles of Chimay, pints of Guinness and mixed drinks along with no-fuss fare like fish 'n' chips and bangers and mash at "ye good olde pub", regarded by some Gaelic groupies as the "perfect neighborhood spot"; still, a minority takes the liberty of saying that it's a "bit dull and snobby for the Mission."

Liberty Cafe & Bakery

| | 20 | 17 | 20 | $8 |

Bernal Heights | 410 Cortland Ave. (Bennington St.) | 415-695-1311 | www.thelibertycafe.com

Thursday through Saturday, the bakery behind this "warmly welcoming" Bernal Heights eatery morphs into a "sweet" wine bar, an

APPEAL DECOR SERVICE COST

"earthy", "calm", no-reservations "oasis off Cortland Avenue" offering a "decent" vino selection and "nibbles"; in the "slightly upscale" restaurant itself, "good for dinner, not for a crazy night out", everything is "delightful", including the famed chicken pot pie, which is "worth the sale of your firstborn."

Z Lime
21 | 24 | 18 | $11

Castro | 2247 Market St. (bet. Noe & Sanchez Sts.) | 415-621-5256 | www.lime-sf.com

The "super-groovy" *Buck Rogers*–meets-*Barbarella* "futuristic" decor at this "flashy", "zany" "place to be seen" in the Castro attracts an "interesting mix" of "queers, metrosexuals and hip straight girls"; "cheers to the chef" for the "smashing small plates" and to the "cocktails that pack a punch" served by a "sexy (if slow) staff"; still, a few snark that its initial popularity has faded, making it a "has-been that barely ever was."

Lingba Lounge
18 | 16 | 17 | $8

Potrero Hill | 1469 18th St. (bet. Connecticut & Missouri Sts.) | 415-355-0001 | www.lingba.com

"Watch out for that flaming" 'Bowl of Monkeys' drink at Potrero Hill's "jungle-themed" "low-key tiki bar" with Thai food – it's just one of many "good libations" you'll feel as you groove to the almost nightly "upbeat DJ music"; if the drinks don't "kick-start a slow conversation", perhaps the "interesting nature videos" flickering on the wall – or Sunday's slightly "scary" 'Karaoke Shark!' night – will.

Lion Pub, The ⊄
21 | 19 | 18 | $8

Pacific Heights | 2062 Divisadero St. (bet. California & Sacramento Sts.) | 415-567-6565

"Originally a gay hangout", this "small", "homey" pub is now the "go-to bar for strawberry mojitos and pints of Stella Artois for the Pacific Heights crowd"; "cozy up to the fireplace" with "must-have" "drinks made with fresh-squeezed juices" and "free nightly nibbles" and you just might find a date, since it's a "serious singles scene"; good thing the jukebox is "not too loud, so conversations are easy to hear."

Li Po ⊄
22 | 17 | 19 | $6

Chinatown | 916 Grant Ave. (Washington St.) | 415-982-0072

"Straight out of *Big Trouble in Little China*", the cult flick, that is, this "mysterious Chinatown dump" that "smacks of days gone by" "beckons you in, and the next thing you know, you're hammered"; the big red booths, "large Buddha" and "eclectic jukebox" are all part of the charm, as are some of the city's "nicest bartenders", who pour potent drinks that just may "knock you on your keister."

Z Little Shamrock ⊄
25 | 20 | 24 | $6

Inner Sunset | 807 Lincoln Way (9th Ave.) | 415-661-0060

"With an odd assortment of young" "UCSF students" and "old-timers who look like they've been warming those barstools since the place opened" in 1894, this Inner Sunset Irish bar "hasn't changed in years", which suits regulars just fine; with "friendly service", "comfy chairs", backgammon and darts, it's the "homiest" haunt to "hang after a romp" in Golden Gate Park, and "if you snag one of the couches, you're set for hours."

	APPEAL	DECOR	SERVICE	COST

Liverpool Lil's
21 | 19 | 22 | $8

Cow Hollow | 2942 Lyon St. (bet. Greenwich & Lombard Sts.) | 415-921-6664 |
www.liverpoollils.com

"Beloved" for its "diverse crowd", this "nice little nook" in Cow Hollow "hidden next to the Presidio" and now owned by Brazen Head's proprietor "pulls in neighborhood regulars, from scruffy windsurfers and über-polished socialites", to young "dinks" and "blue hairs", with the promise of "meat-and-potato dishes accompanied by lots of beer"; "awesome" bartenders (perhaps the city's "wittiest") and an "old-school ambiance" make you feel as if you've stumbled upon a "tiny hidden pub in London."

☑ Lobby Lounge at Ritz-Carlton
25 | 26 | 26 | $16

Nob Hill | Ritz-Carlton | 600 Stockton St. (Pine St.) | 415-296-7465 |
www.ritzcarlton.com

It's "very ritzy" indeed in the "swank" Ritz-Carlton lounge, the perfect "place for self-indulgence", "to impress your date" or "to seal a deal"; on the weekends, "charming tea-time treats" are on tap, but when the live harpist performs on weekends, this "highfalutin" "class" act "demands a flute of champagne" or a hard-to-find scotch; the "fantastic" service and "elegant decor" come at a price, though, so "bring a full wallet."

☑ Lobby Lounge at the St. Regis Hotel
25 | 27 | 25 | $13

SoMa | St. Regis Hotel | 125 Third St. (Minna St.) | 415-284-4000 |
www.stregis.com

The "sleek, modern" lobby of SoMa's St. Regis Hotel, with its "conversation-instigating art", is a "very elegant, hip spot to gather" for an after-work or pre-dinner cocktail; "some of the best drink mixology in the city is going on here" maintain enthusiasts who also nosh on "nibbles like cheese straws, wasabi peas and spiced almonds"; "everything's top-shelf", so "be prepared to pay handsomely."

NEW Local Kitchen & Wine Merchant
- | - | - | M

SoMa | 330 First St. (bet. Folsom & Harrison Sts.) | 415-777-4200 |
www.sf-local.com

Once you figure out how to operate the enormous glass doors, you'll find yourself in a slick SoMa outpost of postmodern cool (think stark white walls, wooden banquettes, communal tables, barstools overlooking the open kitchen); the regionally sourced Californian-Mediterranean menu, featuring thin-crust pizzas blistered in the wood-burning oven, is dwarfed by the global wine list, with selections from France and Italy, plus unexpected places like Greece, Japan and even India.

London Wine Bar
18 | 15 | 18 | $10

Downtown | 415 Sansome St. (Sacramento St.) | 415-788-4811

"Billed as the first wine bar in America" (and "looking like it hasn't been updated since"), this "snug", "unpretentious" Downtowner is a "real find" for grape nuts; the "wonderful" staffers "really know their stuff", "helping you through the long" California-centric list, including "different, obscure" vinos; but while it's "good for an after-work drink", crushed winos wail "sadly, it closes" around 9 PM weeknights and isn't open on weekends.

	APPEAL	DECOR	SERVICE	COST

Lone Palm

22 | 18 | 21 | $7

Mission | 3394 22nd St. (Guerrero St.) | 415-648-0109 | www.lonepalmbar.com

With a "sophisticated, retro feel", "white tablecloths" and "lots of couples holding hands and cuddling", this "classy" yet "amazingly laid-back" bar is "as fancy as it gets in the Mission"; it's "worth checking out" for the "cheap and strong" cocktails shaken and stirred by "very nice bartenders", especially since it's "a great respite from the Valencia Street strip" and "often has tables when its competitors are packed."

Lone Star Saloon

20 | 15 | 21 | $7

SoMa | 1354 Harrison St. (bet. 9th & 10th Sts.) | 415-863-9999 | www.lonestarsaloon.com

"Bears and cubs and boys, oh my!" sigh "big burly men", "trapper guys" and "chubby chasers" who "rub bellies with local and traveling" grizzlies at this "no-frills SoMa" lair, "a little mecca known worldwide among the hairy crowd"; the 'Beer Bust' on Sunday is as "mandatory as going to church that morning, and perhaps as ritualistic" – just "get there early" before it gets swamped.

NEW LookOut, The

- | - | - | M

Castro | 3600 16th St. (bet. Castro & Market Sts.) | 415-703-9750

At this casual Castro hangout, a largely gay (but straight- and women-friendly) crew keeps a constant lookout for strong cocktails and affordable bar bites; the bare-bones interior hasn't changed much from its Metro City Bar days, but neither has the balcony's streetside view, which makes it a popular spot for cruising without leaving your barstool.

Lou's Pier 47

22 | 18 | 22 | $12

Fisherman's Wharf | 300 Jefferson St. (Al Scoma Way) | 415-771-5687 | www.louspier47.com

"Even if you've never heard of the band", you're bound to hear "fabulous" "authentic blues" seven nights a week at this "classic" spot on the water at Fisherman's Wharf; after chowing down on Cajun cuisine, music lovers mosey upstairs to the club, where the "friendly crowd" is "having "far too much fun to be legal" (maybe it has something to do with the house specialty, an astounding 60-ounce margarita).

Lucky 13 ₪

24 | 17 | 20 | $6

Castro | 2140 Market St. (bet. Church & Sanchez Sts.) | 415-487-1313

"Loud, hip and grungy", this Upper Market mainstay offers a "punk vibe for grown-ups", thanks in part to the "best jukebox in the city"; yeah, it's "a little rough around the edges", but the "fantastic assortment of European beers on tap", "knowledgeable bartenders" and "really cool clientele" make it "my kinda place" "for meeting up with boozin' buddies" and "sparking up a conversation."

Luella

▽ 23 | 22 | 24 | $14

Russian Hill | 1896 Hyde St. (Green St.) | 415-674-4343 | www.luellasf.com

When you're looking for a "more adult scene", stop into this "soothing" Mediterranean restaurant in Russian Hill run by "the nicest couple" for a pre-dinner libation; "they think of everything to make it a lovely experience" sigh habitués who nibble on pizzetta and polenta fries while clinking "classy" cocktails; but others shrug it's "not someplace to just go for a drink", preferring to sit down over a "terrific" meal.

Luna Park
20 | 20 | 19 | $10

Mission | 694 Valencia St. (18th St.) | 415-553-8584 | www.lunaparksf.com

"They put the fun back into cocktails" applaud Luna-tics, over the moon about the "top-notch mojitos" made with "fresh ingredients" and poured by a "cheerful staff" at this Mission restaurant; park yourself in the "cool bar" with a "lively", "real San Francisco feel", order a drink (and "at least a bit of food, it's definitely worth it") and enjoy the equally "homey, delicious atmosphere"; P.S it's a "scene on weekend nights."

Lush Lounge ⊅
21 | 21 | 22 | $8

Polk Gulch | 1092 Post St. (Polk St.) | 415-771-2022 | www.thelushlounge.com

What a "great mix of people" – every "age, gender, sexual orientation and race", including a number of "gender benders" – "hangs out and enjoys the evening", sipping "inventive cocktails and drink specials", like "lemondrops made with fresh-squeezed lemons" at this "low-key but stylish" Polk Street pub; "cute bartenders" add to its "all-time favorite" status – this "upbeat" lounge spilleth over with "great personality."

Lusty Lady ⊅
▽ 13 | 7 | 15 | $6

North Beach | 1033 Kearny St. (Broadway) | 415-391-3991 | www.lustyladysf.com

"No need to bring your quarters anymore – the dollar machines are more than happy to take your money" at the country's first union-organized "independent strip club" in North Beach; no drinks are served but horny peeps can peer through the spy holes ("don't touch anything – you'll stick to the walls") and watch girls disrobe on the dance floor; still, even lusty lads guffaw "how gross can one place be?"

Mad Dog in the Fog ⊅
18 | 14 | 18 | $6

Lower Haight | 530 Haight St. (bet. Fillmore & Steiner Sts.) | 415-626-7279

This "comfortable British pub" in the Lower Haight "does the trick" for sports fans ("mostly U.K. transplants") looking to "watch *real* football" (that's soccer to you Yanks); it's a "friendly" place "to meet up with friends", especially on Tuesday and Thursday nights when trivia "night is happening" – and "always consistent – like the family dog waiting at the door when you come home from work"; P.S. "no full bar."

Madrone Lounge
21 | 20 | 18 | $7

Western Addition | 500 Divisadero St. (Fell St.) | 415-241-0202 | www.madronelounge.com

A "young", "bouncy" crowd fills this "inviting" space somewhat reminiscent of a "cool, random New York bar" with "eclectic furniture"; maybe it's the "funky art" that changes frequently, or the "tasty" "infused vodkas" or the "comfy couches", but admirers muse "it may not get any better than this"; still, some Mad-sters aren't glad about the "ridiculous" cover charge on some nights, griping "what's the Marina doing in the Western Addition?"

	APPEAL	DECOR	SERVICE	COST

Magnolia Pub & Brewery

| 23 | 18 | 20 | $8 |

Haight-Ashbury | 1398 Haight St. (Masonic Ave.) | 415-864-7468 | www.magnoliapub.com

"If you consider yourself a beer connoisseur, you know" this "Haight-hip" haunt with an "old-fashioned hippie vibe" – or should – confirm suds-meisters who bubble enthusiastically about the "wittily named brews" handcrafted on-site; "get lost in" the "psychedelic art" on the walls, and chow down on "wonderful" wings and things too; still, fence-sitters shrug it "won't blow you away but will always leave you satisfied."

Make-Out Room ⇗

| 22 | 19 | 20 | $6 |

Mission | 3225 22nd St. (bet. Mission & Valencia Sts.) | 415-647-2888 | www.makeoutroom.com

With its "creepy yet appealing '70s hunting lodge feel – or is it a rec center dancehall?" – this Mission "meet market" is "where the cool kids go"; "interesting" bands play on the "raised stage with a red curtain backdrop", while on other nights DJs "throw down beats you can dance to"; if some kissy faces confide "never made-out with anyone here", they can't blame their scoreless status on the "strong, cheap" drinks.

ⓩ Mandarin Lounge

| 27 | 27 | 26 | $15 |

Downtown | Mandarin Oriental Hotel | 222 Sansome St. (Pine Sts.) | 415-276-9888 | www.mandarinoriental.com

The piano player quietly noodles in the background at this cocktail lounge attached to the ground-floor lobby of Downtown's Mandarin Oriental Hotel; there's "not much of a scene beyond hotel guests" and middle-age suits unwinding after a day's work or finishing up business with clients over a quick one – but "exquisite" potables like the lychee martini make this a "very cool place for a drink and people-watching."

Mario's Bohemian Cigar Store Cafe

| 23 | 18 | 19 | $8 |

North Beach | 566 Columbus Ave. (Union St.) | 415-362-0536

"Wonderful" sandwiches made with "friggin' fantastic focaccia" – the "best panini in San Francisco by a wide margin" – and the "signature" cappuccino are what lure locals to this "magical" "institution" overlooking Washington Square; "don't tell the tourists" whisper bohemians who "cherish" "watching North Beach pass them by" at one of the "inviting window-side tables" or while sitting outside and drinking "affordable red wine" or a "great beer on tap."

MarketBar

| 18 | 18 | 15 | $10 |

Embarcadero | Ferry Bldg. | 1 Ferry Bldg. (Market St.) | 415-434-1100 | www.marketbar.com

What a "wonderful place to play hooky" and "waste away" a "sunny Friday afternoon" rave ray-seekers who quaff Cosmos during the "awesome happy hours" on the outdoor patio of this restaurant/bar, located along the Embarcadero in the "beautiful" Ferry Building; but it's also an "ever-popular watering hole for commuters" and visitors, which may account for the "tourist-class service" and "ridiculously loud" chatter.

Marlena's ⇗

| 18 | 15 | 19 | $7 |

Hayes Valley | 488 Hayes St. (Octavia St.) | 415-864-6672 | www.marlenasbarsf.com

"One part neighborhood bar, one part transvestite haunt", this Hayes Valley "hoot" and a half is the "real thing, folks"; put yourself in the hands of "Marlena, the high priestess of drag, and her following who call" this "divey trannie bar" home, and make everyone feel like they "belong" – and "be sure to catch the show" on Saturdays (yes, the "dude looks like a lady") and the seasonal decorations – what a "riot."

Mars Bar

| 17 | 12 | 20 | $7 |

SoMa | 798 Brannan St. (7th St.) | 415-621-6277 | www.marsbarsf.com
Bartenders that are "friendlier than most" serve "strong drinks" at this SoMa spot, ensuring that everyone can kick back and have a "good time"; it's out of this world for "big groups and parties", thanks in part to the closed-in patio with "powerhouse heaters" that "keep it comfortable" all year long; still, gripers grumble, it's "beyond its prime."

Martuni's

| 22 | 17 | 22 | $8 |

Civic Center | 4 Valencia St. (Market St.) | 415-241-0205 |
www.martunis.ypguides.net

The "sing-along piano bar" is the "hallmark" of this "dimly lit" "Rat Pack–style" Civic Center "must for the cabaret crowd"; it's a "friendly place that welcomes gay and straight alike", and "even the mutest wallflower would be hard-pressed to not strike up a conversation" – or even join in the show tunes – especially after a few "strong" drinks ("it's all about" the "flavored martinis") served by the "sassy staff."

Mas Sake Freestyle Sushi

| 19 | 18 | 17 | $9 |

Marina | 2030 Lombard St. (bet. Fillmore & Webster Sts.) | 415-440-1505 |
www.massake.com

"Hot waitresses" sling "shots and sake bombs" along with "quality" fin fare while a DJ spins "awesome music" in the background at this "extremely loud" Marina hideout where you can "hang out and see beautiful people"; the formula works for "guys on the prowl" who come to "drink and flirt", but detractors hiss "don't forget your tight clothes or fake boobs" – "it's like Hooters for sushi."

NEW Matador

| - | - | - | M |

SoMa | 10 Sixth St. (Market St.) | 415-863-4629
Although it's still a bit of a dive, this SoMa addition has spruced up predecessor Arrow Bar's cavelike decor with dark crimson walls and (naturally) portraits of gender-bending bullfighters; an upgraded sound system and DJs encourage dancing, especially on Friday nights, when the music tends toward house and techno.

☑ MatrixFillmore

| 21 | 24 | 16 | $10 |

Cow Hollow | 3138 Fillmore St. (bet. Filbert & Greenwich Sts.) |
415-563-4180 | www.matrixfillmore.com

This "sleek" lounge is "still the 'it' place in Cow Hollow", thanks to its "snazzy" decor, "super-cool fireplace that casts the perfect light" and "über-fashionable" flock of "pretty twentysomethings" sipping "pricey potions"; but jaded jet-setters jeer that service can be "slow and attitude-y" on "busy" weekend nights, when there are "too many people" of the "self-important variety" "trying too hard."

Mauna Loa ⌿

| 17 | 11 | 17 | $6 |

Cow Hollow | 3009 Fillmore St. (Union St.) | 415-563-5137
Perhaps "the closest thing to a dive bar in Cow Hollow", this "dark" "hole-in-the-wall" is where locals "come to let their hair down after

APPEAL | DECOR | SERVICE | COST

primping for the other spots in the area"; there are "lots of toys", like a "basketball hoop, pool tables and table hockey", to keep you entertained, which helps explain why the "friendly, fun regulars" overlook that "it smells a bit like spilled beer."

Maya
20 | 20 | 21 | $10

SoMa | 303 Second St. (bet. Folsom & Harrison Sts.) | 415-543-2928 | www.mayasf.com
Truly "the best happy hour around" boast buffs of botanas, the "delicious free" bite-size south-of-the-border snacks served weekdays with five-buck drinks at this "modern Mexican" spot in SoMa; you "can't go wrong with the mojitos" or the margaritas in "various flavors", some served with fresh muddled fruit – "I adore Maya!"; but not everyone idolizes this civilized standby – a few faultfinders feel it's a "bit suburban."

McCormick & Kuleto's
20 | 21 | 20 | $13

Fisherman's Wharf | Ghirardelli Sq. | 900 N. Point St. (Larkin St.) | 415-929-1730 | www.mccormickandkuletos.com
An "appealing" "place to duck into to escape the fog" when you're at Fisherman's Wharf, this "lovely" chain link offers "floor-to-ceiling windows overlooking the Bay"; sure, you "pay for the beautiful view" in the form of "pricey" potions served by the "extremely entertaining" bartenders, and some sniff it's a "little stuffy", but vista-ficionados insist it's "not just for tourists."

Mecca
22 | 24 | 19 | $13

Castro | 2029 Market St. (bet. Church & Delores Sts.) | 415-621-7000 | www.sfmecca.com
Slip into your "latest Dolce & Gabbana" get-up and "check out the other guppies parading their designer" duds at this "stylish" restaurant/bar in the Castro that's even more "slinky" following a major renovation; though the "staffers can pitch attitude, all is forgiven" since they're "so very easy on the eyes", and they leave "killer cocktails" and "tasty appetizers" in their wake; "do expect to pay top dollar", but "it's worth it" considering "just being there makes you sexier."

☒ Medjool
23 | 22 | 15 | $9

Mission | 2522 Mission St. (bet. 21st & 22nd Sts.) | 415-550-9055 | www.medjoolsf.com
The charm of the Survey's Most Popular spot, "a bar, lounge, restaurant and deck" all in one that's definitely the Mission "place of the moment", "can be summed up in three words: the rooftop view"; on warm nights, "hordes descend" for a "full-on" gander at the "awesome" Downtown skyline while down below, the "hip" "international crowd" orders Mediterranean meze or lingers on the "low, plush couches" in the "cavernous" interior; the "only downside": servers "slower than slugs"; N.B. the Sky Terrace is cash only.

Men's Room ⊘
16 | 12 | 18 | $9

Castro | 3988 18th St. (bet. Noe & Sanchez Sts.) | 415-861-1310
It's the "perfect pit stop" when you want to have a "personal conversation with friends or new friends" "before moving on to the next attraction" affirm admirers of this "nice quiet" dive in the Castro; forget the flashing video screens and thumping music of neighboring clubs:

	APPEAL	DECOR	SERVICE	COST

a couple of TVs, a fireplace and a jukebox are the enticing attractions at this low-key "neighborhood spot."

Mercury Appetizer Bar

| - | - | - | M |

Marina | 1434 Lombard St. (bet. Franklin St. & Van Ness Ave.) | 415-922-1434 | www.mercurysf.com

When that urge for a drink kicks in, park yourself at this small Marina restaurant/lounge, one of the late-night entrants helping to resuscitate long-gritty Lombard Street; brick walls and a stainless-steel bar create a cozy yet edgy lair that's just right for relaxing with lovely libations (many made with homemade syrups) like the honey-lychee daiquiri, noshing on Asian small plates – and shutting out the outside world.

Metro

| 17 | - | 18 | $9 |

Castro | 2124 Market St. (Church St.) | 415-703-9751

This "no-frills" Castro "hangout" may have relocated to Market Street digs, but it remains the kind of place where you can "unleash your catty queen" among a "mostly gay" but "women-friendly" crowd; sure, it's "crammed with people-watchers", but there's "ample seating" and the vibe is "laid-back" (i.e. "without a lot of attitude"), so you can feel free to relax over a game of pool or "chat with friends" while sipping "strong drinks."

NEW Mexico DF

| - | - | - | M |

Embarcadero | 139 Steuart St. (bet. Howard & Mission Sts.) | 415-808-1048 | www.mex-df.com

The brains behind the restaurants Maya (Felipe Sandoval) and Fonda Solana (David Rosales) dreamt up this urbane Embarcadero newcomer that pairs Mexican *botanas* (appetizers) like quesadillas and duck flautas with south-of-the-border beers and a long list of top-shelf tequilas and margaritas; the warmly lit front lounge is often packed during the 4-6 PM weekday happy hour, when drink specials come with salty snacks on the house.

Mezzanine

| 21 | 16 | 17 | $9 |

SoMa | 444 Jessie St. (bet. Mint & 6th Sts.) | 415-625-8880 | www.mezzaninesf.com

"If you're looking for love, you're in the wrong place", but "if your only love is music", then embrace this "well-apportioned", multi-level "loft on steroids" where "huge acts in hip-hop and electronica" – both musicians and DJs – take center stage; with its "great sound system", "super TV screen with concert effects" and balcony bar that offers another "vantage point" ("can't get a better close-up feel"), it's "hard to resist."

Z Michael Mina

| 24 | 24 | 25 | $15 |

Downtown | Westin St. Francis | 335 Powell St. (bet. Geary & Post Sts.) | 415-397-9222 | www.michaelmina.net

Yes, you "feel like royalty" "splurging" at the "super-cool cocktail lounge" of this "drop-dead gorgeous" restaurant in the Westin St. Francis mew Mina minions who also deem the "flawless" service "outstanding"; what a "first-class" "place to be seen" sipping "expensive", "interesting signature cocktails", ordering "fantastic bottles" from the "killer wine list" or sampling "fabulous truffle popcorn", "so good it makes me weep" – this is "definitely not your standard hotel lobby bar!"

APPEAL | DECOR | SERVICE | COST

Midnight Sun ⌐

17 | 16 | 18 | $7

Castro | 4067 18th St. (Castro St.) | 415-861-4186 | www.midnightsunsf.com

"You gotta be young" and "you gotta be pretty (or at least think you are)" at this Castro "meat market" where "bored-looking twenty-somethings" "crane their necks up to the many video screens", "pretending to watch" while "getting liquored" up; it's a "classic" "standby" agree Midnight cowboys, but those with a less sunny disposition decare it's "absolutely a stand-and-let-other-men-ogle-you bar" – "some things never change", but hello, "the '80s are over."

Mighty ⌐

23 | 21 | 17 | $9

Potrero Hill | 119 Utah St. (bet. Alameda & 15th Sts.) | 415-762-0151 | www.mighty119.com

"Arty" but "not pretentious", this loft/warehouse space with "soaring ceilings, massive columns, dramatic lighting and exposed-brick walls" in "mighty out of the way" Potrero Hill exudes a "New York feel"; it's "what a club should be": "big and intimate at the same time", "so you don't bump up against too many sweaty bodies" as you "get your groove on" until 4 AM dancing to "phenomenal DJs" while the "loud sound system belts out the beats."

Milk Bar

19 | 17 | 17 | $9

Haight-Ashbury | 1840 Haight St. (Stanyan St.) | 415-387-6455 | www.milksf.com

It's "aptly named" muse cineastes – the "decor reminds me of *A Clockwork Orange*" – but, of course, the "relaxed" scene at this Upper Haight club is anything but Kubrick-ian; "get your dance on" Tuesday-Saturday, moving with the "diverse" crowd to reggaeton and dancehall beats – it's a "decent space to party"; but others skim by intermittently, confiding it's "hit-or-miss – either empty or hip-hopping off the hook."

⛇ Millennium

26 | 22 | 24 | $10

Downtown | Hotel California | 580 Geary St. (Jones St.) | 415-345-3900 | www.millenniumrestaurant.com

This "hip spot" in the Hotel California Downtown is a "renowned" vegan restaurant, so in addition to "fantastic" meatless and dairy-less dishes you'll find "biodynamic and sustainably grown wines", "innovative infused spirits" and "small-batch liquors" – even the "garnish in your cocktail is organic"; true, it's not a big nightlife destination, but with "creative" liquor-free libations like the "Love Potion #9", it "appeals to non-drinkers and drinkers alike."

Mint Karaoke Lounge, The ⌐

▽ 21 | 9 | 14 | $6

Castro | 1942 Market St. (Duboce St.) | 415-626-4726 | www.themint.net

There's "a long wait to sing" at this "crazy karaoke" dive on Upper Market between Hayes Valley and the Castro, "but you won't mind" lingering once you get a gander at the other performers, like the "amazing" "60-year-old guy channeling Robert Plant"; though "the bar is 'whatever'", if your moxie is in mint condition, it's "lots of fun."

Mitchell Brothers O'Farrell Theatre

17 | 13 | 16 | $15

Tenderloin | 895 O'Farrell St. (Polk St.) | 415-776-6686 | www.ofarrell.com

"Drunk investment bankers" and other randy clubbers fork over a fistful of dough to "get their soft porn fix", complete with "full-contact lap dances" at this Tenderloin house of titillation; "who cares" that there's no booze – the compensation is babes in the buff and there's "nothing else like" it – in fact "if this place were any raunchier, it would be illegal."

Mix ⋑

17 | 12 | 17 | $7

Castro | 4086 18th St. (Castro St.) | 415-431-8616 |
www.sfmixbar.com

"Meet up with friends or make new ones" at this "small", "crowded" gay bar in the Castro that's "super-fun, even for a straight girl"; whether it's Wednesday 'Chick Night', when lesbians break out of their shells, 'T.G.I. Monday' when there's free pool and cheap beer or basically any evening, when mixmasters hang on the back patio, "there are always people whooping it up" (maybe it's the "strong" drinks).

Moby Dick ⋑

19 | 14 | 18 | $7

Castro | 4049 18th St. (bet. Castro & Noe Sts.) | 415-861-1199 |
www.mobydicksf.com

"Cute and young, old and hung, fat and thin . . . you name it, you got it" at this "crowded, dark" "neighborly" hangout that's "definitely less 'stand and pose' than other Castro bars"; the location "off the main drags seems to add to its intimacy" – this is "where the gays, I mean guys, are on Friday night", shooting pool on the "always popular" tables; still, it's "loud so it's not the best place for conversation."

Molotov ⋑

17 | 12 | 17 | $5

Lower Haight | 582 Haight St. (Steiner St.) | 415-558-8019

With "punk on the jukebox and a pool table in the back", it's little wonder that this "grungy" hangout with the "cool name" is full of "the young and the pierced"; "honestly, it's a dive", and you might wonder how can a place "with all those windows be so dark", but it's the rare "spot in the Lower Haight that has a full bar", and besides, they make "a strong drink."

MoMo's

20 | 18 | 17 | $10

South Beach | 760 Second St. (King St.) | 415-227-8660 | www.sfmomos.com

"Packed when the Giants are at home, empty when the baseball team is out of town", this "nicely decorated restaurant" with a "fabulous heated patio" just a fly ball away from AT&T Park is where "the beautiful people" "meet before a game and continue the celebration after"; fans root for the "flavorful drinks" and "even better bar food", but unforgiving umps pout the "nearly nonexistent service" and "high-priced" potables strike out.

NEW Monk's Kettle

– | – | – | E

Mission | 3141 16th St. (Albion St.) | 415-865-9523 | www.monkskettle.com

Beer worshipers could cloister themselves for weeks at this cozy Mission tavern and still not make their way through the five-page menu, which features 24 brews on tap and around 100 in the bottle; it's hopping at all hours with suds lovers who pair their porters with the likes of chedder-ale-topped pretzels and goat-cheese salads.

Mr. Bing's ⋑

17 | 11 | 21 | $7

Chinatown | 201 Columbus Ave. (Pacific Ave.) | 415-362-1545

A "classic old-time SF bartender" makes "cheap, stiff drinks" at this "no-frills" "hole-in-the-wall" that's "meant for boozing" – or at the

| | APPEAL | DECOR | SERVICE | COST |

very least a "mellow drink on a weeknight"; no matter that "they should renovate the decor", those who insist Bing's the thing tout it as "the ultimate dive bar", and a "must-stop on a North Beach/ Chinatown pub crawl."

Mr. Smith's
22 | 20 | 19 | $9

SoMa | 34 Seventh St. (bet. Market & Mission Sts.) | 415-355-9991 | www.maximumproductions.com

While "you can't tell from the exterior", standing on Seventh Street in a "dodgy" part of SoMa, inside is a "swanky little" three-level club with "very friendly" service and a "sexy ambiance", from a "sweltering" basement dance floor that "really gets going on weekends" to a "chill, loungey" mezzanine; if you "don't mind the pickup scene", it could be the "perfect place to find Mrs. Smith", especially if she's a "well-heeled", *très jolie* "twentysomething."

Mucky Duck ⊽
16 | 11 | 20 | $6

Inner Sunset | 1315 Ninth Ave. (Irving St.) | 415-661-4340

You can "chill all evening" at this "typical sports bar" with "fantastic bartenders"; "if you hear a blues band bumping, swing by for a fun night" suggest Inner Sunset regulars who catch the occasional live performance; but ducks who aren't so daffy for this "completely random" dive squawk "there's not much to recommend it", while still other muckety-mucks cluck "yuck."

Murio's Trophy Room ⊽
12 | 10 | 15 | $5

Haight-Ashbury | 1811 Haight St. (bet. Shrader & Stanyan Sts.) | 415-752-2971

"Can you say drink and dive?" this "rough and tumble" Upper Haight hole-in-the-wall with the "great punk rock–filled jukebox" is full of "serious pool players", some of whom look like they "never left" since the joint opened in 1959; yup, the bar has "history", but still, it's unlikely to bring home any beauty prizes since "it makes other dives look good."

🅉 Nectar Wine Lounge
23 | 22 | 21 | $12

Marina | 3330 Steiner St. (bet. Chestnut & Lombard Sts.) | 415-345-1377 | www.nectarwinelounge.com

"Everything I ever wanted in a wine bar, and then some!" assert admirers abuzz over this "always packed", "wonderfully intimate" Marina hangout (and its Burlingame offshoot); "snuggle with your honey" on a "swanky couch", sip "extraordinary" vino from the "serious list" (a "must-read for its exotic, poetic descriptions") and graze on "small plates of the Californian/fusion persuasion", delivered by a "staff that knows its stuff"; still, claustrophobes carp it's "way too small to fit even the super-skinny" regulars.

NEW Nickie's
- | - | - | M

Lower Haight | 466 Haight St. (bet. Fillmore & Webster Sts.) | 415-255-0300 | www.nickies.com

What was once a sweaty Lower Haight hole-in-the-wall has been spruced up with wooden tables, banquette seating and sleek Japanese-style stools; a comfort-food menu is served until 10 PM, after which DJs spin funk, reggae, mashups and more and though it offers a bevy of beers and wines, cocktails are limited to concoctions made with either soju or Asian vodka.

	APPEAL	DECOR	SERVICE	COST

Nihon Whisky Lounge

| | 23 | 24 | 20 | $13 |

Mission | 1779 Folsom St. (14th St.) | 415-552-4400 |
www.nihon-sf.com

"Happy hour is a must" at this "friendly" Mission lounge offering a "hip take on the clubby scotch scene" with "too many top-shelf" whiskeys to mention, a "fantastic drink selection", izakaya-style food and a staff that's "beautiful in an approachable sort of way"; spirits-seekers assert that the "remarkable Japanese interior" including a bottle-service room, "beautiful river rock floor" and "perfect lighting" gives plenty more "reasons to go."

Noc Noc

| | 20 | 23 | 17 | $6 |

Lower Haight | 557 Haight St. (bet. Fillmore & Steiner Sts.) | 415-861-5811 |
www.nocnocs.com

"If Timothy Leary could have built a bar" it might have looked like this "*Flintstones* acid trip", a "psychedelic cavern" with "Anasazi-punk hieroglyphs"; like some "David Lynchian nightmare", it's "just plain strange", but this "hipster hangout", offering beer, wine and sake, is also a "favorite" "place to kick back and dance without worrying about who's watching", while the "low seating comes in handy when you might otherwise fall off the stool."

Noe Valley Ministry ⊅

| | 24 | 17 | 19 | $9 |

Noe Valley | 1021 Sanchez St. (23rd St.) | 415-454-5238 |
www.noevalleymusicseries.com

It's definitely "not a bar, but any music here is guaranteed to be excellent" enthuse followers of this Presbyterian church in Noe Valley that doubles as a neighborhood performance venue; there's no smoke, no booze, but, hey, no worries: the "diverse performances and events" ranging from independent singer-songwriters to tango dancers are "not found elsewhere" – and worshipers say they're "worth" checking out.

nopa

| | 24 | 24 | 23 | $10 |

Western Addition | 560 Divisadero St. (bet. Fell & Hayes Sts.) |
415-864-8643 | www.nopasf.com

"Love that even if you waltz in at 11:30 PM the staff is just as friendly as if you'd had a reservation at 6:30" muse night owls who find the service "as strong as the food and drink" at this "crowded", "trendy" late-night Western Addition hot spot; it's got a "nice buzz", "pitch-perfect Manhattans" and a "cutting-edge wines-by-the-glass" list, so if you don't want to "fight for a barstool", "get there early."

North Star Cafe

| | 21 | 15 | 22 | $8 |

North Beach | 1560 Powell St. (bet. Green & Vallejo Sts.) |
415-397-0577

"Regular folks – cab drivers, construction workers", "rugby players and Marina transplants" – "intermingle" at this North Beach "dive" where everyone "feels at home"; sure, it "doesn't offer much in terms of decor", but the "friendly, chill" bartenders and "great jukebox" "set the mood for a good time", plus there's a pool table and "tabletop Pac-Man – need I say more?"; P.S. "avoid the crammed weekend nights."

	APPEAL	DECOR	SERVICE	COST

Occidental Cigar Club
▽ 24 | 17 | 25 | $8

Downtown | 471 Pine St. (bet. Kearny & Montgomery Sts.) | 415-834-0485 | www.occidentalcigarclub.com

"One of the few cigar-friendly places in San Fransisco" "where you can light up with impunity while having a drink indoors", this "small" Downtown club with a "big liquor selection" is puff heaven for stogie aficionados; follow the "regulars, a sort of *Cheers* meets *One Flew Over the Cuckoo's Nest* crowd" and let the "friendly" bartenders "set you up" with a single-barrel bourbon or a single-malt scotch to maximize the smoking experience.

NEW O Izakaya Lounge
- | - | - | E

Japantown | Hotel Kabuki | 1625 Post St. (Laguna St.) | 415-614-5431 | www.jdvhotels.com/dining

Inspired by Japanese izakaya houses, where food is shared at large tables, this sports-themed lounge in the revamped Hotel Kabuki bridges East and West with a menu that puts a California spin on yakimono (grilled meats); in addition to wines and specialty cocktails, the bartenders pour Japanese beer, shochu and sake, and the flat-screen TVs are as likely to broadcaset games played in Tokyo as those in Toronto.

Olive Bar & Restaurant
19 | 18 | 18 | $9

Tenderloin | 743 Larkin St. (O'Farrell St.) | 415-776-9814

Surveyors are split on this "mellow" little cocktail lounge "in the heart of the 'loin'"; supporters stand behind the "strong post-work drinks" featured on the "interesting cocktail menu" and totally "love the waiters" that tote "tasty pizzas" and small plates to table; but a minority cites "nonexistent service" and skewers the artwork on the walls.

Z 111 Minna
22 | 23 | 17 | $8

SoMa | 111 Minna St. (bet. New Montgomery & 2nd Sts.) | 415-974-1719 | www.111minnagallery.com

"If Andy Warhol were alive, this would be his West Coast hangout" muse Minna-sters of SoMa's "mashup bar/gallery"; the "artwork is cutting-edge" – there's always "one piece to kick off a conversation" – while the "fresh beats" attract "hipsters, artists and the occasional Downtown suit monkey"; 111 can seem "like the decibel level", but Wednesday's 'Qool' happy-hour parties provide "a great midweek way to blow off steam."

O'Neill's
- | - | - | M

NEW Fisherman's Wharf | Ghirardelli Sq. | 900 N. Point St. (Larkin St.) | 415-771-8560

SoMa | 747 Third St. (bet. King & Townsend Sts.) | 415-777-1177 www.tisoneills.com

See review in South of San Francisco Directory.

One Market
21 | 20 | 21 | $12

Embarcadero | 1 Market St. (Steuart St.) | 415-777-5577 | www.onemarket.com

"Corporate guys in gray suits" who "take off their ties" to "look casual" gather at this "high-end" restaurant/bar along the Embarcadero for after-work cocktails; yeah, it's a bit "stuffy", and it can be "way too

	APPEAL	DECOR	SERVICE	COST

crowded during Friday happy hour", but the "professional crowd" that doesn't dig "annoyingly hip and trendy places" appreciates that "you can actually get a drink here without having to wait 30 minutes."

Oola
23 | 22 | 20 | $12

SoMa | 860 Folsom St. (5th St.) | 415-995-2061 | www.oola-sf.com
"Very cool and modern" with an "intimate" "neighborhood vibe" and "flattering lighting", this SoMa "destination for drinks at the small bar, dinner in a sexy booth or both" attracts a "perfect little mix of urban dwellers and a smattering of cool tourists"; it's one of the "most relaxing" places to sip "expensive" cocktails (you'll find "some completely original combos") and grab "late-night eats", plus the staff is "attentive."

Orbit Room Cafe, The ⊟
24 | 21 | 22 | $7

Castro | 1900 Market St. (Laguna St.) | 415-252-9525
"You may have to wait a while for your custom-made drink to be mixed" at this "very cool spot" on Upper Market, but it's "well worth" the time "if you're into serious cocktails" "made with seasonal fruit"; the "eclectic crowd adds to the hipster fun", as do "funky tables" that are out of this world so "hang a while and soak up the vibe."

O'Reilly's Holy Grail
22 | 23 | 20 | $10

Polk Gulch | 1233 Polk St. (Bush St.) | 415-928-1233 | www.oreillysholygrail.com
"With truly authentic" churchlike stained-glass windows from Ireland, this "high-end" Polk Street pub (and O'Reilly's sister) boasts a "stunning interior" that's "as blasphemously fun as the name of the place"; the crowd's "a bit older", but the "atmosphere is off the charts", especially when the live acts, from "good blues and rock" to "quality jazz" and traditional Irish tunes perform in what may be the "coolest room in town."

O'Reilly's Irish Pub & Restaurant
20 | 18 | 19 | $7

North Beach | 622 Green St. (Columbus Ave.) | 415-989-6222 | www.oreillysirish.com
Everyone at this "excellent Irish pub" is "in a happy, friendly, social mood"; chalk it up to the "fantastic folks" who work here or the "great Bloody Marys", or maybe it's the outside seating where you can "take in North Beach's never-dull street life"; expats "homesick for a plate of bangers and mash" "grab a table" in the restaurant and hunker down when the "boisterous" "bar area is too crowded."

Otis
- | - | - | E

Downtown | 25 Maiden Ln. (Kearny St.) | www.otissf.com
This sign-free sliver of a space was formerly a members-only affair after 10 PM, but these days it's open to the hoi polloi at all hours; downstairs the ornate walls look as if they're covered with Egyptian hieroglyphs crossed with a Klimt painting, while in the low-ceilinged upstairs, DJ decks are squeezed into a corner; the Lilliputian bar means the stock of spirits is on the slim side, still the bartenders are skilled at their craft.

Ottimista Enoteca-Café
23 | 20 | 19 | $11

Cow Hollow | 1838 Union St. (Octavia St.) | 415-674-8400 | www.ottimistasf.com
Thirtysomethings looking for a "terrific hideaway" to escape the Cow Hollow "frat-party" scene hole up over "country-style tables" at this

APPEAL | DECOR | SERVICE | COST

"excellent wine bar" serving mostly Northern Italian and California vinos and "delicious" small plates; servers "know their stuff" and are "happy to have you sample" their wares, plus the "cozy outdoor seating area" ups the "romance"; still, misanthropes mope that "it's always packed"

Ozumo

| 23 | 24 | 21 | $12 |

Embarcadero | 161 Steuart St. (bet. Howard & Mission Sts.) | 415-882-1333 | www.ozumo.com

"Wearing black appears to be de rigueur" at this "pricey" Embarcadero restaurant/lounge that's "Japanese chic right down to the artfully plated sushi"; after work it can be "asses-to-elbows" with a FiDi crowd of "good-looking men and beautiful ladies" taking advantage of the "amazing happy-hour" prices on fin fare and the "more than plenteous collection" of sakes, while later on "DJs provide sexy grooves", ensuring there's "plenty of zoom-zoom in Ozumo."

Palomino

| 19 | 18 | 18 | $11 |

Embarcadero | 345 Spear St. (bet. Folsom & Harrison Sts.) | 415-512-7400 | www.palominosf.com

A "yuppie crowd" "meets, mingles" and orders "good nibbles" and libations from the "endless assortment of cocktails" during the "busy happy hour" at this "lively place" on the Embarcadero; saddle up a seat on the "nice, wide patio", but take heed: the "spectacular views" of the Bay Bridge may be obscured by the recent rise of new eateries nearby.

Paragon Restaurant & Bar

| 21 | 22 | 19 | $11 |

SoMa | 701 Second St. (Townsend St.) | 415-537-9020 | www.paragonrestaurant.com

The SoMa outpost of this pair, "just a home run away from the Giants' ballpark", is "packed during baseball season" with fans sipping "creative martinis" and chowing down "decent food", but it can be "quiet as a library" otherwise; at the Berkeley branch, "crowds fight for a table on the deck", a "perfect break from the everyday" where the reward is "one heck of a sunset" and "gorgeous" vistas across the Bay.

Paréa Wine Bar & Café

| - | - | - | M |

Mission | 795 Valencia St. (19th St.) | 415-255-2102 | www.pareawinebar.com

"An oasis in the middle of the hectic Mission", this "mellow" "little jewel" is "worth stopping by" for "tasty Mediterranean munchies" and a glass or two of red, white or bubbly or on Greek Night once a month; "remember: this isn't your chic Marina wine bar", but if you're just looking "to have a relaxed drink with a few friends or a date", the "unusually solicitous" servers will make you feel right at home.

Peña Pachamama

| - | - | - | M |

North Beach | 1630 Powell St. (bet. Green & Union Sts.) | 415-646-0018 | www.penapachamama.com

Once the North Beach "stomping ground for Joe DiMaggio and Marilyn Monroe", not to mention famous mugs like Dean Martin and Rocky Marciano, the former speakeasy Amelio's "turned South American world music club" is a "fun place for a group outing"; graze on Bolivian fare served by a staff that's actually part of the "awesome" "high-energy" entertainment ranging from samba, salsa and merengue to flamenco dancing – it's definitely "something unique in SF."

	APPEAL	DECOR	SERVICE	COST

Perbacco

| - | - | - | E |

Downtown | 230 California St. (Battery & Front Sts.) | 415-955-0663 | www.perbaccosf.com

A well-heeled after-work and waiting-for-a-table crowd frequently jams into the bar area situated just inside this sleek and spacious Downtown Italian restaurant, meeting for fine cocktails and upscale snacks like *finochiona* and truffled egg toast; a mix of exposed brick, wood and clean light colors lend an airy hospitality to the long room, which is packed all the way back with eager diners.

Perry's

| 19 | 16 | 20 | $10 |

Cow Hollow | 1944 Union St. (bet. Buchanan & Laguna Sts.) | 415-922-9022 | www.perryssf.com

Although it "used to be the prime singles spot in San Francisco", these days this "reliable" "standby" in Cow Hollow attracts an "odd mix of old and young" mingling over a "satisfying post-dinner drink"; if trendwatchers scoff it's "tired, tired, tired" – the "person sitting next to you might be your granddad" – supporters swear this "classic joint" "still delivers" – and hope that its recently relocated new sibling, due to open summer 2008, at 155 Steuart Street, will too.

Phoenix

| 19 | 14 | 18 | $6 |

Mission | 811 Valencia St. (bet. 19th & 20th Sts.) | 415-695-1811 | www.phoenixirishbar.com

"Relive your time in Ireland" at this "solid", "surprisingly authentic" Mission pub with "plentiful" seating that just may be the "perfect place to watch football (aka soccer)", guzzle a Guinness or groove to the "amazing jukebox"; the "Brits favor Newkie on tap and the birds go for the Boddingtons", but everyone, especially the "comfort-food freaks", gets behind the "nightly blackboard specials."

Phone Booth ⊄

| ∇ 20 | 16 | 22 | $5 |

Mission | 1398 S. Van Ness Ave. (25th St.) | 415-648-4683

The mixed crowd of "hip lesbians and hip hipsters", you know, the "kids in black pants with aspirations of being an artist/musician/DJ/etc.", makes this "dark", "divey" Mission hangout the "last place they hit on the way home"; the "intimate" environs are "aptly named", "nonetheless there's a pool table wedged into the tiny space", and it's dialed in with "free popcorn" and "quality beers" – "what else would you want?"

☒ Pied Piper Bar

| 26 | 26 | 23 | $10 |

Downtown | Palace Hotel | 2 New Montgomery St. (Market St.) | 415-512-1111 | www.sfpalace.com

Maybe it's the "fantastic" Maxfield Parrish mural for which the "old-world bar" is named, but this "sophisticated San Francisco landmark" in Downtown's Palace Hotel just "oozes history"; "upscale" "without being pretentious", it's a "good place to wet the whistle", and with "expert" bartenders mixing up "great martinis", it's a "nice escape" – even a "quiet, romantic" retreat – from "bustling" Market Street.

Pier 23 Cafe

| 21 | 13 | 17 | $8 |

Embarcadero | Pier 23 | The Embarcadero (Battery St.) | 415-362-5125 | www.pier23cafe.com

"On a sunny day", "you can't beat" "sitting on the deck watching the boats on the Bay" at this "friendly, funky spot" along the Embarcadero;

"what a way to pass" the time – add in "excellent jazz", DJs, salsa lessons and other entertainment and it's no wonder it's "incredibly" packed; if a few find the crowd "weird" ("unless you're into chicks with Harleys"), most maintain "no written description does justice to how much fun" it is.

Pig & Whistle

23 | 17 | 23 | $5

Inner Richmond | 2801 Geary Blvd. (Wood St.) | 415-885-4779 | www.pig-and-whistle.com

With an international array of "great beers on tap" and in bottles, you "can't beat the Pig" agree tickled pink brewmeisters who sing the praises of this Inner Richmond hangout; there's a "pool table in back that's usually available and darts" too but bear in mind that it's "jammed with crazed soccer fans" during "important sporting events" – "one can barely move."

Pilsner Inn ⌂

▽ 19 | 14 | 18 | $5

Castro | 225 Church St. (Market St.) | 415-621-7058 | www.pilsnerinn.com

"Not your typical gay bar", this "no-attitude", "easygoing" "local dive" with a "working-class vibe" welcomes a mixed crowd to the Castro with ice-cold draft beers on the "nice patio out back"; it's a "comfortable neighborhood bar to meet friends", and regulars reveal that it also "doubles as the waiting room for the restaurant Chow next door."

Pink

21 | 20 | 16 | $10

Mission | 2925 16th St. (bet. Mission St. & S. Van Ness Ave.) | 415-431-8889 | www.pinksf.com

"Once you get past the snooty people working the door" and join the "eclectic" crowd within, this "very chic" yet "cozy" Mission dance club is a "fun and very sweaty" spot for "shaking some tail" to the "best house music" around; "yes, it is pink inside", and you can "ask the cute bartender for the Pink Drink", "but the decor isn't over the top" – it's just a "visually appealing oasis" for "red-hot late nights."

Place Pigalle

21 | 12 | 17 | $6

Hayes Valley | 520 Hayes St. (bet. Laguna St. & Octavia Blvd.) | 415-552-2671 | www.place-pigalle.com

"Low-key, hip" Hayes Valley locals fill this "steady standby", "relaxing" with wine and "great beers on tap" on "frat-house couches" and "listening to neo-punk and garage bands on the jukebox" ("there's no hard stuff, so maybe it's the place to bring your friends who can't handle their liquor"); admirers give a "thumbs-up" to bartenders who "always make you feel at home" concluding, "in some subtle way, it's perfect."

Plouf

20 | 17 | 19 | $12

Downtown | 40 Belden Pl. (bet. Bush & Pine Sts.) | 415-986-6491 | www.ploufsf.com

Almost everyone at this "teeny-tiny bar" Downtown is "waiting for a table, which is what you should be doing too" at this "fabulous" French seafooder that satisfies that "mussels and Sancerre" craving; servers get varied appraisals, from the "friendliest garçons in town" to "slow" and "snotty", nonetheless the ambiance is "delightful", especially "on a warm evening" when you can "sit outside cafe-style."

	APPEAL	DECOR	SERVICE	COST

Plough and Stars, The
18 | 12 | 17 | $5

Inner Richmond | 116 Clement St. (2nd Ave.) | 415-751-1122 | www.theploughandstars.com

"A bit o' the old Irish" in the Inner Richmond, this "very traditional" pub is somewhat "plain", but it's a "solid, unpretentious" place "to hear authentic traditional music" sing fans of the fiddles and the pipes; Gallic groupies also gush that the "friendly, professional bartenders" pull pints of the "best Guinness", suggesting "don't miss it"; still, the bleary eyed "can't tell it apart" from every other Dublin dive in town.

Poleng Lounge
▽ 22 | 22 | 19 | $8

Western Addition | 1751 Fulton St. (Masonic Ave.) | 415-441-1751 | www.polenglounge.com

There's a "cool vibe" at this sleek Balinese-inspired multitasker in the Western Addition, a combination restaurant, tea lounge and nightclub where the "beautiful driftwood branch above the bar" is only one aspect of the stylish "modern decor"; it's "too hip for words", and "good hip-hop acts are booked" in the Temple Room, but a few mutter about the "weird clash" between the "front room and back room dynamics."

Ponzu
20 | 22 | 20 | $12

Downtown | Serrano Hotel | 401 Taylor St. (bet. Geary & O'Farrell Sts.) | 415-775-7979 | www.ponzurestaurant.com

The "comfy" "oversized velvet couches" and "subdued lighting" "lead to intimate conversations" over "fun specialty cocktails", "flights of sake" and "exotic" Asian-inspired appetizers at this Downtown lounge in the Serrano Hotel; though "service can be a little slow" during peak hours, it's so "dark, sexy and sultry", awash in "reds and purples", that you'll be too busy "making out with your date to notice."

Postrio
22 | 21 | 23 | $13

Downtown | Prescott Hotel | 545 Post St. (bet. Mason & Taylor Sts.) | 415-776-7825 | www.postrio.com

Executive chef Wolfgang Puck "can still turn on the charm", as evidenced by the "professionals, well-heeled tourists" and "famous people" who eat and drink at the "popular bar" of his "beautiful restaurant" attached to Downtown's Prescott Hotel; it's "worth bucking the crowd" – indeed, the "lively" throngs are "worthy of the price of a show"; still, a handful lament that it's "lost its luster", calling it "a faded vestige of the boom era."

Power Exchange ⊄
18 | 13 | 10 | $12

SoMa | 74 Otis St. (Gough St.) | 415-487-9944 | www.powerexchange.com

True, there's "no alcohol" at this SoMa sin city, but it's still a "fun place for the uninhibited" to let loose "after the bars close"; with separate floors for straight and gay pleasure-seekers, "it's the biggest sex club" around, "but as mama used to say, 'size isn't everything'", in fact, the turned-off would "rather be celibate" than brave the sketchy conditions; P.S. since it's something of a "trannyland", "beware – that girl you're playing with might be a dude."

Powerhouse ⊄
▽ 21 | 16 | 18 | $7

SoMa | 1347 Folsom St. (bet. 9th & 10th Sts.) | 415-552-8689 | www.powerhouse-sf.com

"Pump those pierced pecs and show off your latest tats" to the other "nocturnal bears and Levi's"-clad lotharios at "one of the last remain-

ing leather bars in San Francisco"; this SoMa place "may have toned
down a bit over the years", but the bartenders are still "hot", "the music is loud, the videos are porn" and "the back room attracts those in
search of anonymous physical encounters."

Pres a Vi
- | - | - | E

Presidio | Letterman Digital Arts Ctr. | 1 Letterman Dr. (Lombard St.) |
415-409-3000 | www.presavi.com

"Deliciously decorated in dark wood", this "cavernous" new wine bar/
restaurant, a sibling of Walnut Creek's Va de Vi bistro, has a "beautiful
location" in the Presidio's Letterman Digital Arts Center with views of
the Golden Gate Bridge and the Palace of Fine Arts; "be prepared to be
amazed at the selection" of vino, creative cocktails and global small
plates, and "best yet, it has parking" in an underground garage.

Presidio Social Club
- | - | - | E

Presidio | The Presidio | 563 Ruger St. (Letterman Dr.) | 415-885-1888 |
www.presidiosocialclub.com

At ease, private, as this historic former army barracks in the Presidio
is now an informal and inviting destination for lunch, dinner or drinks
at the long bar – no membership or enlistment required; from the ceiling fans to the white-wood trim, the atmosphere evokes vintage
Singapore, inspiring among other things classic cocktails like crisp
martinis and old-world pisco punches.

Puerto Alegre
21 | 11 | 16 | $6

Mission | 546 Valencia St. (bet. 16th & 17th Sts.) | 415-255-8201

"Swarming crowds" of Missionites amiably "look past the rough fa-
cade" of this "loud" "local favorite" and "keep coming back" for the
"great vibe" and, of course, the "cheap and good" "old-style margaritas" that pack a punch ("pitchers, please!"); but the under-
whelmed dis the "decent" Mexican *comida* and wonder "why
people love this mediocre place", suggesting have a drink and
"ponder for yourself."

Punchline Comedy Club
22 | 14 | 16 | $10

Downtown | 444 Battery St. (bet. Clay & Washington Sts.) | 415-397-7573 |
www.punchlinecomedyclub.com

"Funny + food? – how can you miss?" ask amused attendees of this
Downtown comedy venue that's "great" for laughs and entertaining
"guests from out of town"; it's "a bit tight", but "the way the stage is
set up", "all the seats are good seats" whether you're there to "see un-
knowns or some very knowns"; still, a few knock the servers, sniping
they "need to pick up the speed a little bit."

Purple Onion
18 | 15 | 18 | $11

North Beach | 140 Columbus Ave. (bet. Jackson & Kearny Sts.) |
415-956-1653 | www.caffemacaroni.com

An eclectic lineup of musicians and "underground comics" performs at this "fun old-school venue for live acts" "in the heart of
North Beach"; no, it's "not swank", and some comedians joke that it
"looks worse than Phyllis Diller" (who, incidentally, got her start
here), but "decent drink prices" and the "club's classic SF history" are
"a winning combination" declare devotees who find it "still funky after
all these years."

	APPEAL	DECOR	SERVICE	COST

Ramblas

Mission | 557 Valencia St. (bet. 16th & 17th Sts.) | 415-565-0207 | www.ramblastapas.com

19 | 20 | 20 | $9

Bring your "friends" so you can "enjoy at least one pitcher" of the "tasty sangria" ("love the white" version), along with "delicious tapas" assert admirers who ramble into this "lively, appealing Mission" spot; "inventive cocktails" like the "fantastic pomegranate margaritas" and beer from brother Thirsty Bear Brewing Company help some forget it's a "little pricey for their palate."

Ramp, The

China Basin | 855 Terry Francois St. (Mariposa St.) | 415-621-2378 | www.ramprestaurant.com

21 | 12 | 14 | $8

"Come early on a sunny weekend to battle hoards of hipsters" who "recover from a hangover with the hair of the dog" at China Basin's "waterfront dive"; sure, the barbecue is "average", decor means "plastic furniture" and the "servers are too few for the crowds" – still, there's nothing like "dancing next to the waves of the Bay" May–October, when salsa and international music light up the "awesome deck."

Rasselas Jazz Club & Ethiopian Restaurant

Western Addition | 1534 Fillmore St. (Geary Blvd.) | 415-346-8696 | www.rasselasjazzclub.com

▽ 23 | 15 | 19 | $7

"Jazz is the name of the game" at this "unique" club "full of history" in the Western Addition that combines "outstanding" Ethiopian food and "top-notch" live music; the "atmosphere is wonderful and draws you in" – no wonder it's "hopping" every night with "cool cats"; N.B. there's a cover on weekends and a two-drink minimum Sunday–Thursday.

R Bar

Polk Gulch | 1176 Sutter St. (Polk St.) | 415-567-7441

17 | 11 | 19 | $7

Though it "resembles a tough motorcycle bar" from the outside, inside a "fun crowd" of Polk Gulch "villagers" along with folks "escaping the Marina" mix and mingle with "people in the restaurant and bar industry"; "ask and ye shall receive", since the "top-notch bartenders" are "what makes this place super laid-back", but beware weekends, when it "tends to be too loud to talk" and "turns into a meat market."

Red Devil Lounge

Polk Gulch | 1695 Polk St. (Clay St.) | 415-921-1695 | www.reddevillounge.com

18 | 14 | 15 | $7

The "style of music" on tap nightly – from Chuck Prophet to Dramarama – "determines who the crowd might be" at this "outstanding" Polk Street venue where the "sexy" Gothic red decor and "dim lighting" make it "great for a date"; thanks to the "genius" upper level with a second bar "you don't have to feel like a salmon swimming upstream to get a drink" – yes, "this place is A-ok" concur Devil worshipers.

Red Jack Saloon

Fisherman's Wharf | 131 Bay St. (Stockton St.) | 415-989-0700

18 | 18 | 21 | $11

"There's nothing flashy or fancy" about this "end-up" place where "waiters have a drink after working" a shift nearby in Fisherman's Wharf; a "good jukebox and board games provide entertainment", ensuring a "comfortable vibe" when you "want to escape from all the touristy places in the area" and just "relax with a group of friends."

⊠ Redwood Room
24 | 28 | 17 | $13

Downtown | Clift Hotel | 495 Geary St. (Taylor St.) | 415-929-2372 | www.clifthotel.com

"Did I somehow end up in LA?" wonder barhoppers "lucky" enough to get past the "snooty" door staff and inside the "ritzy" Philippe Starck-designed "swank central" in Downtown's Clift Hotel boasting "funky furniture", a "beautiful bar" carved from a redwood tree and "museum-looking portraits" ("they do change – you're not crazy"); the "original drinks" and "classy ambiance" give you an "excuse to dress up and parade amongst the pretty people" – just "bring a fat wallet"; still, kvetchers bark it's "too big for its britches."

Restaurant LuLu
20 | 21 | 18 | $10

SoMa | 816 Folsom St. (bet. 4th & 5th Sts.) | 415-495-5775 | www.restaurantlulu.com

This SoMa "standby" has "got everything", from a "warm, welcoming atmosphere" to a separate wine bar serving "two-ounce tastes" and a selection of 70 vintages by the glass, plus the "very friendly" bartenders know how to "mix a good drink"; still, the "comfort-food" diners nearby "make so much noise" in the "gymnasium"-like warehouse space that "barflies need earmuffs" so steel yourself to "shout to be heard."

Retox Lounge
– | – | – | M

Dogpatch | 628 20th St. (3rd St.) | 415-626-7386 | www.retoxsf.com

Distant Dogpatch is more accessible since the introduction of the Third Street MUNI rail line, giving venues like this industrial lounge a boost in business; front-facing windows offer an outlet to the outside world, but there's lots to entertain you within, from the $2 beers during happy hour to the exuberant mix of DJs and live music.

Revolution Café ⊟
22 | 18 | 20 | $7

Mission | 3248 22nd St. (Bartlett St.) | 415-642-0474

Acoustic acts, "live jazz and lively discussions on the veranda" lend a "real urban", "bohemian touch" to these "funky, unpretentious digs" in the Mission that make you "feel like you're visiting a smaller, warmer and slightly less capitalistic foreign land"; whether you park yourself near the front that opens onto the street or view the "artwork that's either disturbing or inspiring", it's a "friendly" forum for "meeting people in a totally nonthreatening way."

Rick's
∇ 19 | 16 | 22 | $9

Outer Sunset | 1940 Taraval St. (bet. 29th & 30th Aves.) | 415-731-8900 | www.ricksaloha.com

"A good place to get your Jimmy Buffet on", or sway to Hawaiian music, this "unpretentious" neighborhood bar and "cozy restaurant" in the Outer Sunset deals in "delicious" tropical cocktails like 'Pele's Flaming Potion' and mai tais; it's a "fun place overall", but "don't expect great people-watching, unless you're into blue-haired women and middle-aged men"; N.B. karaoke follows live music several times a week.

	APPEAL	DECOR	SERVICE	COST

Rickshaw Stop
20 | 17 | 19 | $6

Civic Center | 155 Fell St. (bet. Franklin St. & Van Ness Ave.) | 415-861-2011 | www.rickshawstop.com

"Perfect sight lines" from the mezzanine allow even "those of smaller stature" to check out the "independent and underground" bands and "good DJs" at this "quirky yet comfortable" Civic Center bar with an "off-the-hook sound system" and a "super-nice staff"; after standing "shoulder-to-shoulder" with the "funky hipster crowd" through opening acts, "you'll want to fight to sit" in the "cozy rickshaws" while sipping your "affordable drink."

Riptide ⌗
▽ 17 | 15 | 19 | $5

Outer Sunset | 3639 Taraval St. (47th Ave.) | 415-681-8433 | www.riptidesf.com

Yes, the fireplace is "always burning" at this "sleepy surfer bar" a block from the beach, where you can "warm up from the bitter cold and ocean wind" over a cocktail; though it's a "little out of the way", and the thrice-weekly bands "can be hit-or-miss", the "unique" "mountain lodge resort" vibe and "awesome" bartenders are worth the trek; besides, "when you're way out in the Outer Sunset, where else can you really go?"

Rite Spot Cafe
▽ 22 | 17 | 20 | $6

Mission | 2099 Folsom St. (17th St.) | 415-552-6066 | www.ritespotcafe.net

Yes, "the name says it all" suggest supporters of this "funky hideaway" for "alternative" types on a quiet block of the Mission; there's "rarely much of a crowd" for the "sometimes interesting live music" (usually singer-songwriters), but the "friendly staff" and "nice vibe" (check out the "original art" on the walls) mean it's a "cool place to chill."

Roccapulco
▽ 20 | 18 | 20 | $8

Mission | 3140 Mission St. (Cesar Chavez) | 415-648-6611 | www.roccapulco.com

The "place to dance" with some "friendly, talented" movers and shakers on Wednesday, Friday and Saturday, this "fabulously sparkly salsa club" in the Mission even offers early evening lessons that help the "uninitiated feel more comfortable" out on the "spacious" floor; get "dressed to the nines" before coming out, because "everyone else will be", and after your class, "stick around" for the "excellent" live music.

Rockit Room
19 | 15 | 17 | $7

Inner Richmond | 406 Clement St. (bet. 5th & 6th Aves.) | 415-387-6344 | www.rock-it-room.com

"Get away from the pubs", so popular in the Inner Richmond, here at the "city's best unknown music venue"; groups of every stripe (including "non-bippy-boppy bands") frequently perform upstairs, while downstairs there's "cheap pool" and foosball in the "kind of sparse" room; still, a few feel it "lost its appeal" following a change of hands and retrofit.

Roe Lounge
20 | 23 | 20 | $10

SoMa | Roe Restaurant | 651 Howard St. (Hawthorne St.) | 415-227-0288 | www.roerestaurant.com

"Dressed to impress", the "glam" group matches the "beautiful surroundings" at this "versatile" tri-level SoMa venue that was recently revamped, rendering the decor burgundy-and-gold and even more chic; after dancing to DJs in the "crowded", "hip-hopping" upstairs, take a "breather" and "chill" in Roe Restaurant, now offering a new contemporary Asian menu, or any of the three bars on each level; still, a few fuss about the "hit-or-miss" crowd that's "clearly crossed a bridge" into town.

Rogue Ales Public House   21 | 16 | 20 | $8

North Beach | 673 Union St. (Columbus Ave.) | 415-362-7880 | www.rogue.com

A rotating number of "excellent" Rogue brews plus "guest taps" are the attractions at this ale heaven, where the "large back patio" is suited for "summer swilling"; while a few mugs quibble about an ambiance that's "typical beer hall, without much charm", and food that can be "pretty average", even they admit that the "fun quiz night on Thursdays" steps up its sudsy charms.

RoHan Lounge   19 | 20 | 20 | $9

Inner Richmond | 3809 Geary Blvd. (2nd Ave.) | 415-221-5095 | www.rohanlounge.com

The mood at this "hip" Korean cocktail bar "off the beaten path" in the Inner Richmond veers from "vibrant and lively" to "exotically romantic", "depending on the crowd"; DJs spin funk, soul and hip-hop while the "mostly late 20s" patrons order up "late-night bites" of "small Asian fusion plates" and drinks from the "personable bartenders"; P.S. there's no hard liquor, but "beware of the soju cocktails – they sneak up on you."

Rose Pistola   22 | 19 | 20 | $13

North Beach | 532 Columbus Ave. (bet. Green & Union Sts.) | 415-399-0499 | www.rosepistolasf.com

"Even if you're not eating" a "delish" dinner, it's "worth the trip" to the "busy" bar of this trattoria, a "lovely" spot to "start or end your North Beach evening"; the "sexy" environs provide a "modern contrast to much of traditionally Italian" area, the "martinis rock, specialty vodkas abound" and there's an "excellent selection" of wines too, plus there's live jazz on weekends – no wonder fans deem it a "favorite."

Rosewood   21 | 21 | 15 | $10

Chinatown | 732 Broadway (bet. Powell & Stockton Sts.) | 415-951-4886

"Everything comes out roses" at this "tiny", *très chic* bar, "one of the last bastions of hipness left in the North Beach"–Chinatown area that's "easy to hang out in"; petal-pushers give the "cleanly designed" digs, "good-looking crowd" and "stiff" cocktails a thumbs-up, adding that the garden is the "perfect spot to host your own soiree"; but kvetchers knock on Wood, wailing it "can be tough to get a drink during peak hours."

Rouge et Blanc   - | - | - | E

Downtown | 334 Grant Ave. (Bush St.) | 415-391-0207

Aqua chef Laurent Manrique and partners recently revitalized the Downtown space formerly occupied by Enoteca Viansa, converting it into a casual, modern wine bar/lounge with high ceilings and comfortable seating; by day it's a cafe, by night, a sophisticated spot to sip reds or whites, choosing from an international selection of about 15 wines by the glass, accompanied by snacks like charcuterie and cheese plates.

Rouge Nightclub

| 13 | 14 | 14 | $10 |

Russian Hill | 1500 Broadway (Polk St.) | 415-346-7683 | www.rougesf.com

There's no doubt the "lush" blush-colored velvet decor is a "bit over-done", but red-blooded revelers say it creates a "fun ambiance" for "shaking your groove thing" on the "fair-sized dance floor" at this Russian Hill romping ground; still, foes fume that the "tacky" surroundings and "suburbanites in for a big night in the city" make it "more cheesy than Tillamook County."

Route 101 ⇗

| 13 | 7 | 18 | $6 |

Polk Gulch | 1332 Van Ness Ave. (bet. Bush & Sutter Sts.) | 415-474-6092

"Scraggly men rooted to the barstools" comprise a fair "number of regulars" you'll find at this "funky" "grade-A dive" on Van Ness; though it's definitely a "dump", this "no-frills biker bar" gets points for a "good jukebox" and "pretty cool" bartenders, making it a "very welcoming" spot when you just want a "cheap beer" – and when you'd rather not "be seen by anyone you know."

Royal Exchange, The

| 17 | 14 | 16 | $7 |

Downtown | 301 Sacramento St. (Front St.) | 415-956-1710 | www.royalexchange.com

"The absolute best place to pick up a young hot investment banker" laud loyalists who join the "fun social" after-work crowd, a "healthy mix of babes" and stockbrokers, at this Financial District watering hole; yeah, it's a "madhouse during happy hour" and "crazy crowded" "during big game weekend", when Cal and Stanford alums are in full force, "but the booths in the back make it much more cozy, with less pushing."

Royal Oak ⇗

| 19 | 18 | 15 | $9 |

Russian Hill | 2201 Polk St. (Vallejo St.) | 415-928-2303

"Lots of plant life" lends this "cozy fern bar" an "intimate" ambiance, while the "bombshell bartenders" ratchet up its appeal, making it a longtime "favorite" "for Russian Hill singles", especially midweek, when the noise level is "tolerable" and it's easy to snag one of the "Victorian-style couches" ("hello darling, come sit next to me" . . .); still, a handful huff it has the "odd feel of your grandmother's home."

Roy's

| 24 | 23 | 23 | $14 |

SoMa | 575 Mission St. (bet. 1st & 2nd Sts.) | 415-777-0277 | www.roysrestaurant.com

What a "cool spot to sip" "nifty", "exotic" tropical libations like the "to-die-for Hawaiian martini" – it's "as much fun as eating" here – so "do both" rave island gals and guys who breeze into this "refined, inviting" SoMa chain link; the Pebble Beach–bound also find the outpost in the Inn at Spanish Bay a "chill" place to "unwind after a round of golf with friends", advising "go before sundown for fabulous ocean views."

NEW Rrazz Room

| - | - | - | M |

Downtown | Hotel Nikko | 222 Mason St. (Ellis St.) | 415-394-1189 | www.therrazzroom.com

The Plush Room, one of the city's most venerable cabaret venues, closed last year, and now its bookers are bringing similar acts to this intimate 190-seat space on the lobby level of Downtown's Hotel Nikko; the former meeting room has been revamped so whether you sit at the cocktail tables or in booths you're guaranteed a good view of the jazz, blues and pop vocalists and occasional drag queen performers; N.B. in addition to the ticket price, there is a two-drink minimum.

Rubicon

| 21 | 21 | 24 | $12 |

Downtown | 558 Sacramento St. (bet. Montgomery & Sansome Sts.) | 415-434-4100 | www.sfrubicon.com

The "superb" wine list, with over 40 by the glass and 1,700 by the bottle, is the siren song of this Downtown destination for fine "wining and dining"; have a seat at one of the two small bars, upstairs and down, or go all out and "get the tasting menu" paired with vinos by the sommelier; a few surveyors, though, are diametrically opposed on the experience, calling it both "overrated" and "underrated."

Ruby Skye

| 20 | 21 | 16 | $11 |

Downtown | 420 Mason St. (bet. Geary & Post Sts.) | 415-693-0777 | www.rubyskye.com

"Taking its cue from similar spots in NYC and London", this "gorgeous" multilevel club in a "beautifully restored" "old theater" Downtown is usually "worth the high cover charge" what with "headliner DJs" and a "large dance floor" where you can shake it till 4 AM; but cynics who'd rather not "pay the big $$$ for a booth" and bottle service refrain from love letters, scrawling "Dear Ruby Skye, get over yourself already!"

Rye

| 23 | 25 | 21 | $9 |

Tenderloin | 688 Geary St. (Leavenworth St.) | 415-786-7803 | www.ryesf.com

Go for the "terrifically imaginative drinks", "as complicated as a meal (but more fun)", and the free pool table – "you will not be disappointed" by this "very chill" cocktail lounge with the "stunning" "New York style" that's a "definite repeat" stop; the "knowledgeable bartenders" are "truly nice people" – you can't "beat that" – but a few scotch the clientele, scoffing it's "full of Marina-like yuppies" slumming it in the "seedy" Tenderloin.

Sadie's Flying Elephant ⊅

| 22 | 15 | 20 | $6 |

Potrero Hill | 491 Potrero Ave. (Mariposa St.) | 415-551-7988

A mix of "professional drinkers" and "hipster" Potrero Hill habitués appreciate that "you can be yourself" at this "rockin' dive bar" that's managed to retain it's "kinda seedy", "homestyle" vibe; the "well-stocked jukebox", occasional DJs or live music, free popcorn and pool, pinball and tabletop Ms. Pac-Man make it just the "place to while away your Friday, your birthday or the day you sneak out from work" – "what could be better?"

Saloon, The ⊅

| 21 | 12 | 15 | $5 |

North Beach | 1232 Grant Ave. (Columbus Ave.) | 415-989-7666

"If you're in the business of drinking" head to this circa-1861 North Beach "honky-tonk" and line 'em up while listening to live "gritty blues" with an "eclectic, very friendly" crowd; "legend has it that it was saved from the 1906 quake because firemen liked to hang out here", so "savor the atmosphere" and remember that though the bartenders seem "mean", they're "bringing the Barbary Coast character to life."

	APPEAL	DECOR	SERVICE	COST

Salt House
▽ 25 | 24 | 22 | $14

SoMa | 545 Mission St. (2nd St.) | 415-543-8900 | www.salthousesf.com
The "sassy younger sister" to the successful Town Hall, this "airy" industrial-chic destination set in a former printing press warehouse in SoMa is already "bustling" with "lots of well-dressed thirtysomethings flirting" over drinks and raw bar platters; although the "fun" crowds "can cause major gridlock" in the "small bar area", it's worth the wait to "enjoy a modern twist on the salty dog or a fine glass of wine" before a "casual-chic dinner."

San Francisco Brewing Company
21 | 17 | 20 | $7

North Beach | 155 Columbus Ave. (Pacific Ave.) | 415-434-3344 | www.sfbrewing.com
Although there are "tons of clubs within a block" of this North Beach bar, lager lovers lean toward this historic hangout with an "old-time feel" that opened in 1907 as the Andromeda Saloon; "some of the best micro-brews around" are made on-site, plus the "happy hour rocks" with 10-ounce beers for $1, so grab a sidewalk table and "watch the world go by" or stop by on select nights for live entertainment.

Sauce
20 | 18 | 21 | $9

Hayes Valley | 131 Gough St. (Lily St.) | 415-252-1369 | www.saucesf.com
"Love it! – it's so fresh and inviting" exclaim enthusiasts who "could spend the whole night" sipping "well-researched custom cocktails" and "nice wines by the glass" at this "Hayes Valley hot spot"; the bartender is "charming" and the "delicious" bites are "reason enough to be a regular"; but the few who fail to pour on the accolades find seating "limited" and much prefer the "intimate dining room."

Savanna Jazz
21 | 18 | 20 | $13

Mission | 2937 Mission St. (bet. 25th & 26th Sts.) | 415-285-3369 | www.savannajazz.com
"If you dig jazz" head to this "honest-to-goodness, back-to-the-'50s, beboppin' club" that's "classier than your usual Mission hangout" where staffers are dedicated to "educating you about the history" of the genre; the bar is "lively", the crowd "slightly older" and you can wash down "good cocktails" with Caribbean–West African chow; still, purists pout that while it has "so much potential" the "fusion-y" music and "jam band nonsense" seem "subpar."

Savoy Tivoli ⊄
19 | 15 | 16 | $8

North Beach | 1434 Grant Ave. (bet. Green & Union Sts.) | 415-362-7023
A "cool crowd" (well, "at least in their own minds") of "chill", "good-looking" locals hangs out at this North Beach neighborhood "legend" dating back to 1906; sure, it can be a "total pickup joint" "reminiscent of fraternity row", but savvy Savoy-ers, "happy" to sip $1.50 schnapps and retreat to the heated patio to shoot some pool have a "good time nonetheless"; P.S. "go for the Saturday afternoon jazz" from 3-6 PM.

Scala's Bistro
22 | 21 | 22 | $10

Downtown | Sir Francis Drake Hotel | 432 Powell St. (bet. Post & Sutter Sts.) | 415-395-8555 | www.scalasbistro.com
Despite its "tourist central" location "smack in the middle of Union Square", you'll still find "lots of locals" at this "very friendly" French-

Italian restaurant next to the Sir Francis Drake Hotel; the bar is "often packed tight" with "mature" diners waiting on a table ("take your parents, or better yet, your grandparents"), but "if you crave the feel and buzz of a New York bistro", wade on in for a "strong drink."

☑ Seasons Bar
| 26 | 26 | 28 | $14 |

Downtown | Four Seasons Hotel | 757 Market St., 5th fl. (bet. O'Farrell & Stockton Sts.) | 415-633-3737 | www.fourseasons.com

When you need a "refined break from the Market Street hubbub" slink into this "elegant" lounge on the fifth floor of Downtown's Four Seasons and treat yourself to a "sophisticated drink"; it's "quite pricey", but the "picture-perfect" setting and "top-notch" staff, voted No. 1 in the SF Survey for Service, make "you feel like a million bucks" – just don't expect a "pickup scene", because seasoned sorts here tend to be "old and rich"; P.S. "the piano player is amazing."

NEW Serpentine
| - | - | - | M |

Dogpatch | 2495 Third St. (bet. 22nd & 23rd Sts.) | 415-252-2000 | www.serpentinesf.com

More New American restaurant than nightspot, this newcomer with a minimalist industrial look is sister to the Slow Club in the outer Mission; the area near the 25-ft.-long slate bar may be tight, but the classic cocktails, including the popular Whiskey Smash, are reason enough to pop in for a pre- or post-dinner drink; even better, the Dogpatch location means that street parking is easy to come by in the evening.

Shanghai Kelly's
| 17 | 14 | 20 | $7 |

Polk Gulch | 2064 Polk St. (Broadway) | 415-771-3300

The "late 20s, early 30s crowd" at this "casual" Polk Street "place for a pint" is "lively and friendly"; good thing, since "it doesn't have much room to maneuver", especially during football season, when it's "lousy with Steeler fans" and "a few too many frat boys watching the game"; otherwise count on a "chill" "neighborhood watering hole" with "charming" bartenders who "have a strong right arm when pouring."

Shanghai 1930
| 23 | 23 | 20 | $12 |

Embarcadero | 133 Steuart St. (bet. Howard & Mission Sts.) | 415-896-5600 | www.shanghai1930.com

"Drift into beautiful Shanghai without having to buy an expensive airline ticket" at this "sexy" if "slightly sleepy jazz venue" near the Embarcadero serving "wildly delicious" Chinese food and "cool cocktails"; service is "attentive" and you don't have to "fight obnoxious scenesters" for a seat in the "underground, swanky setting", making it a "perfect" place to "wind down from a busy day"; N.B. members can puff in the Guanxi Lounge, the private cigar area.

Sheba Piano Lounge
| - | - | - | M |

Western Addition | 1419 Fillmore St. (O'Farrell St.) | 415-440-7414 | www.shebalounge.com

All you need are "some good looking men fanning you with a giant feather and feeding you peeled grapes" to complete the picture say would-be Mae Wests who slink over to this Ethiopan restaurant's cozy jazz piano lounge in the Western Addition; the live bop and swing accompanied by soft lighting and a lengthy list of bar snacks makes it a "wonderful place to chill out, relax and enjoy the good life."

	APPEAL	DECOR	SERVICE	COST

Shine
24 | 19 | 22 | $9

SoMa | 1337 Mission St. (bet. 9th & 10th Sts.) | 415-255-1337 | www.shinesf.com

If "someone decorated their parents' basement and invited all of Burning Man over for a drink", the scene might resemble this "intimate" SoMa club with an "upbeat vibe", "such friendly service" and "solid DJs" spinning a "mix of musical options"; it's a "funky" spot for scenesters turned off by "big nightclubs", plus the photo booth is a "nice bonus" – just beware that the pics are posted on Flickr.com nightly.

Silver Clouds
- | - | - | M

Marina | 1994 Lombard St. (Webster St.) | 415-922-1977

Twentysomethings come to this unglamorous Marina karaoke bar in large groups, the better to egg on their friends to belt out 'Total Eclipse of the Heart' and other cheesy '80s tunes; it isn't the spot for serious crooners, but fueled with enough liquid courage (in the form of more than 25 beers on tap, strong cocktails and cheap tequila shots), everyone at least thinks they're a star; weekend brunch and dinner are served in the adjoining restaurant.

Simple Pleasures Cafe ⊉
- | - | - | I

Outer Richmond | 3434 Balboa St. (bet. 35th & 36th Aves.) | 415-387-4022

Locals who live in this stretch of the Outer Richmond are "sure to recognize a friendly face" at this "relaxed" cafe offering wine, beer and "decent food" along with "traditional" coffee drinks; it's a bit of a "small town in the city" so "feel free to play" one of the board games, "chat with friends on the comfy couches" or drop in to enjoy the "occasional" live acoustic jazz or folk acts.

Sip Bar & Lounge
17 | 17 | 18 | $9

North Beach | 787 Broadway St. (Powell St.) | 415-699-6545 | www.siploungesf.com

"Not too big" and "usually not too crowded", this "slightly upscale", "laid-back lounge" in North Beach is just right for a "chill night" nod night owls who sip the evening away, and despite a "layout that's a little quirky", groove to "fairly good music" on the dance floor; but critics carp that the "movies playing on the screen" are "distracting", adding that it "tries to be cooler than it is."

Skylark
14 | 13 | 15 | $7

Mission | 3089 16th St. (Valencia St.) | 415-621-9294 | www.skylarkbar.com

On weekends the "tiny dance floor" gets "packed, packed, packed" with "sweaty" sorts grooving to hip-hop DJs, while on Sundays (when there's live Brazilian music) and weekdays, it's "loungelike" making it "one of the few Mission bars in the 16th and Valencia area where you can chill, dance" or sip $2 beers during happy hour; still, the jaded jibe that "classless snobs drink here", though cocktails can be "hard to find" (feels like "100 people and one bartender").

☑ Slanted Door, The
24 | 23 | 21 | $12

Embarcadero | Ferry Bldg. | 1 Ferry Plaza (Market St.) | 415-861-8032 | www.slanteddoor.com

Should you be "lucky enough to sneak a seat at the bar", order a "mighty refreshing", "expensive" "exotic mixed drink" from the "knowledgeable bartender" before "chasing your poison down" with "the most exquisite Vietnamese food" anywhere; "young, hip" locals, the "commuter crowd" and tourists alike all adore this "fabulously sexy" restaurant in the Embarcadero's Ferry Building, where you can "check out the lights on the Bay", so don't be surprised if the "background buzz" veers toward "deafening."

Slide
22 | 23 | 18 | $9

Downtown | 430 Mason St. (Geary St.) | 415-421-1916 | www.slidesf.com

When "you're so inclined", scoot feet first down the "kitschy slide" and "into a night of fun" at this "fabulous" Downtown "throwback to the Prohibition era" with a "fun speakeasy atmosphere"; what a "comfortable layout" – the "backlit bar" is "definitely not lacking in tasty drinks", there's an "energetic dance floor" and "cozy nooks and booths" too; but the less-electrified vent that the "velvet rope is a nightmare" – it's "hard to get in" if you don't reserve bottle service.

Slim's
20 | 11 | 14 | $8

SoMa | 333 11th St. (bet. Folsom & Harrison Sts.) | 415-255-0333 | www.slims-sf.com

"Come for the bands, not the bar" because the "music rocks" at this "cool SoMa" spot, a "marvelous venue" owned by '70s sensation Boz Scaggs; "love being cramped into this place and listening to some great tunes" declare diehards who catch "interesting" alternative, blues, roots and R&B acts; still, a slim few cite "small", "expensive" drinks and "surly stagehands"; N.B. make a dinner reservation to guarantee a table.

Slow Club
21 | 18 | 19 | $8

Mission | 2501 Mariposa St. (Hampshire St.) | 415-241-9390 | www.slowclub.com

A "casual, hip" hangout "lit by candlelight" (or so it seems), this Outer Mission restaurant with a "small bar" is a "sexy" spot to enjoy a "few intimate drinks" (try the "fabulous" Bloody Mary) "away from the hustle-bustle"; but while acolytes adore the "über-cool" decor and deem the "ambiance priceless", especially for a "first date", others are slow to come around, kvetching that the decor boasts a "wee" bit "too much concrete."

S.N.O.B.
17 | 15 | 16 | $12

Polk Gulch | 1327 Polk St. (bet. Bush & Pine Sts.) | 415-440-7662 | www.sfsnob.com

"Don't let the name fool you", because this "rustic yet hip" vino bar on Polk Street is "very down-to-earth and friendly" confide followers who favor "sitting on a wine barrel" and "nibbling on some cheese and crackers" with a glass from the "extensive list" "away from the hullabaloo of the city"; but detractors describe the selection as "subpar" and assert that prices are "too high for this neighborhood."

Space 550 ⊉
20 | 14 | 14 | $10

Bayview | 550 Barneveld Ave. (bet. Industrial St. & Oakdale St.) | 415-550-8286 | www.space550.com

"Secluded from the city" in "middle-of-nowhere" Bayview, this bi-level 15,000-sq.-ft. club with DJs spinning house, hip-hop and new wave lures a mostly gay and lesbian crowd that likes to "get lost in the fantastic space"; three "spacious" dance floors and four hangout areas allow "lots of room to breath", even during "popular" parties, but on off nights it can make you feel like you're "stranded on a desert isle."

🅉 Specs Bar ⊉ `25` `20` `21` `$6`

North Beach | 12 William Saroyan Pl. (bet. Broadway & Columbus Ave.) | 415-421-4112

"Ginsberg, Cassady and Italian fishermen ooze from the decor" of this "not-to-be-missed" "beatnik 'museum'" in North Beach "where locals actually go" for "great beer" and to "go with your pint, a wedge of cheese and a sleeve of crackers"; "no pretenses here", just a "world-class dive with class" and "character that makes it shine"; no wonder diehards dig in their heels, taunting "stay away – this is my place."

Steps of Rome `20` `14` `17` `$10`

North Beach | 348 Columbus Ave. (bet. Grant Ave. & Vallejo St.) | 415-397-0435 | www.stepsofrome.com

"If you're looking for a late-night snack and a beer – and perhaps someone's number, this could be your place" confide female fans who also dish about the "outrageous", "flirty" Italian waiters that "make you feel like the most beautiful girl in the world"; but the less-smitten step off, carping it's a "tourist trap" that "brings Cancún to North Beach" – plus the staff's shtick "gets annoying after about five minutes."

Stray Bar ⊉ `-` `-` `-` `M`

Bernal Heights | 309 Cortland Ave. (bet. Bennington & Bocana Sts.) | 415-821-9263 | www.straybarsf.com

Showpiece purebreds and floppy-eared mongrels alike all flock to this cozy Bernal Heights homebody, which picks right up where previous owner Chaise Lounge left off; with a daily happy hour until seven and a welcome attitude toward canine companions (meaning it's a dog-friendly venue), it's no wonder that it's already captured a loyal audience of gay and straight regulars.

Stud, The `19` `11` `17` `$7`

SoMa | 399 Ninth St. (Harrison St.) | 415-863-6623 | www.studsf.com

"Usually totally packed and sweaty", this "landmark alternative queer" club in SoMa boasts a "funky, revolving buffet" of "men, men, men, manly men" every night, from "bears" to "punkers" to "chubs" who "shake their big ol' booty" during a twice-monthly party; still, it's the "revolutionary, twisted" and yes, "famous", Tuesday drag show, 'Trannyshack', that nails this dive's rep as the "funnest gay bar in town."

Suede `17` `17` `15` `$11`

Fisherman's Wharf | 383 Bay St. (Mason St.) | 415-399-9555 | www.suedesf.com

"Lots of stairways and many bars make it easy to get lost if you're drinking" at this "packed" Fisherman's Wharf club with "lush decor" and "hopping tunes (depending on the night)", but stepmasters insist that "just adds to the fun, especially if you're trying to avoid your boyfriend"; still, touchy types hammer home it's a "subterranean maze", citing a "swanky crowd" that "knows it's hot" and makes you "feel looked down upon."

	APPEAL	DECOR	SERVICE	COST

Sugar Café

	-	-	-	E

Downtown | 679 Sutter St. (bet. Mason & Taylor Sts.) | 415-441-5678 |
www.sugarcafesf.com

Get your sugar high on during the day while devouring fresh baked
goods with a cuppa joe by the huge granite fireplace, then come back
for a different kinda buzz (and bar bites too) after dark when this
Downtown sophomore transforms into a sleek, modern nightspot; the
finishing touch: sliding mirror doors that open to reveal an eight-ft.-
high liquor display stocked with all the makings of a tasty cocktail.

Sugar Lounge

	20	22	19	$10

Hayes Valley | 377 Hayes St. (bet. Franklin & Gough Sts.) | 415-255-7144 |
www.sugarloungesf.com

"Sweet, sweet Sugar" – "love" this "hip bar" that took over the old
Hayes and Vine space sigh Hayes Valleys habitués who pour on the
accolades, kvelling over the "cool and sexy" ambiance suited for
"snuggling on the couches" or dancing to DJs Tuesdays–Sundays;
sure, it can be "crowded as hell on weekends", but pocketbook-pluses
like a free "generous happy-hour spread", and "cocktail prices that
won't break the bank" help make it the "perfect" weeknight "retreat."

suite one8one

	18	18	15	$10

Tenderloin | 181 Eddy St. (bet. Mason & Taylor Sts.) | 415-345-9900 |
www.suite181.com

"Perhaps the hottest Miami-style" spot in town quip suite-talkers,
wooed by the "constant beat and rhythm of great music" and three "always packed" dance floors at this "popular", 16,000-sq.-ft. Tenderloin
venue where you're bound to "meet friends or make new ones"; but
jaded jet-setters jibe the "mix of people" leaves room for "improvement", scoffing that the "loungey upstairs attempts classy, but the
basement reveals the trashy."

Suppenküche

	22	17	19	$8

Hayes Valley | 601 Hayes St. (Laguna St.) | 415-252-9289 |
www.suppenkuche.com

"Sprechen zie beer?" if so, then head to this slice of "Berlin by the Bay",
a Hayes Valley hophouse and "Teutonic eatery" mit "saucy service";
though the "insufferable" crowds can make it "feel like an Eastern bloc
interrogation room", the "phenomenal" selection of "hard-to-find"
German beers "poured in glasses taller than small children" offers
compensation aplenty; P.S. stay for dinner and you may "make new
friends at the communal tables."

supperclub

	22	24	18	$11

SoMa | 657 Harrison St. (bet. 2nd & 3rd Sts.) | 415-348-0900 |
www.supperclub.com

"Populated by beautiful people and the occasional green-haired
stilt-walker", this SoMa supper club with a "blinding white interior"
feels like a "psychedelic experience without the psychedelics"; drink
and "dine in a beautiful bed and watch" as the "bizarre" "theatrical entertainment" unfolds – it's "like having a slumber party with Cirque du
Soleil" – then get into the "nice dance grooves"; it's so "surreal" you
"gotta try it once" – even if a few hiss it's "sometimes too cool for
its own good."

Sushi Groove South

23 | 21 | 19 | $10

SoMa | 1516 Folsom St. (bet. 11th & 12th Sts.) | 415-503-1950
Get your sake cocktail groove on at the "small" bar in this "hip" SoMa restaurant where "expensive" drinks are served in "large martini glasses"; true, most mill around and sip "while waiting for a table", where they order "awesome, creative sushi", but since the bartenders are "friendly" and DJs spin every night of the week, it's worth a stop, plus you may meet some "really cool people."

Swig

19 | 20 | 17 | $9

Tenderloin | 561 Geary St. (Taylor St.) | 415-931-7292 | www.swigbar.com
On weekdays, join the "beautiful" people sipping "fabulous" "strawberry basil cocktails" at this Tenderloin lounge; "shake your tail" to "eclectic" DJs and live bands on the "bumping dance floor" or relax by the "cozy fireplace" and dig the "chill" vibe that's "a little New York and a little San Francisco" "but without affectation"; but on "crazy-insane" weekends it can be a "meat market and proud of it", with a "slew of single men hoping to get lucky."

Syn Lounge

- | - | - | E

Mission | 2730 21st St. (Bryant St.) | 415-647-6546
Lust, Pride and Envy are here along with the likes of Floozy and Fornication – in cocktail form, of course, at this den of iniquity deep in the Mission; a painted planetary landscape marks the building's entrance (leftover from the space's previous owners, Cosmos and Monkey Bar) while behind the velvet curtains you'll find a sultry mix of laid-back sounds, low tables and moody lighting.

Tadich Grill

22 | 19 | 21 | $11

Downtown | 240 California St. (bet. Battery & Front Sts.) | 415-391-1849
A trip to this Downtown "classic", open since 1849, is "like going back in time" to "old-tyme San Francisco", when bartenders in "white jackets" were the norm; "surly is always the special of the day", thanks to the "crotchety waiters", the best of whom "have been working here since the Gold Rush", but that only "adds to the charm" say traditionalists who quaff "stiff drinks" with "quality seafood."

NEW Temple

- | - | - | E

SoMa | 540 Howard St. (bet. 1st & 2nd Sts.) | 415-978-9942 | www.templesf.com
After months spent wrangling the proper permits, this green-minded 20,000-sq.-ft. SoMa megaclub in the same complex as Prana restaurant is finally thumping, with big-name DJs spinning house, hip-hop and other beats over a first-rate sound system; the over-the-top decor – think Buddhist temple-meets-*Indiana Jones* – includes one virginal white-on-white room, and the Las Vegas-style excess extends to the strong drinks.

Ten15 Folsom
(aka 1015)

16 | 15 | 11 | $10

SoMa | 1015 Folsom St. (6th St.) | 415-431-1200 | www.1015.com
"Variety is the key" at this "dark" SoMa "megaclub", where the "multiple room setup means you'll never get bored" and "excellent DJs", an "awesome sound system" and five dance floors explain why it "always

gets a huge crowd" that just "wants to dance, dance, dance"; but nixers not into the numbers game declare it's "way past its prime"; N.B. it's only open Friday and Saturday, but doesn't wind down until the wee hours.

NEW Terroir Natural Wine Merchant   – | – | – | E

SoMa | 1116 Folsom St. (7th St.) | 415-558-9946 | www.terroirsf.com
A cavernous warehouse with an unfinished look houses SoMa's newest wine bar/retail store, which specializes in organic and biodynamic bottles; the young owners spin their favorite tunes on the record player while they tell the tales behind their vino options, many of which aren't found elsewhere in the city, and serve them with a small selection of cheese, charcuterie and foie gras.

Thee Parkside   17 | 14 | 14 | $6

Potrero Hill | 1600 17th St. (Wisconsin St.) | 415-503-0393 | www.theeparkside.com
"There's always something cool going on" at this "funky" dive, a "fine wall-hole" in Potrero Hill, now under new ownership, where you can park yourself for "great" live pop or alternative acts and on Sundays, "the coolest country music in the city", from rockabilly to bluegrass; the "semi-enclosed" back patio is an "unexpected treat", offering outdoor Ping-Pong tables, 'Punk Rock BBQ Happy Hour' shows and every now and then, a "nice respite from the noise."

Thirsty Bear Brewing Company   18 | 16 | 17 | $9

SoMa | 661 Howard St. (bet. 2nd & 3rd Sts.) | 415-974-0905 | www.thirstybear.com
"Enjoy your suds" at SoMa's "upbeat" "after-work watering hole" with an "industrial feel", serving "wonderful" "home-brewed" varieties that "will excite your beer belly", especially when consumed with "tasty tapas", the "ultimate accompaniment"; after "loosening up" at the bar, head upstairs where "pool tables galore" and darts "keep you entertained"; still, grumpy grizzlies growl that the "cavernous" warehouse digs are "loud, loud, loud."

13 Views Lounge   ▽ 21 | 19 | 19 | $14

Embarcadero | Hyatt Regency Hotel | 5 Embarcadero Ctr. (Market St.) | 415-788-1234 | www.hyatt.com
As luck would have it, you'll find one of the city's "best" "panoramic views" of Justin Herman Plaza, the waterfront and "SF's skyline" at this "calm, relaxing" "traditional" hotel bar in the "big atrium"-dominated lobby of the Hyatt Regency Hotel; it's the "place for out-of-towners", who choose from more than a baker's dozen of specialty cocktails, beers on tap and wines by the glass.

330 Ritch   19 | 13 | 18 | $10

South Beach | 330 Ritch St. (bet. Brannan & Townsend Sts.) | 415-541-9574
It may be "hard to find", but once you track down South Beach's happy-hour bar/club combo, "you'll wonder how the hell you'd never heard of it"; "rotating theme nights", including Thursday's 'Popscene', "can be a lot of fun", luring Brit- and mod-music-loving diehards to the "decent-sized dance floor", but it's also a "cool place to see up-and-coming bands" and DJs – and even more so following a recent renovation that's injected a modern, industrial feel.

	APPEAL	DECOR	SERVICE	COST

Tokyo Go Go

19 | **19** | **18** | **$9**

Mission | 3174 16th St. (bet. Guerrero & Valencia Sts.) | 415-864-2288 |
www.tokyogogo.com

"Go go here" root rabid fans of this "funky local spot" in the Mission
with "fine sushi", a "good sake selection" and "fun" specialty cocktails
from the full bar; though it's more restaurant than bar, regulars report
"happy hour is the way to do this joint", when the "small place" offers
"big satisfaction" in the form of "cheap" food and drink.

Tommy's Joynt ⌀

17 | **15** | **16** | **$7**

Polk Gulch | 1101 Geary Blvd. (Van Ness Ave.) | 415-775-4216 |
www.tommysjoynt.com

"If you have never been to a hofbrau", "steer for the bar" of Polk Gulch's
circa-1947, "one-of-a-kind" family-run "San Francisco institution"
with "cheesy", even "random and strange" decor; you'll find "a beer
from every country – how can you beat that?" – "fairly small" cocktails
("no alco-pops here"), plus "meat galore", including the "hearty" signature buffalo stew that tastes particularly "terrific" in the wee hours
when "you're a starvin' Marvin."

Tommy's Mexican Restaurant

22 | **16** | **21** | **$8**

Outer Richmond | 5929 Geary Blvd. (bet. 23rd & 24th Aves.) | 415-387-4747 |
www.tommystequila.com

Ask Tommy's son, sommelier Julio Bermejo, "for the special stuff"
suggest samplers who covet the "incredible" range of over 275 "quality"
100% blue agave tequilas "in or out of a margarita" at the "tiny bar" of
this "divey Mexican restaurant in the Richmond"; join the tasting club
and become an "expert" or "just go early (or expect to push your way
through)" and sip an "amazing selection" with "great grub."

Tonga Room

22 | **24** | **19** | **$13**

Nob Hill | Fairmont Hotel | 950 Mason St. (bet. California & Sacramento Sts.) |
415-772-5278 | www.fairmont.com

For "a taste of the tropics in San Francisco", an "odd mix" of "surprised
conventioneers, ironic hipsters and Japanese businessmen" heads to
this recently renovated "freaky tiki" bar in Nob Hill's Fairmont Hotel;
where else can you find hourly "indoor rainstorms" and "terrible lounge
acts" "playing cheesy tunes" from a "bandstand in the artificial lagoon"?;
just "order something with an umbrella" (yes, it's "insufferably expensive") and get into the "over-the-top kitsch" – it's "so bad it's good."

Tonic

17 | **14** | **17** | **$9**

Russian Hill | 2360 Polk St. (Union St.) | 415-771-5535 | www.tonic-bar.com

"When empty it's great for conversation, when full, great for partying
around" – add in "pretty cool" bartenders, "a jukebox with a mix of new
and old songs" and gummi bear bowls (a "refreshing alternative to the
traditional bar snack") and you've got a "laid-back" watering hole with
a "loungey NYC feel"; but while Russian Hill locals insist it's a "smart
choice" on weeknights, bubble-bursters believe it's "loosing its fizz."

Tony Nik's

23 | **19** | **22** | **$9**

North Beach | 1534 Stockton St. (bet. Green & Union Sts.) | 415-693-0990

A "tiny little spot" "tucked away" on a side street in North Beach, this
"friendly" lounge maintains a "low tourist factor", leading some surveyors to plead "please don't tell anyone about this place . . . it would

spoil it"; a visit is like "stepping back" to "the '50s", when you could "enter a relaxed bar, and leave hours later after befriending the bartenders and likely your neighbors as well."

☑ Top of the Mark   25 | 23 | 20 | $14

Nob Hill | Mark Hopkins InterContinental Hotel | 1 Nob Hill, 19th fl. (bet. California & Mason Sts.) | 415-616-6916 | www.topofthemark.com
The "scenery outside rivals the inside" at this "ritzy" skyline bar on the 19th floor of Nob Hill's Mark Hopkins Hotel that's "worth every extra dollar" for the "five-star view of San Francisco" from the "wraparound windows"; the "old-style elegance" hints at retro "Hollywood", while the live jazz and "impressive" "100-martini menu" "take you back" "to the days of Frank Sinatra", making it the "perfect" "dress up" place to "take your honey" to "rekindle the flame."

☑ Toronado ⊄   25 | 15 | 17 | $6

Lower Haight | 547 Haight St. (bet. Fillmore & Steiner Sts.) | 415-863-2276 | www.toronado.com
"If you're looking for some random, rare" brews, check out this "dark, dingy", "loud" Lower Haight "beervana" where the "best selection" "anywhere in town" (about 50 on draft and 100 bottles) means "you can pretty much drink your way around the world"; "enjoy your pint" with a "scrumptious sausage" ordered from Rosamunde next door – and just "ignore the bartenders' surliness" ("they hate everybody", even the "rough"-looking and "prominently tattooed" regulars).

Tosca Cafe ⊄   23 | 19 | 21 | $10

North Beach | 242 Columbus Ave. (Broadway) | 415-986-9651
"Channel your inner Rat Pack" entertainer at this "beyond cool" classic that's "retro without the kitsch"; operatic arias on the jukebox, "great red booths", a "gorgeous antique bar" and bartenders who "ritualistically pour" "satisfying" "spiked" cappuccino drinks establish an "Italian vibe"; despite the "swarms of tourists" its North Beach location inevitably attracts, "don't be surprised" to find celebs "elbowing up to the bar" or playing pool in the "secret room in the back."

Town Hall   23 | 22 | 23 | $12

SoMa | 342 Howard St. (bet. Beale & Fremont Sts.) | 415-908-3900 | www.townhallsf.com
The "brick interior adds just the right ambiance" to this "warm, inviting" SoMa "hot, hot, hot" spot; because the "buzzing" bar is "always crowded" during happy hour and beyond, and "it gets very loud" ("bring earplugs"), consider "kicking back" at the "awesome communal table" for some "interesting conversation" and "amazing" regional American food; no matter where you sit, you'll find a "knowledgeable bar staff" and servers who "make you feel like royalty."

Trad'r Sam's ⊄   22 | 17 | 18 | $7

Outer Richmond | 6150 Geary Blvd. (26th Ave.) | 415-221-0773
Yes, the "oversized" scorpion bowls ("meant to be shared between four people, or so they say") are "always a recipe for trouble" at this "tiny", "cheesy tropical" tiki hut in the Outer Richmond that's "been around for a gazillion years", well, since 1939; never mind the "divey" digs – after a few "frothy, fruity drinks", you'll be ready to "break out the ukulele and the leis" with the rest of the "college kids and drunks."

	APPEAL	DECOR	SERVICE	COST

Trax

| | 19 | 14 | 22 | $6 |

Haight-Ashbury | 1437 Haight St. (bet. Ashbury St. & Masonic Ave.) | 415-864-4213

"A gay dive bar in the Haight? why not?" ask aficionados of this unusually "straight-friendly" "spot for a drink"; obviously it's "nothing fancy", but the "completely unpretentious, attitude-free atmosphere" attracts "friendly" folks who want to "get away from the clones of the Castro" and shoot a game of pool at the "table that no one ever uses"; P.S. some of the "cheap drinks" get even cheaper during the extra-long happy hour.

Tres Agaves

| | 22 | 20 | 19 | $10 |

South Beach | 130 Townsend St. (bet. 2nd & 3rd Sts.) | 415-227-0500 | www.tresagaves.com

"Celebrate or lick your wounds after a ball game" at AT&T Park at this "loud, packed", "happening" Mexican restaurant/lounge that adds a "sophisticated splash of margarita madness" to South Beach; order a flight from the "commanding" tequila list and "enjoy in true aficionado fashion" or a "pricey, potent" cocktail from the "knowledgeable" agave gurus behind the bar – you "can't have just one!"; still, prickly sorts snipe the bartenders have *très* "attitude" (it's "not rocket science").

Truck

| | - | - | - | M |

Mission | 1900 Folsom St. (15th St.) | 415-252-0306 | www.trucksf.com
The former resident of this Outer Mission space, Wilde Oscar's, had an unfortunate meeting with the business end of a wayward truck; the result though is this aptly named new venue, where an easy-mix gay-straight crowd gathers in the casually kitschy, transporation-themed space for pinball and pool, drinks and late-night eats like burgers and doughnut holes (served until 1 AM nightly).

Tunnel Top ⌦

| | 18 | 12 | 18 | $6 |

Downtown | 601 Bush St. (Stockton St.) | 415-986-8900
You could "walk by" this "dark", "swanky dive" on top of the Stockton Tunnel "a million times and not realize it's there", but it's "definitely worth stepping inside"; yeah, it sometimes swarms with "well-paid tech types posing as bicycle messengers" and a handful huff it's "grittier than most bars in the area", but it's also undoubtedly "hip" and "full of character", plus there are DJs nightly – "you can't help but get swept up by it."

12 Galaxies

| | 21 | 13 | 17 | $7 |

Mission | 2565 Mission St. (22nd St.) | 415-970-9777 | www.12galaxies.com
"Sometimes the acts are brilliant, sometimes not so much" at this "divey" live music venue in the "hipster-flooded" Mission with a "great sound" system and a "sassy staff"; the "upstairs mezzanine is a nice way to get out of the crush", play pool, down "cheap drinks" and "spy your cutie below watching the band"; P.S. given its "size you can dance anywhere" – but you might not be able to drink as its license was temporarily revoked in early 2008.

21st Amendment Brewery Cafe

| | 20 | 17 | 19 | $7 |

South Beach | 563 Second St. (bet. Brannan & Bryant Sts.) | 415-369-0900 | www.21st-amendment.com
"Creative" "craft beer brewed on-site" is the "specialty at this loud urban alehouse", a "cool loft space" in South Beach near AT&T Park;

there's no prohibition on "tasty" food, either, as evidenced by the "great wings" and other "innovative" items; yup, the outside garden is a bit of a "zoo" before Giants games, but off-season the "mellow atmosphere", "interesting mix of people" and events like iPod Night on Wednesdays make it a neighborhood hangout.

2223 Restaurant & Bar
21 | 20 | 21 | $12

Castro | 2223 Market St. (bet. Noe & Sanchez Sts.) | 415-431-0692 | www.2223restaurant.com

"Relaxed and elegant", this "swanky restaurant/bar" – a "rare find in the Castro" – may be the "perfect place to mingle before dinner" or for a "weeknight date"; the "crowd is hip" and the "eye candy's not bad either" "courtesy of the servers", who not only dress up the venue but are also "friendly and very knowledgeable", whipping up "divine drinks" to help you wash down those "great small plates."

Twin Peaks Tavern ⊖
14 | 14 | 18 | $7

Castro | 401 Castro St. (17th St.) | 415-864-9470 | www.twinpeakstavern.com

Perhaps the first homosexual "bar in San Francisco to open up its insides to the outside world with full-length picture windows", this "affordable place" with "affable" "bearlike bartenders" provides a "ringside seat for Castro Street people-watching"; if some fresh whippersnappers give it a "bad rap", deriding its "Rogaine crowd" of "mostly middle-aged and older men", supporters who regard it as the 'gay *Cheers*' retort "glad it's there" – it's "kind of a beacon for the neighborhood."

TWO
- | - | - | M

SoMa | 22 Hawthorne St. (bet. Folsom & Howard Sts.) | 415-777-9779

Hawthorne Lane may be history, but the restaurant's resident bartenders remain, nimbly mixing cocktails made with fresh-squeezed juices and house-infused spirits like vodka and tequila for a boisterous happy-hour crowd at this recently reborn SoMa spot funkified with a copper/concrete bar and eye-catching light fixtures; TWO's also a magic number for oenophiles who order 15 wines by the glass or carafes of barrel-aged wines at rock-bottom prices to match the hearty $2 bar bites.

222 Club ⊖
∇ 22 | 19 | 22 | $8

Tenderloin | 222 Hyde St. (bet. Eddy & Turk Sts.) | 415-440-0222 | www.222club.net

"Don't tell anyone about the 'loin's best hideout" confide conspirators who brave the somewhat "seedy area" to "unwind" at "this inconspicuous place" that's "hip to spinners and DJ aficionados"; small plates, thin-crust pizzas and a "limited but well-selected" cocktail menu make it a "nice place" to kick back "for those looking to take a night off" from the bustling bar scene.

Umami
- | - | - | E

Cow Hollow | 2909 Webster St. (Union St.) | 415-346-3431 | www.umamisf.com

No sign on the door does not translate to no crowds at this swanky, low-lit Pan-Asian newcomer in Cow Hollow boasting rustic woods, smooth stone and clean lines; dinner customers settle into tables upstairs, ordering bitter, sour, salty and sweet dishes, with some seeking

	APPEAL	DECOR	SERVICE	COST

'umami,' an elusive 'fifth taste' that's somewhere in between these flavors; but the party bunch that fills the sake bar seems more preoccupied with drinks, small plates and dancing.

Underground SF

	18	13	18	$8

Lower Haight | 424 Haight St. (Webster St.) | 415-864-7386
A "nice alternative" to the "Castro and SoMa scenes", this Lower Haight "home away from home" for "in-the-know homos" "from all walks of life" has "lots of divey appeal"; check out the "black light graffiti art" and the "theme nights to match any taste" (the 'Drunk and Horny' parties on Saturdays "totally live up to their name"); still, old-school sorts sigh "it was a heck of lot more fun" back when it was The Top.

Uptown ⊄

	23	12	21	$5

Mission | 200 Capp St. (17th St.) | 415-861-8231
"Hipsters looking for cheap drinks" and working-class Mission-ites populate this "lovably dowdy old place" boasting booths and decrepit couches and on occasion, live music; it's so low-key (the "way a dive bar ought to be") you could practically "drink in your PJs", but you might look silly if you choose to challenge someone to pool or play pinball; N.B. barbecue is available most weekend afternoons.

NEW Uva Enoteca

	-	-	-	M

Lower Haight | 568 Haight St. (bet. Fillmore & Steiner Sts.) | 415-829-2024 | www.uvaenoteca.com
Sommelier Boris Nemchenok, who once worked alongside Mario Batali, brings a bit of *Italia* to the Lower Haight with this traditional enoteca, where antipasti, charcuterie plates and panini are paired with vinos from all along the Italian peninsula; belly up to the Carrera marble bar to quaff wine by the quartino (one-third bottle) or three-ounce pour or press on to the more sedate dining room in the back; though there's no hard liquor, celebrity cocktail consultant Camber Lay has concocted a drinks menu drawing on sparkling wines.

Varnish Fine Art & Wine Bar

	21	23	20	$9

SoMa | 77 Natoma St. (2nd St.) | 415-222-6131 | www.varnishfineart.com
Truly a "great place to get your art on", this "funky, offbeat", bi-level gallery space in SoMa showcases "interesting" exhibitions (mostly sculpture) sure to "spark conversation with new acquaintances" over a beer, glass of wine or a sake or soju cocktail; the "lovely owners" and "awesome" bartenders who "know how to treat customers" add a "warm" finishing touch; P.S. call ahead, because they're "often closed for special events."

Velvet Cantina

	-	-	-	I

Mission | 3349 23rd St. (Bartlett St.) | 415-648-4142 | www.velvetcantina.com
Though most brave the long wait for a table, the better to enjoy huge helpings of nachos, tacos and chile con queso, night owls pack into the small bar area, content to quaff killer cocktails like pineapple margaritas and cilantro gimlets until 2 AM; the two low-ceilinged dining rooms, each lit with a dim amber glow, recall a Mexican saloon transplanted to the Mission, but instead of Guadalajarans you'll probably see gringos and gringas swilling pitchers of sangria during raucous birthday celebrations.

Vertigo ⏸

			M

Polk Gulch | 1160 Polk St. (Sutter St.) | 415-674-1278

The lighting is so dim in this South Seas–themed Polk Gulch bar that you may miss the hundred-plus tiki masks on the walls, but the larger-than-life Polynesian potions, like the Volcano, hit you between the eyes; still, most enjoy the chill scene with traditional cocktails and draft beers, before hitting the dance floor (Wednesday–Saturday), when the DJs get busy, or taking a breather in the enclosed smoking patio.

Vessel

			VE

Downtown | 85 Campton Pl. (Stockton St.) | 415-433-8585 | www.vesselsf.com

If you want to skip the velvet rope and waltz straight into this Downtowner in the basement of a Niketown store, a sleek package done up with brick walls, a glowing orange interior and even a petrified juniper tree in the V.I.P. area, reserve a table on the weekends; the seat is certain to come in handy after dancing all night with a techie bigwig crowd to booming hip-hop and house music.

❏ Vesuvio

24	22	19	$8

North Beach | 255 Columbus Ave. (Jack Kerouac Alley) | 415-362-3370 | www.vesuvio.com

"Discuss literature, poetry and film over a pint" just like Jack Kerouac at this "beat generation hangout" near City Lights bookstore in North Beach; no matter how many tourists pass through, it remains an "iconic" SF landmark that's "worth the legendary hype", thanks in part to the "walls covered with interesting stuff in full crazy color"; P.S. "sit upstairs and watch the hustle and bustle of Columbus Avenue" below.

❏ View Lounge

26	21	20	$11

SoMa | Marriott Hotel | 55 Fourth St., 39th fl. (bet. Market & Mission Sts.) | 415-896-1600 | www.marriott.com

Yes, "the name says it all" at this "elegant" lounge with a "relaxed ambiance" "high up" on the 39th floor of SoMa's Marriott; "it's definitely better when it's dark", when peering through the "massive" panes is "like looking out the Death Star window", though during the day a "melting pot of people" "watch the fog roll in"; but while the vistas are "fantastic", some scoff that the "rest is mundane"; N.B. live jazz on weekends.

Vino Rosso

			M

Bernal Heights | 629 Cortland Ave. (Anderson St.) | 415-647-1269

Oenophilic fever has made it to the cozy hilltop neighborhood of Bernal Heights with the opening of this new enoteca; the space is small but the atmosphere warm and the Italian-centric selection by the glass, taste or bottle an invitation to exploration (helped along by occasional vino-tasting classes too); N.B. parents can roll in with strollers on 'Wine and Whiner' Wednesdays.

Voda

19	19	19	$10

Downtown | 56 Belden Pl. (bet. Bush & Pine Sts.) | 415-677-9242 | www.vodasf.com

"*Très* chic" with "international appeal", this recently renovated "temple" to the clear stuff, "fittingly tucked" into "very Euro" Belden Place, seems to stock "every vodka known to humankind", served by a "saucy" staff; the "relaxed atmosphere" "does the trick" for desk jock-

	APPEAL	DECOR	SERVICE	COST

eys, and later, when "DJs spin good music", it becomes "loud", "energetic" and the "hippest" bar around; still, a handful huff that a "lame" "drunk" crowd sometimes "ruins what could be a sexy spot."

Warfield, The

| 20 | 20 | 15 | $10 |

Downtown | 982 Market St. (bet. 5th & 6th Sts.) | 415-775-7722 | www.bgp.com

"You're never too old or too young to fit in with the eclectic crowd" at this circa-1922 "grand palace" Downtown, a former vaudeville theater and "piece of San Francisco heritage" that remains a "great smaller venue" for "top rockers"; "if you want to feel like you're really a big part of the concert, then don't sit in the balcony" confide insiders who "bring good standing shoes"; still, bashers boo the "stressed out" bartenders and hiss it's an "unsatisfying" experience.

NEW Waterbar

| - | - | - | E |

Embarcadero | 399 Embarcadero (bet. Folsom & Harrison Sts.) | 415-284-9922 | www.waterbarsf.com

At Pat Kuleto's Embarcadero newcomer with a Walt-Disney-meets-Jules-Verne theme, live fish flap around two floor-to-ceiling cylindrical aquariums, an upbeat crowd clinks glasses beneath a glittering hand-blown chandelier and the Bay Bridge looms large outside the windows; it's a splashy setting for a sophisticated seafood supper, or for just sipping a well-crafted cocktail and slurping oysters at the raw bar; tables on the waterfront patio are coveted during warm weather.

Whiskey Thieves ⇌

| 23 | 19 | 25 | $7 |

Tenderloin | 839 Geary St. (bet. Hyde & Larkin Sts.) | 415-409-2063

"What's not to like" about a dive with a "good pool table" and as the name suggests, a "wall full of whiskeys" (about 175 in all) muse scotch aficionados who also light up inside the premises of this owner-operated 'loin hang equipped with a high-tech ventilating system; the "friendly" bartenders who "always remember a face" pour "strong drinks", though, so don't expect to be able to do the same.

Whisper

| ▽ 15 | 16 | 11 | $13 |

Mission | 535 Florida St. (bet. 18th & Mariposa Sts.) | 415-356-9800 | www.whispersf.com

A "restaurant by day and a nightclub at night", this "huge" "venue with multiple rooms" and outdoor decks is a "surprise find" on the edge of the Mission; the "crowd depends on which promoter throws the event", so it's "sporadically fun", but the bartenders who are "poor at best" and dole out "drinks that are just ice with barely any liquor" get few shout-outs from those in-the-know.

Wild Side West ⇌

| 22 | 20 | 21 | $6 |

Bernal Heights | 424 Cortland Ave. (Wool St.) | 415-647-3099

"On a sunny afternoon", "it's all about drinks" in the "secret garden" at this "welcoming" "lesbian stomping ground" that "takes all comers" ("no straight hate" here); if you're not gay, "being a 25- to 35-year-old hipster is a close second", especially if a "low-key Burning Woman vibe" is your thing; yup, it's a "little out of the way" in Bernal Heights, but hey, it's the "perfect neighborhood" place to "kick back with a beer."

NEW Wine Bar, The

- | - | - | M

Russian Hill | 2032 Polk St. (bet. B'way & Pacific St.) | 415-931-4307

With such a straightforward name, it's no wonder this narrow nook in Russian Hill is one of the city's least snooty vino bars: it offers wines by the glass, flight and bottle, but there are also bottles of oatmeal stout and even some Pabst Blue Ribbon; the chocolate-hued room is equally unpretentious, with industrial-style light fixtures offering a dim glow.

NEW Wine Jar

- | - | - | E

Western Addition | 1870 Fillmore St. (Bush St.) | 415-931-2924 | www.winejar-sf.com

Though the menu isn't huge – at any given time about 30 wines by the bottle and 25 by the half and full glass are on offer, as well as a cheese plate for the peckish – the space is even smaller at this new Western Addition *vin* venue; low-slung suede sofas and black-and-white photos on the wall make it a comfy place to hang out while waiting for your table at SPQR, the wildly popular restaurant about a block away.

Wish

22 | 19 | 22 | $8

SoMa | 1539 Folsom St. (bet. 11th & 12th Sts.) | 415-278-9474 | www.wishsf.com

"Lighting that is oh-so-flattering" and "consistently great music spun by San Francisco's top DJs" make this "SoMa mainstay" "in the hoppin' 11th and Folsom area" "a sure hit"; "extremely attentive" mixologists help ensure it's "always packed" with the "young and beautiful" "from all over the city", but wishful thinkers yearn for more room in the "narrow bar", whining "sometimes it can be too packed."

Woody Zips

- | - | - | M

North Beach | 1609 Powell St. (Green St.) | 415-982-8898 | www.woodyzips.com

It's not just die-hard sports sorts who have reason to cheer about this North Beach tavern that pairs its televised action with DJs, "nice, stiff cocktails", decent eats (think housemade corn dogs) and an "arty" atmosphere; surfing, skiing and soccer all share plasma-screen space with the NFL, making it an "enjoyable" destination for the "professional crowd after work and a fun mix of cute girls and guys on the weekends."

Would You Believe . . . Cocktails ⌷

11 | 8 | 19 | $7

Inner Richmond | 4652 Geary Blvd. (bet. 10th & 11th Aves.) | 415-752-7444

While the female bartenders "always have a moment to get to know you" at this "funky" Inner Richmond watering hole, would you believe that they also "range from not knowing what vodka is to being very good" at their craft?; locals don't mind that's it's "not super-exciting" and that the crowd is an "odd assortment" of "Asian people" and "drunk blokes from Ireland", shrugging "if you like dives" then "this is the place."

NEW Wunder Brewing Co.

- | - | - | I

Inner Sunset | 1326 Ninth Ave. (bet. Irving & Judah Sts.) | 415-681-2337 | www.wunderbeer.com

An SF fixture from 1896–1909, this esteemed name in beerdom is dormant no more thanks to brewmaster John Wonder (pure coincidence) and partners who've resurrected the handle at this bi-level Inner Sunset brewery, where stainless-steel vats of housemade beers are visible

	APPEAL	DECOR	SERVICE	COST

through the window; sit at the butcher paper–topped tables and order one of eight or so suds on tap (say, a stout, pilsner or IPA) and pub grub or at the curvaceous bar and watch the game on the TVs.

XYZ
20 | **23** | **18** | **$12**

SoMa | W Hotel | 181 Third St. (Howard St.) | 415-817-7836 | www.xyz-sf.com

The "beautiful people", "trendy" locals and "convention" attendees on the "company expense account" are "dressed to kill" at this "sleek, dark", "right-out-of-a-movie" "hot spot" in SoMa's W Hotel; but while some quip "XYZ is where you'll find me" sitting in a "big comfy booth" with a martini or a glass of biodynamic wine, others lament it's not letter-perfect, musing "don't we all have a friend who's more impressed with herself than she should be? – this is the bar equivalent."

Yancy's ⊅
20 | **15** | **18** | **$6**

Inner Sunset | 734 Irving St. (bet. 8th & 9th Aves.) | 415-665-6551

"A strange combination of sports bar and fern bar", this Inner Sunset spot mixes it up with a jumbo-screen TV and tons of potted plants; UCSF upperclassmen and "working stiffs" bring in food from nearby restaurants, then "chill and watch the big game"; you also "can't beat the dartboard" and pool table – yup, this "homey" hangout is just as "comfy" as a "college student's living room."

Yield Wine Bar
▽ **25** | **23** | **27** | **$10**

Dogpatch | 2490 Third St. (22nd St.) | 415-401-8984 | www.yieldsf.com

Giving the wine-inclined another "reason to go to Dogpatch", this "welcome" sophomore delivers "organic, sustainable and biodynamic" reds, whites and sparklers in a "cozy setting"; yes, "there are tasty 'green'" choices out there enthuse eco-oenophiles, who find it a "perfect place" for "an intimate conversation" (it's like "having friends over to your own private cellar") and appreciate that the "knowledgeable staff" also serves up a small menu of snacks; N.B. closed Sundays.

ⓩ Yoshi's San Francisco
24 | **22** | **21** | **$11**

NEW **Western Addition** | Fillmore Heritage Ctr. | 1330 Fillmore St. (Eddy St.) | 415-655-5600 | www.yoshis.com

See Yoshi's Jack London Square review in East of San Francisco Directory.

Zam Zam ⊅
23 | **22** | **18** | **$8**

Haight-Ashbury | 1633 Haight St. (bet. Belvedere & Clayton Sts.) | 415-861-2545

Offering "a welcome respite" from the surrounding "hempy" hippie scene, this "surprisingly elegant" Upper Haight hideaway with a "hip Moroccan vibe" is "reminiscent of a bygone era"; though a few feel it was "even better" when the late "martini Nazi" Bruno Mooshei "ruled the roost", even they admit that at least now you don't have to face his unpredictable "moods"; indeed, many believe the bartenders still "mix a mean cocktail here" ("close to frozen, but not crunchy").

Zebulon
21 | **18** | **16** | **$11**

SoMa | 83 Natoma St. (bet. 1st & 2nd Sts.) | 415-975-5705 | www.zebulonsf.com

A lunch spot for FiDi suit monkeys by day, this "chic, comfortable" SoMa "loft space" morphs into the "perfect" "happy-hour gathering point with affordable drinks and good bar food snacks" when the sun goes down; but while aesthetes agree that "high ceilings, brick walls and interesting huge paintings add to the atmosphere", grouches growl it "tries too hard to be SF arty" and the "music gets waaay too loud."

☑ Zeitgeist ⊅ | 23 | 13 | 15 | $5

Mission | 199 Valencia St. (Duboce Ave.) | 415-255-7505

"Divey biker bar meets German beer hall" in the Mission, where "tattooed punk rockers", "grandmas" and "Japanese tourists" "cross-pollinate"; buy your pitcher inside, then head to the "sea of picnic tables" in the "legendary" garden; if the "BBQ smoke wafting through the air" makes your stomach rumble, order food, but steel yourself for the "comically rude" servers who "yell at you when your order's ready."

Zeke's Sports Bar & Grill | - | - | - | M

SoMa | 600 Third St. (Brannan St.) | 415-392-5311 | www.zekesbar.com

What a "great place for alums to gather" – "few places rival" this SoMa sports bar "when it comes to watching the Ohio State Buckeyes" and other college and national leagues; it's a "favorite for a burger and brew" cheer fans who swing by after the ballpark to tune in to games on the multiple screens courtesy of the six satellite dishes; but it's not win-win for all – cynics maintain it's "mediocre" and needs an "upgrade."

☑ Zuni Café | 24 | 22 | 22 | $11

Hayes Valley | 1658 Market St. (bet. Franklin & Gough Sts.) | 415-552-2522 | www.zunicafe.com

"Rub shoulders with SF's movers and shakers" who "still pack in" to Hayes Valley's "venerable" hangout that's "never out of style", even after over 29 years in this "odd-shaped" space that "anchors Market Street"; whether you sip a "fantastic Bloody Mary" at the "beautiful" copper-topped bar, nab a corner table and "enjoy views" through the "huge windows" or best yet, stay for a "full-blown meal", "it fits all the bills" for a "good night's entertainment"; N.B. closed Mondays.

East of San Francisco

Albany Bowl
17 | 10 | 14 | $7

Albany | 540 San Pablo Ave. (Clay St.) | 510-526-8818 |
www.albanybowl.biz

It "isn't the classiest of places" but this "old-fashioned", "classic"
Albany alley "from another era" (1949, in fact) boasting "lanes as
smooth and flat as a tuna casserole" is definitely a "fun" spot "to
spend an evening"; after tallying your strikes, join the local crowd at
the "pretty funky" pool tables and the arcade games or roll over to the
sports bar for a beer.

❷ Albatross Pub ⌿
25 | 18 | 20 | $7

Berkeley | 1822 San Pablo Ave. (bet. Delaware St. & Hearst Ave.) |
510-843-2473 | www.albatrosspub.com

This "cozy, warm" Berkeley hangout "acts as a community living
room" for a "diverse crowd" of "laid-back grad students", "Cal profes-
sors and assorted locals" that finds "the draw of drinking and playing
Trivial Pursuit" or other board games "irresistible" (hard-core buffs
"flaunt their knowledge at Sunday's pub quiz"); it's also "heaven for
dartboard fans" while the "never-ending popcorn bowls" and "excellent" brew selection "make it easy to become a regular."

Alley, The ⌿
22 | 19 | 19 | $5

Oakland | 3325 Grand Ave. (Mandana Blvd.) | 510-444-8505

"Rod Dibble, an Oakland institution", "tickles the keys" while "local
virtuosos" croon to his "melodic stylings" at this "classic dive piano
bar"; while some find it "very strange", with "drunk" "lounge lizards"
singing and "70 years of business cards on the wall", others call it
"charming", citing "cheap, stiff cocktails", including a "pretty and potent" mai tai; no one can deny, though, it's a "unique" spot for warbling
"your worries away."

Ashkenaz ⌿
18 | 15 | 15 | $9

Berkeley | 1317 San Pablo Ave. (Gilman St.) | 510-525-5054 |
www.ashkenaz.com

"The spirit of hippies and flower children lingers" at this "funky
Berkeley tradition" with a "soulful, gritty atmosphere" where you can
hear an "unbelievable" variety of "great live music, particularly of the
world beat variety", from African to Zydeco and everything in between; "when you have no desire for pretense and want to dance till
your heart's content", this "eclectic", kid-friendly "community place"
is a "great place to be."

Beckett's Irish Pub
22 | 21 | 20 | $8

Berkeley | 2271 Shattuck Ave. (bet. Bancroft Way & Kittredge St.) |
510-647-1790 | www.beckettsirishpub.com

Pints of "Guinness pulled properly" beckon Beckett-ites to Berkeley's
"quintessential Irish pub", set in a "wonderful old fairy-tale building"
boasting "warm rooms with fireplaces and wood paneling" that may
"make you want to stay all night"; entertainment varies nightly thanks
to the rotating roster of "lively" honky-tonk, acoustic rock, pop and
world music acts, but regulars confide "don't miss the brainiacs" on
Tuesday's quiz night.

APPEAL | DECOR | SERVICE | COST

Ben & Nick's
18 | **13** | **13** | **$7**

Oakland | 5612 College Ave. (bet. Keith Ave. & Ocean View Dr.) | 510-923-0327

Rockridge locals "love to sit by the windows on a summer evening" and "watch the yuppies go by" while enjoying the "excellent selection of craft beers" and "great fried calamari" at this "casual" hangout; it's "funky and fun" and a "good place to start or wrap up an evening" – just overlook the collegiate "hipster" crowd that "can get overprotective" of their "grungy" neighborhood spot.

Blakes on Telegraph
17 | **13** | **16** | **$9**

Berkeley | 2367 Telegraph Ave. (Durant Ave.) | 510-848-0886 | www.blakesontelegraph.com

"Hang with a mainly college-age crowd" at this "long-standing music/cocktail venue" that's "very popular" with Berkeley undergrads; the "kitchen serves passable grub", but telegraphers signal that "it's best known" for its "dim", "kinda grungy" "downstairs scene", where "local artists" do their thing; but not everyone gets the Morse code, taunting "if you like drinking like a student, this is the place for you."

Café Rouge
21 | **19** | **21** | **$11**

Berkeley | Market Plaza | 1782 Fourth St. (bet. Hearst Ave. & Virginia St.) | 510-525-1440 | www.caferouge.net

"Champagne and oysters on a Saturday afternoon? yes!" exclaim "Fourth Street shoppers, foodies and local workers" who pop their corks over this "airy, bright" cafe with a "wonderful ambiance"; when you can't go for a "great" dinner, "go with your lady" or guy and celebrate that red letter day with "wonderful bar nibblies" and a little something from the "good drink selection."

Café Valparaiso
22 | **17** | **18** | **$8**

Berkeley | La Peña Cultural Ctr. | 3105 Shattuck Ave. (Prince St.) | 510-849-2568 | www.lapena.org

"Get out your tie-dye shirt" and head to the La Peña Cultural Center's "intimate", "multiethnic venue" for a "little slice of a Berkeley-gone-by" "not found elsewhere"; the "great" mix of artists and cultural events, many with a Latino bent, from blues to spoken word, "helps to ensure that you're never bored" while the Latin American meals and snacks, plus beer and wine sold at the next-door cafe help stave off the munchies.

Cafe Van Kleef
24 | **25** | **20** | **$8**

Oakland | 1621 Telegraph Ave. (bet. 16th & 17th Sts.) | 510-763-7711 | www.cafevankleef.com

"Pretty kick-back but with good energy" and "chock-full of exotic eclectica", this "crazy-looking place in the heart of Downtown" Oakland "looks a little like an antiques store exploded"; the "welcoming" owner, Peter Van Kleef, imbues the neighborhood with "quirky" "pizzazz" as he serves up specialty libations that are "worth the wait" made with citrus fruits "fresh-squeezed to order" (the "fantastic greyhound" is a "true destination drink").

Caffe Trieste
20 | **15** | **18** | **$7**

Berkeley | 2500 San Pablo Ave. (Dwight Way) | 510-548-5198 | www.caffetrieste.com
See review in City of San Francisco Directory.

	APPEAL	DECOR	SERVICE	COST

Cato's Ale House

19 | **15** | **17** | **$6**

Oakland | 3891 Piedmont Ave. (Montell St.) | 510-655-3349 | www.mrcato.com

Some of the "most knowledgeable 'beertenders' around" man 22 "taps flowing with great brews" at this "brother to Ben & Nicks", also in Oakland; it's a "serve-yourself kind of place", so stand in line, order a pint, soju cocktails and "tasty pub food", then take it to the "funky patio" that makes you feel like you're "kickin' it in your own backyard" and enjoy the "casual vibe."

Cerrito Speakeasy Theater

- | **-** | **-** | **M**

El Cerrito | 10070 San Pablo Ave. (bet. Central & Fairmount Aves.) | 510-814-2400 | www.cerritospeakeasy.com

Fill your belly with pizza, beer or wine at this art deco movie house that's set in the restored El Cerrito theater, run by the couple behind Oakland's Parkway Speakeasy Theater – and fast becoming a runaway suburban hit; grab a comfy seat and scope out classic and repertory titles on two screens, and on Tuesdays bring newborn critics (under one year) along for 'Baby Brigade' screenings.

☒ César

25 | **23** | **23** | **$11**

Berkeley | 1515 Shattuck Ave. (bet. Cedar & Vine Sts.) | 510-883-0222
Oakland | 4039 Piedmont Ave. (bet. 40th & 41st Sts.) | 510-985-1200 | www.barcesar.com

"What's this? a bar for grown-ups in Berkeley?" quip seasoned supporters who suggest "bring your tweed" jacket, because this "happening" "gem in the Gourmet Ghetto" is a "favorite of the professor set"; the staff is "delightful" and the "classic Spanish tapas rule", especially when washed down with wine from the "lovely list" – just brace yourself for a "hefty bill"; P.S. a few prefer the newer "trendy" outpost in Oakland.

Club Mallard

23 | **20** | **24** | **$6**

Albany | 752 San Pablo Ave. (Washington Ave.) | 510-524-8450

"Inside, outside, upstairs, downstairs" – choose your scene at Albany's "quirky, friendly locals' bar" with a "clubhouse atmosphere"; the "super-cozy" interior, complete with multiple pool tables, feels like "some eccentric friend's hunting lodge", while the "wonderful" alfresco tiki area may be "one of the East Bay's best patios"; wherever you land, the "drinks, made expertly" by "fun bartenders", contribute to the "great energy and vibe."

Compadres Bar & Grill

18 | **16** | **18** | **$9**

Oakland | 4239 Park Blvd. (Wellington St.) | 510-482-3663 | www.compadresrestaurants.com

See review in South of San Francisco Directory.

Conga Lounge

23 | **22** | **18** | **$11**

Oakland | 5422 College Ave. (Manila St.) | 510-463-2681 | www.congalounge.com

You "feel like you're in an island hut" at Oakland's "cozy", "hidden tropical cocktail club" with the "crazy retro-kitsch" tiki decor that's "super fun, in that unique College Avenue way"; though it's so "small" it seems "impossible to find a square inch" to rest your "strong but sweet" drink, that doesn't deter Conga-liners, who order pizza from the restaurant downstairs and "hang ten, Hawaiian-style."

	APPEAL	DECOR	SERVICE	COST

downtown

| | | 21 | 24 | 20 | $13 |

Berkeley | 2102 Shattuck Ave. (Addison St.) | 510-649-3810 |
www.downtownrestaurant.com

"This is Berkeley, hold the granola" laud locals who sip "big dry marti-nis" and graze on "excellent" small plates in the new bar area of this "sleek", "chic" eatery; it's a "great fallback spot when you don't want to leave" town – and "wonderful jazz" or DJs on Friday and Saturday nights makes it even more "appealing", especially for the "stylish the-ater crowd"; still, a few fret that service is a bit "snooty."

Easy Lounge

| | | - | - | - | E |

Oakland | 3255 Lakeshore Ave. (Lake Park Ave., off I-580) | 510-338-4911 |
www.easy510.com

Join a mixed crowd that's mostly dressed down in jeans and hip hoodie sweatshirts at this Oakland lounge where the Abita beer and a few of the fine specialty drinks (like the French Quarter martini) give a nod to the Big Easy; two large booths by the DJ decks are coveted perches, especially since the music is subdued enough for a civilized conversa-tion, while smokers can retreat to the concrete-bound patio out back.

Elephant Bar & Restaurant

| | | 16 | 18 | 16 | $10 |

Concord | 1225 Willow Pass Rd. (Diamond Blvd.) | 925-671-0119
Emeryville | 5601 Bay St. (Shellmound St.) | 510-601-1001
Fremont | 39233 Fremont Blvd. (Gateway Dr.) | 510-742-6221
www.elephantbar.com

See review in South of San Francisco Directory.

Fat Lady, The

| | | 19 | 21 | 20 | $10 |

Oakland | 201 Washington St. (2nd St.) | 510-465-4996 |
www.thefatladyrestaurant.com

Victorian decor and memorabilia collected from old SF breweries set the scene at this "bordello-modern roadhouse", a onetime brothel set in a circa-1884 building near Oakland's Jack London Square that nowadays draws a "lovely crowd"; what a "cozy, timeless spot for an East Bay rendezvous" agree regulars who appreciate this "ol' gal's" "very spir-ited" vibe, not to mention its "great, great burgers and Bloody Marys."

NEW Franklin Square Wine Bar

| | | - | - | - | M |

Oakland | 2212 Broadway (Franklin St.) | 510-251-0100

The wine bar craze has finally reached Oakland in the form of this spot that supplements its after-hours imbibing with weekday lunches (sal-ads, sandwiches and small plates) from Jake Alioto, the chef from its across-the-street sibling, Luka's Taproom; the mainly French and Californian wines are sold by the glass, half-glass and bottle.

Freight & Salvage ⊘

| | | 21 | 13 | 17 | $7 |

Berkeley | 1111 Addison St. (San Pablo Ave.) | 510-548-1761 |
www.freightandsalvage.com

A "treasure" for "folk music aficionados", this Berkeley "mecca for pick-ers and players" is a "wonderful venue" to see "bluegrass, Americana and related music" "up close"; no alcohol is served – instead you'll find "ok coffee" and "good snacks" – which means the focus is squarely on the performances; no wonder fans speculate that musicians must "love playing here"; N.B. plans are underway to relocate nearby to 2020 Addison Street mid-2009.

	APPEAL	DECOR	SERVICE	COST

Heinold's First and Last Chance Saloon ⌷

▽ 23 | 21 | 21 | $5

Oakland | Jack London Sq. | 48 Webster St. (Embarcadero W.) | 510-839-6761 | www.heinoldsfirstandlastchance.com

At this "tiny", historic nook with "friendly bartenders", a "rustic feel" and perhaps the "most character" of any of Oakland's Jack London Square spots, "it's easy to imagine London" himself "snapping down a few shots before boarding the *Snark*" – and, indeed, the author used to write here; expect a "new slant on drinking": the floor "slopes like a ski run, so the fellow five stools over is head-high to your feet."

Jupiter

21 | 19 | 16 | $8

Berkeley | 2181 Shattuck Ave. (Center St.) | 510-843-8277 | www.jupiterbeer.com

"Summer nights in Berkeley are synonymous" with this "chilled-out biergärten", housed in a sprawling livery stable that dates back to the 1890s; sit on the "killer" outdoor patio "by the fire and heat lamps for optimal enjoyment of the home-brewed beers" and choose from a "nice selection of wood-fired pizzas" – but "don't expect them quickly", as the "slow" "servers move in their own orbit"; N.B. live music rotates from jazz to bluegrass.

Kingman's Lucky Lounge

▽ 21 | 18 | 19 | $6

Oakland | 3332 Grand Ave. (bet. Mandana Blvd. & Santa Clara Ave.) | 510-465-5464

Lucky be the loungers that snag a spot on one of the "comfortable couches" at this "klassy, kool" "hip urban retreat" near Oakland's Grand Lake Theater endowed with a happy hour that "rocks"; the "eclectic mix of DJs" spins "well-chosen music" almost every night, establishing a "chill yet popping vibe" to "match the equally diverse crowd."

⧫ Left Bank

20 | 21 | 18 | $11

Pleasant Hill | 60 Crescent Dr. (Contra Costa Blvd.) | 925-288-1222 | www.leftbank.com

Perhaps the "nicest mainstay in Pleasant Hill" laud Francophiles who also file into this brasserie chainlet's other Bay Area links for "consistently great martinis" or an after-work "glass of Burgundy" with "cheeses and appetizers to accompany" the libations; the occasional "jazz combos are just right" for the "Parisian"-inspired space, creating a "lively atmosphere to connect with friends", and during the summer, the outside seating makes a "perfect people-watching" perch.

Levende East

22 | 23 | 18 | $11

Oakland | 827 Washington St. (9th St.) | 510-835-5585
See Levende review in City of San Francisco Directory.

Luka's Taproom & Lounge

23 | 19 | 21 | $8

Oakland | 2221 Broadway (Grand Ave.) | 510-451-4677 | www.lukasoakland.com

"Is it a bar with great food or a restaurant with a great bar?" whatever you call this "cool Oakland hangout", you'll find a "diverse crowd" downing "awesome" Belgian beers and craft brews, plus "perfect" fries ("heaven wrapped in grease-soaked paper"); in fact, it's "single-handedly revitalized upper Broadway" – it "bustles at almost all hours" with "DJs spinning fresh tracks" and a "back room for playing pool" or pinball – what a "breath of fresh air."

	APPEAL	DECOR	SERVICE	COST

924 Gilman

▽ 26 | 20 | 18 | $7

Berkeley | 924 Gilman St. (8th St.) | 510-525-9926 | www.924gilman.org
"AFI got its start" at this "nonprofit, all-ages" Berkeley club (aka Gilman) as did its most famous alum, Green Day – and hardcore, thrash and death metal bands still take the stage on Fridays, Saturdays and sometimes Sundays, playing to an audience of "fresh-faced and aging punkers alike"; P.S. "no liquor is allowed" at this collectively organized music and performance venue.

☑ Oliveto Cafe & Restaurant

25 | 22 | 23 | $12

Oakland | 5655 College Ave., upstairs (Keith St.) | 510-547-5356 | www.oliveto.com
A "fabulous" triple threat, this "cute laid-back" Oakland spot boasts an "informal and comfortably casual downstairs" cafe and bar that are "favorite after-work meeting places" and "ideal for lazy Sunday afternoons" as well as a more "elegant upstairs" restaurant; it's a "cozy" place for "intimate interludes" over a "creative cocktail" or a glass of "wonderful Italian wine", but most can't resist the "delicious edibles" too.

Pacific Coast Brewing Company

19 | 17 | 18 | $7

Oakland | 906 Washington St. (10th St.) | 510-836-2739 | www.pacificcoastbrewing.com
Spend "happy hour with your co-workers" sampling the "spectacular home brews" and "guest selections" at this "hidden gem" that also offers "good food choices" and "easy access to BART"; the outdoor patio is "fairly pleasant considering it's adjacent to a parking lot in Downtown Oakland", but surveyors are split on the staffers, who are called "mega-friendly" by some, but painted as "ultraslow" by the impatient.

Paragon Bar & Cafe

21 | 22 | 19 | $11

Berkeley | Claremont Resort & Spa | 41 Tunnel Rd. (Claremont Ave.) | 510-843-3000 | www.paragonrestaurant.com
See review in City of San Francisco Directory.

☑ Paramount Theater

26 | 29 | 18 | $7

Oakland | 2025 Broadway (bet. 20th & 21st Sts.) | 510-465-6400 | www.paramounttheater.com
What an "architectural delight" – this truly "grand", "remarkably restored" "art deco palace" in Oakland with "plush seats" and a "stunning interior" makes you "feel like a 1930s movie star as soon as you enter the door" – no wonder night owls voted it No. 1 in the SF Survey for Decor; "wear a vintage outfit", "slug down" a cocktail, then catch your "favorite act" (it's a "great alternative to crowded SF joints"), be it The Oakland East Bay Symphony or The Swell Season.

☑ Parkway Speakeasy Theater

26 | 14 | 21 | $6

Oakland | 1834 Park Blvd. (E. 18th St.) | 510-814-2400 | www.picturepubpizza.com
"Order a pitcher of beer and a pizza instead of your standby popcorn and a Coke" at Oakland's movie theater/pub/restaurant where you can "kick back" with a flick; true, the food's "not gourmet", and it's probably "good that it's so dark" given the somewhat "grungy", "funky decor", but film buffs who "almost feel like going in their pajamas" love that "it's like being at home"; N.B. infants welcome during Monday's 'Baby Brigade.'

	APPEAL	DECOR	SERVICE	COST

Pyramid Brewery & Alehouse

| | 19 | 16 | 18 | $7 |

Berkeley | 901 Gilman St. (8th St.) | 510-528-9880
Walnut Creek | 1410 Locust St. (Cypress St.) | 925-946-1520
www.pyramidbrew.com

"Go with a group" suggest beer buffs who appreciate the "excellent" selection of brews made on the premises at this "Berkeley institution" and its Walnut Creek cohort, both branches of a West Coast chain; though it's "loud, loud, loud", thanks to a "jumble of screaming toddlers and twentysomethings", a "friendly staff" and "fantastic Hefeweizen" help dull the pain.

Radio Bar

| | ▽ 23 | 20 | 17 | $7 |

Oakland | 435 13th St. (bet. Broadway & Franklin St.) | 510-451-2889

A "cool, hip" "hiding spot" with a "speakeasy vibe", this "sweet, stylish" stomping ground "fills a much-needed niche in the Downtown Oakland bar scene"; the "tiny" dance floor is "always crowded" with movers and shakers tuned in to the "deafening techno", but grooving might be better than gabbing here since it's "too loud" "to have deep conversations with your company."

Raleigh's

| | 24 | 18 | 20 | $8 |

Berkeley | 2438 Telegraph Ave. (Haste St.) | 510-848-8652

"Beer is king at this Berkeley student haunt" that's "packed to the gills" during "Cal football games", but otherwise a "relaxed" "environment filled with regulars who always know your name"; it's the "perfect" place "to immerse yourself in your college days" (ah, "memories, or lack thereof" . . .), plus "pool tables and shuffleboard entertain while you tip back reasonably priced pints", while the garden provides an "idyllic escape from the grunge of Telegraph Avenue."

Ruby Room

| | - | - | - | M |

Oakland | 132 14th St. (bet. Madison & Oak Sts.) | 510-444-7224

You're bound to "bump into bike messengers and other Oakland denizens" of the hipster persuasion at this "terrific" hangout, reminiscent of sib Radio Bar, "but slightly darker" and lit with a sexy red glow; a roster of DJs gets the "mostly younger crowd" out onto the tiny dance floor, and on other nights, locals crank up the jukebox and get that party started.

Saddle Rack

| | 21 | 18 | 17 | $8 |

Fremont | 42011 Boscell Rd. (Auto Mall Pkwy.) | 510-979-0477 | www.thesaddlerack.com

"For those who never outgrew *Urban Cowboy*", "the Bay Area's only true honky-tonk" lassos 'em in with line dancing lessons, three themed bars and "even a mechanical bull" (there's "nothing better than a ride after a few trips to the 'dentists chair'", where margaritas are poured down your throat); the "kinda random" Fremont location is A-ok with homesick cowpokes who muse it "truly makes you feel like you're back in the Midwest."

Schmidt's Tobacco & Trading Company ⊄

| | - | - | - | I |

Albany | 1492 Solano Ave. (Santa Fe Ave.) | 510-525-1900

Sip your "British pub–style" pint and puff to your heart's content on the patio of this Albany hangout that's not technically a cigar bar, but

APPEAL DECOR SERVICE COST

still sells a few stogies; "comfy couches", a lit fireplace and board games heighten the feeling that you've "stepped into someone's living room" – it's so homey, in fact, that you may even "feel somewhat like an intruder."

Shattuck Avenue Spats

15 | 17 | 17 | $8

Berkeley | 1974 Shattuck Ave. (University Ave.) | 510-841-7225

"Even the guys can try" the "froufrou drinks" that are "more dessert than cocktail" at this "funky", "kitschy Victorian" Berkeley grogshop since to "have anything else is to miss the point" of the "experience"; while it's "never crowded", it remains "popular with college kids camping it up" – shucks, the cocktails are "fun to order, and dates will be amused."

Shattuck Down Low

16 | 15 | 15 | $8

Berkeley | 2284 Shattuck Ave. (Bancroft Way) | 510-548-1159 | www.shattuckdownlow.com

There's "room to get your groove on" at this Berkeley club with the "huge dance floor"; Sundays are for reggae, while on Tuesdays it's "crowded" with karaoke lovers and on Wednesdays it "gets extremely hot" "once the salsa dancing starts"; other nights expect eclectic DJs and live bands; still, naysayers snipe this is where "undergrads go to think they're cool" and suggest "it only survives because there are no alternatives near Cal."

Skates on the Bay

21 | 21 | 18 | $10

Berkeley | 100 Seawall Dr. (University Ave.) | 510-549-1900 | www.skatesonthebay.com

If you need to be "reminded why tourists come to the Bay Area", drop anchor and "watch the sailboats coming and going" in the Berkeley Marina and soak up the "breathtaking" waterfront view; the time to "get the lowdown" on what this "spacious" spot is about: at "sundown with small plates at the bar"; if a few skate by, citing "pricey" tabs, vaunters divulge the vista "makes up for many shortcomings."

Starry Plough

20 | 15 | 18 | $8

Berkeley | 3101 Shattuck Ave. (bet. Prince & Woolsey Sts.) | 510-841-2082 | www.starryploughpub.com

"Inspires one to write Irish jigs" or odes "about the open seas" assert starry-eyed surveyors who hail this "funky" "Berkeley institution" as "an authentic Irish pub experience"; the "arts are thriving here", with "poetry slams, Celtic music, open mikes and rock music" performances drawing the "Birkenstock crowd", plus it's an "always amusing" spot to get a "good buzz" on, that is, if "inexpensive" beer and wine is your bag.

Stork Club ⇗

19 | 19 | 16 | $6

Oakland | 2330 Telegraph Ave. (bet. 23rd & 24th Sts.) | 510-444-6174 | www.storkcluboakland.com

With a "weirdo Barbie doll collection behind the bar" and "Christmas decor year-round", this "funky", "no-attitude" Oakland "institution" is somehow both "goofy and badass"; there's a "nice variety of entertainment" on offer, from "good" alternative rock acts to "young, bottom-of-the-barrel" performers, so kick back with "bad mixed drinks" and "Rolling Rock longnecks" and enjoy the "cheap, interesting live music."

Townhouse Bar & Grill
| 20 | 18 | 21 | $10 |

Emeryville | 5862 Doyle St. (bet. 59th & Powell Sts.) | 510-652-6151 | www.townhousebarandgrill.com

Enjoy the "early bootlegger atmosphere" at this "funky old-time Emeryville" roadhouse, which was constructed in 1926 and has been racking up a colorful history ever since; Townies tout the "exotic drinks" (and "surprisingly good food"), noting you can always expect "a friendly smile at the bar" and consider the "casual yet classy" ambiance fitting for live jazz shows on Wednesdays and Thursdays; P.S. locals "love the outdoor area in the summertime."

Trader Vic's
| 19 | 21 | 19 | $13 |

Emeryville | 9 Anchor Dr. (Powell St.) | 510-653-3400 | www.tradervics.com

For a "sweet taste of Polynesia without having to get on a plane" mai tai mavens sail on over to these "ultimate tiki temples", links in legendary Victor Bergeron's international chain that serve up a heavy dose of "nostalgia" to the "blue-hair crowd" in Emeryville and Palo Alto; the "giant foofy drinks" "with seemingly twice the amount of rum" definitely don't come "cheap", but hey, chances are "you won't leave sober."

Triple Rock Brewery
| 21 | 15 | 18 | $7 |

Berkeley | 1920 Shattuck Ave. (Hearst Ave.) | 510-843-2739 | www.triplerock.com

A "favorite" of UC students, this "no-nonsense" brewpub offering a "fine choice of beer", a few wine selections and "solid" burgers is "so very Berkeley in so many ways"; watch the game on flat-screen TVs, "try your hand at tabletop shuffleboard" and on "those rare hot afternoons", "check out" the roof deck "for *cervezas* alfresco" – you "can't miss here"; still, the rah-rah–resistant retort "it's a little too sporty for my tastes."

Va de Vi
| - | - | - | E |

Walnut Creek | 1511 Mt. Diablo Blvd. (Main St.) | 925-979-0100 | www.vadevibistro.com

Well-heeled Walnut Creek wine lovers pack into Pres a Vi's older sibling, a cozy spot to enjoy vinos by the glass and in flights of three generous three-ounce pours; sit at the chef's counter and watch the cooks concoct international tapas while sipping a specialty cocktail, or, better yet, score a coveted seat on the back patio, shaded by umbrellas and a 350-year-old oak tree; N.B. reserve in advance to avoid waiting in the narrow, crowded bar area.

White Horse Bar ⌀
| 19 | 11 | 19 | $7 |

Oakland | 6551 Telegraph Ave. (66th St.) | 510-652-3820 | www.whitehorsebar.com

Definitely "a very inclusive GLBT-straight-whatever kind of" establishment, this "historic" Oakland club, said to be the country's oldest gay bar, is "where you go to shake your ass" and "raise serious hell" on the dance floor; though the "carpeting and decor are early '70s cruise ship chic", and the "guys could be hotter", the "wonderfully diverse" crowd

	APPEAL	DECOR	SERVICE	COST

and "welcoming" feel mean it's a "good place to make your own fun"; N.B. DJs spin Thursday–Saturday.

☑ Yoshi's at Jack London Square

24 | 22 | 21 | $11

Oakland | Jack London Sq. | 510 Embarcadero W. (bet. Clay & Washington Sts.) | 510-238-9200 | www.yoshis.com

"Sushi and jazz! who came up with this combination? – but somehow it works" at this "helluva" "happening" Oakland club offering "intimate tables" ("for a special evening out"), "world-class" acts and "interesting Japanese food" (eat in the restaurant – that's the "key to better seat selection"); but others muse the music "is the ticket here" – just skip the "mediocre" fare; N.B. the new Western Addition offshoot is housed in a two-story, 720-seat building whose modern, minimalist look places the focus on the local and big-name performers.

North of San Francisco

Ana's Cantina
| 18 | 13 | 18 | $12 |

St. Helena | 1205 Main St. (Spring St.) | 707-963-4921

"When you're sick of wine", it's time to visit "one of the spiciest location in the otherwise staid" town of St. Helena; what a "rockin' joint" – this Mexican "watering hole" with a "friendly staff" is "fun, loud, crowded, alive! and packed on Thursdays" for karaoke night – "you don't want to miss the action here."

☑ Auberge du Soleil
| 28 | 27 | 26 | $16 |

Rutherford | Auberge du Soleil | 180 Rutherford Hill Rd. (Silverado Trail) | 707-963-1211 | www.aubergedusoleil.com

"You'll feel on top of the world" at Relais & Châteaux's "stunning" "Mediterranean-style hillside inn" in Rutherford; head to the deck and "bask in the glory" of the "incredible", "insane view" of the vineyards while sipping champagne – "it's how the other half lives"; the "selection of wines by the glass is what you'd expect from one of Napa's premier spots" (the "list is literally a book") while the servers are "true professionals" – little wonder it's the "place to be", "particularly at sunset."

Boca
| 20 | 21 | 21 | $13 |

Novato | 340 Ignacio Blvd. (Rte. 101) | 415-883-0901 | www.bocasteak.com

This Argentine-inflected steakhouse may seem "out of place next door to a strip mall" but insiders insist it's a Novato "oasis" for a "quiet drink" some nights and "local action" on others; "stop in at happy hour" when bar menu items like "lobster corndogs are half price" or order a "mean burger to wash down" with a "killer wine" flight; still, the less-bewitched bemoan too "small for comfort."

☑ Bouchon
| 25 | 23 | 24 | $14 |

Yountville | 6534 Washington St. (Yount St.) | 707-944-8037 | www.bouchonbistro.com

"Whatever you drink, drink it with the best onion soup this side of Paris" propose Francophiles who fawn over super-toque Thomas Keller's "fabulous food" ("so, so French") and, *oui*, the "amazing wine" list at the "French Laundry's younger, more fun little sister", open till 1 AM; "spend hours at the bar" indulging in "champagne, oysters and a cheese platter" – what a "cozy Napa evening" – or opt for the "street-side patio" where Yountville "restaurateurs are often seen after closing down their own locales."

Buckeye Roadhouse
| 24 | 23 | 22 | $11 |

Mill Valley | 15 Shoreline Hwy./Hwy. 1 (west of Hwy. 101) | 415-331-2600 | www.buckeyeroadhouse.com

"Just what a roadhouse should be!" declare devotees of this "warm, inviting" Mill Valley "getaway" with "old-school service"; the "bar is always packed" with Roadies (including a "quality divorcée crowd") tippling "top-shelf margaritas", but straight shooters also make a beeline for "after-work martinis and appetizers" or a sip "on Sunday after hiking" in Marin (a "great idea" if you don't feel like bucking "horrendous" traffic into the city).

	APPEAL	DECOR	SERVICE	COST

Café Amsterdam
21 | 16 | 20 | $7

Fairfax | 23 Broadway Blvd. (Bolinas Rd.) | 415-256-8020 |
www.cafeamsterdamfairfax.com

Fairfaxers head to this "mellow" "semi-dive" bar/cafe to "sample
the local music scene", the "cheap eats" and the beer and wine too;
"comfy surroundings", a heated patio and a schedule that's
"jammed full" most nights make it "a nice place to relax and listen" to
"below-the-radar groups", but it even "feels good to be here when the
sun is out."

Caffe Cicero
▽ 18 | 15 | 20 | $12

Napa | 1245 First St. (Randolph St.) | 707-257-1802 |
www.caffecicero.com

"I always have fun" at this "casual and cozy" Napa cafe concur propo-
nents who praise the "homey and eclectic menu", "casual" late-night
(for the neighborhood) bar snacks and selection of 25 wines by the
glass; while there may not be "much atmosphere", few mind as revolving art exhibits and frequent live performances of the blues enhance
its largely local allure.

Caffe Trieste
20 | 15 | 18 | $7

Sausalito | 1000 Bridgeway St. (Caledonia St.) | 415-332-7660 |
www.caffetrieste.com

See review in City of San Francisco Directory.

Calistoga Inn Restaurant & Brewery
22 | 18 | 18 | $11

Calistoga | Calistoga Inn | 1250 Lincoln Ave. (Cedar St.) | 707-942-4101 |
www.calistogainn.com

"Honest brews" created at the on-premises Napa Valley Brewing
Company along with "good eats" and "funky music" make this "folksy,
friendly" historic Calistoga inn an "upvalley destination for many locals"; grab a seat in the "popular" pub or when the temperatures rise,
find a spot in the "beautiful creekside garden", then kick back with
your suds and enjoy the live music.

Cole's Chop House
▽ 24 | 25 | 23 | $14

Napa | 1122 Main St. (bet. 1st & Pearl Sts.) | 707-224-6328 |
www.coleschophouse.com

"This is where you go to feel glamorous" in Downtown Napa – the
"martinis are unparalleled, the bartenders are hot" and the bar feel is
a "bit more cosmopolitan" than the rest of the "relaxed" steakhouse;
if you stay and chow down, there are lots of "good grain distillates to
go with your beef" – not to mention a far-reaching wine list emphasiz-
ing the Valley's Cabernet Sauvignons.

COPIA
19 | 19 | 18 | $13

Napa | 500 First St. (Napa River) | 707-259-1600 | www.copia.org

An "ambitious" Napa "monument to food and drink" declare disci-
ples who revel in the ample attractions like the "amazing gardens",
"arty" events, vino museum, casual cafe, new lounge (serving
small plates and drinks) and Julia's Kitchen, the restaurant named for
Julia Child; "taste a variety of wines and learn about them" at daily
classes or spend that "first date" among the "extensive herb"
patches – what an "enjoyable" experience; still, a few can't copia with
the "expensive" prices.

Cork Enoteca ▽ 21 | 17 | 20 | $10

Sausalito | 317 Johnson St. (Bridgeway) | 415-332-2975 |
www.corksf.com

What a "homey" "small town gathering spot" assert admirers who
congregate at this "unintimidating little wine bar" with a "delightful"
atmosphere "off the typical Sausalito tourist track" in Marin; natch,
there are "lots of fine wines" on the "eclectic" list, but don't pass up
the "little nibbles from the locally sourced menu" like the crostini, panini, finger sandwiches and gourmet cheeses.

E&O Trading Company 20 | 21 | 19 | $10

Larkspur | 2231 Larkspur Landing Circle (Old Quarry Rd.) | 415-925-0303 |
www.eotrading.com

See review in City of San Francisco Directory.

Frantoio ▽ 25 | 24 | 23 | $12

Mill Valley | 152 Shoreline Hwy. (west of Hwy. 101) | 415-289-5777 |
www.frantoio.com

If you go when the "neat" working olive press (*frantoio*) at this
"wonderful Italian" eatery in Mill Valley is in operation, "you can have
a free taste" of the fresh oil, whether you're there for the "great pizzas
and pastas" or just stopping by for the "good wine list" boasting more
than 100 bottles; though it's a bit "expensive", fanciers confide it's
a "fabulous experience."

Guaymas 24 | 21 | 19 | $10

Tiburon | 5 Main St. (Tiburon Blvd.) | 415-435-6300

This "lively" Tiburon location with "spectacular views of San
Francisco" and the Bay is a "fantastic place" to "watch the boats slip
into the harbor and their owners slip into a coma" induced by the
"wonderful margaritas" and "eclectic" Mexican-style seafood; there
can be "far too many tourists" on fair days, when everyone wants to
"spend a lazy afternoon sipping cocktails in the sun", but it's "never
disappointing, except for the wait."

Insalata's 22 | 24 | 21 | $10

San Anselmo | 120 Sir Francis Drake Blvd. (Barber Ave.) | 415-457-7700 |
www.insalatas.com

"Mediterranean tapas marry well" with the "innovative mixed
drinks" and a "good" selection of 20 wines by the glass at this "arty,
modern and cozy" restaurant/bar; though it's not exactly a raging
scene, and the "very local" crowd consists mostly of those "waiting
for a table", the "wonderful" fare is "worth a trip" over the Golden
Gate to San Anselmo.

⊠ Lark Creek Inn 26 | 25 | 24 | $13

Larkspur | 234 Magnolia Ave. (Madrone Ave.) | 415-924-7766 |
www.larkcreek.com

"Romantically situated" in a redwood grove, this legendary
Larkspur restaurant housed in a "beautiful" 1888 Victorian is an
"elegant but friendly" "place to meet a date" for a drink, and it's
also a "charming" spot to roost for "cocktails with the girls"; the
"cozy fireplace near the bar" may make you feel like you're "coming
home" – but the "pricey" tabs remind you that you're ensconced in one
of "Marin's finest."

	APPEAL	DECOR	SERVICE	COST

◲ Left Bank — 20 | 21 | 18 | $11

Larkspur | 507 Magnolia St. (Ward St.) | 415-927-3331 | www.leftbank.com
See review in East of San Francisco Directory.

Marin Brewing Co. — 17 | 15 | 17 | $7

Larkspur | Larkspur Landing Shopping Ctr. | 1809 Larkspur Landing Circle
(Old Quarry Rd.) | 415-461-4677 | www.marinbrewing.com
Seasonal craft beer brewed on-site "is the thing here" at this "loud",
"crowded", "twentysomething happy-hour hangout" with a "standard
brewery vibe" set in a shopping center near the Larkspur ferry landing;
"sit on the deck on a sunny day and enjoy" an ale while the live music
plays or drop by for $2 tacos on Mondays or the $3 pints all day on
Tuesdays when it's "quite the meat market."

◲ Martini House — 25 | 25 | 23 | $13

St. Helena | 1245 Spring St. (Money Way) | 707-963-2233 |
www.martinihouse.com
"You could spend all night drinking in front of the fireplace, chatting
with the friendly barkeeps and just enjoying the atmosphere" in the
"wonderful, warm downstairs" area at this "very popular" Pat Kuleto-
designed restaurant in St. Helena; "even when wall-to-wall with people,
the charm's never lost" – "patrons always seem happy and outgoing,
as does the staff", which serves "great" cocktails and "hard-to-find"
vinos; N.B. in fair weather, the patio is equally atmospheric.

Mustards Grill — 23 | 20 | 22 | $13

Yountville | 7399 St. Helena Hwy./Hwy. 29 (bet. Oakville Grade Rd. &
Washington St.) | 707-944-2424 | www.mustardsgrill.com
"A truly perfect ending to a long day" visiting wineries, this Yountville
"must" features chef-owner Cindy Pawlcyn's "not fancy but delicious
food", "fine wines by the glass" and "better versions" of cocktails
"than you've ever tasted"; it can be "sooooo loud" at the "tiny, tiny
bar", where it's also "difficult to get a seat", but once you nab one, the
"saucy" bartender "feels like an old friend."

Mystic Theatre — 22 | 17 | 20 | $10

Petaluma | 23 Petaluma Blvd. N. (bet. B St. & Western Ave.) | 707-765-2121 |
www.mystictheatre.com
"Come and get it live and loud" at Petaluma's "old theater", once a
vaudeville venue, where "wonderful" musical talent – including lots of
rock, blues and singer-songwriters – performs "in a chill and intimate
atmosphere"; though the "seating arrangement is a little awkward",
the "balcony seats are nice if you're looking to get cozy with your
honey", and the adjoining McNear's Saloon offers plenty of local
and imported beer.

19 Broadway — 19 | 12 | 19 | $7

Fairfax | 19 Broadway Blvd. (Bolinas Rd.) | 415-459-1091 |
www.19broadway.com
"You'll know you're in Fairfax" at this "very bohemian", "friendly" "dive"
that's "always good for some local sounds, sights and interesting people-
watching"; some "kick-ass bands roll through" marvel music mavens
who groove to rock, reggae, roots, funk and jazz seven nights a week
and also get their kicks from the thatched-roof tiki lounge that's especially "appealing in summer."

No Name Bar ⌷

▽ 19 | 15 | 21 | $7

Sausalito | 757 Bridgeway (bet. Anchor & Bay Sts.) | 415-332-1392

The name may be 'nonexistent', nevertheless locals declare that this "great little" neighborhood nook feels "like an oasis in the middle of all the shops" "in tourist-thronged Sausalito"; regulars swing by to listen to live jazz, blues or the jukebox, strut their stuff on open-mike nights or hang out in the "nice garden patio"; still, it's not letter-perfect for others who retort it's "nothing to write home about."

ⓩ Pelican Inn

27 | 25 | 23 | $8

Muir Beach | Pelican Inn | 10 Pacific Way (Hwy. 1) | 415-383-6000 | www.pelicaninn.com

A "taste of the English countryside" that's straight "from the story-books", this "very traditional" pub in a cozy inn is the "best retreat" "on those foggy, socked-in nights" so common at Muir Beach; "you never know who you'll meet" here if you "pull over and warm up" with a pint of ale, but rest assured that everyone has a yarn or an "accent" at this congenial grogshop.

Piazza D'Angelo

22 | 19 | 20 | $10

Mill Valley | 22 Miller Ave. (bet. Sunnyside & Throckmorton Aves.) | 415-388-2000 | www.piazzadangelo.com

During the week, this Italian restaurant in Mill Valley is crowded with "casually clad boomer families" and wage slaves who "meet after work for a glass of wine and a thin-crust pizza"; weekends, it's "divorcée heaven", packed with "50-year-old singles" cruising for a date; no matter who you are, though, it's definitely the place to "feel comfortable and taken care of", plus the vino list and "well-stocked bar" "never disappoint."

Rancho Nicasio

23 | 17 | 20 | $9

Nicasio | 1 Old Rancheria Rd. (Nicasio Valley Rd.) | 415-662-2219 | www.ranchonicasio.com

"Bring your boots" and your "cowboy and cowgirl friends" – it's "worth the drive" "way the hell out" to this "Rancho remote" roadhouse in the "one-horse town" of Nicasio in West Marin to see "lots of notable" alt-country, folk, roots and rock bands perform; you'll find "real, genuine folk" and a "mellow scene", especially during the 'Backyard BBQ concert series' – what a "super summer weekend spot" – then again, it's "definitely down home" year-round.

ⓩ Sam's Anchor Cafe

25 | 16 | 16 | $9

Tiburon | 27 Main St. (Tiburon Blvd.) | 415-435-4527 | www.samscafe.com

They take reservations for the restaurant, not the deck, so get to Tiburon "early" if you want to "spend the day sipping drinks in the sun" outside with "to-die-for" views of the Bay advise old salts; the "never-ending bowl of free popcorn" and the "best Ramos gin fizz in the world" (their signature drink) make it worth the inevitable wait, but "watch out" for the marauding seagulls.

Silverado Brewing Company

18 | 15 | 18 | $9

St. Helena | 3020A N. St. Helena Hwy. (Stice Ln.) | 707-967-9876 | www.silveradobrewingcompany.com

"It takes a lot of great beer to make good wine" – just get a load of all the "winery crews knocking back" "fresh" pints at this "raucous" microbrewery "under the valley oaks" in St. Helena; the suds may be merely "fine" and the food "nothing to write home about", but the patio offers "decent views", and the "charming cobblestone building" is an "excellent place to watch football on a rainy winter day."

Silverado Resort Lounge

▽ 24 | 21 | 19 | $14

Napa | Silverado Resort | 1600 Atlas Peak Rd. (Hardman Ave.) | 707-257-0200 | www.silveradoresort.com

When the urge to go "upscale" hits, hit the trail to this "chic" Napa country club, spa and resort; the "elegant" lounge was once the living room of a historic home but nowadays a cocktail crowd cozies up to the stone fireplace, while taking in "great views" of the golf course, then heads to the "tight dance floor" in the glass-enclosed patio terrace room or to the adjacent Royal Oak restaurant.

Silver Peso

14 | 9 | 18 | $6

Larkspur | 450 Magnolia Ave. (Cane St.) | 415-924-3448

Formerly a "seedy, smoke-filled" watering hole, and now a tad "tamed" (puff your butts outside), this "classic biker bar" in "upscale Downtown Larkspur" is nonetheless still an "absolute dive"; "all types", from a "middle-aged crowd" to "scary" regulars to college kids "meeting for impromptu reunions around the holidays", show up for "pool, pinball and people-watching", ensuring this "institution will always be there."

☑ Sushi Ran

25 | 20 | 24 | $12

Sausalito | 107 Caledonia St. (bet. Pine & Turney Sts.) | 415-332-3620 | www.sushiran.com

"Slick across the board" agree "well-heeled" acolytes who engage in "lively exchanges" with "local Sausalito-ites" while sipping 20 "wonderful" wines by the glass and 30 "fabulous" sakes (or "super" soju cocktails) at this "hip", "crowded" Japanese bar "across the walkway from the restaurant"; but don't let the night go by in a blur - for a truly "memorable evening", order some of the "best sushi in the Bay Area."

☑ Sweetwater Saloon

28 | - | 22 | $8

Mill Valley | 32 Miller St. (Sunnyside Ave.) | 415-388-2820 | www.sweetwatersaloon.com

Loyalists who laud this "Mill Valley classic" - it's "like taking a trip through history to the days when harmonicas reigned and going out didn't mean planning your outfit for a week" - hope it maintains its "special feel" once it moves to new digs at 32 Miller Street, slated to open June 2008; since 1972, some of the biggest stars in blues, jazz and R&B performed at its former "laid-back" incarnation, playing for "rock royalty" and locals - no wonder diehards declare it's the North Bay's "best music venue."

☑ Tra Vigne

26 | 26 | 24 | $13

St. Helena | 1050 Charter Oak Ave. (Main St.) | 707-963-4444 | www.travignerestaurant.com

"A fantastic spot to end a day" of visiting vintners in the Valley, this "cozy" but "elegant" St. Helena "favorite" offers a full bar along with its "wonderful" wine list; but "surely you're here for more than a drink" agree acolytes also swayed by this "Napa staple's" Italian fare; meanwhile, alfresco-seekers head to the adjacent enoteca, Cantinetta, select one of the 60 by-the-glass offerings and sip away on the "sunny" patio.

Two AM Club

15 | 9 | 21 | $6

Mill Valley | 380 Miller Ave. (Montford Ave.) | 415-388-6036

A "true Marin classic", "'The Deuce'", "as it's known to those in-the-know", "has a special place in the heart of anyone who's lived" nearby; true, "Huey Lewis doesn't hang out anymore" (the cover to the album *Sports* was shot here), but students still "meet for reunions around the holidays" and sports fans gather to "watch the game" – perhaps because this "homely" dive is the "only real bar in Mill Valley."

South of San Francisco

Agenda Restaurant & Lounge

▽ | 15 | 20 | 19 | $9

San Jose | 399 S. First St. (San Salvador St.) | 408-287-3991 |
www.agendalounge.com

"Wednesday-night salsa dancing", "fun" live jazz bands and a variety
of DJs, from house to hip-hop, are on the agenda of San Jose's tri-level
triple threat restaurant/nightclub/lounge; step up to the "main level
bar for a large selection of drinks", then head to "big dance floors" if
your idea of a "good time" is tripping the light fantastic.

Antonio's Nut House

16 | 9 | 15 | $5

Palo Alto | 321 S. California Ave. (Birch St.) | 650-321-2550

You gotta "love the feeling of peanut shells crushed underfoot" to appreciate this "low-key", "quintessential dive bar", offering "cheap
drinks" and a "good change of pace from the usual Palo Alto club"; "who
can beat the name?" muse "Stanford students on a budget" who "can
be found morning to evening" playing pool and darts; still, aesthetes
sniff it takes the concept of "run-down hangout" to a "new level."

Black Watch ⊨

21 | 12 | 18 | $7

Los Gatos | 141½ N. Santa Cruz Ave. (bet. Hwy. 9 & Main St.) |
408-354-2200

"You'll find this place by looking for the motorcycles parked outside";
inside, though, the crowd is a "good mix of all ages", from "young
preppies to bikers", who down "cheap" "to-die-for kamikazes" by the
pint while "playing liar's dice"; it may be "a dump", but it's a "beautiful
dump" say Los Gatos locals who declare it's the "ultimate dive bar."

Blank Club, The

▽ | 14 | 12 | 13 | $8

San Jose | 44 S. Almaden Ave. (Post St.) | 408-292-5265 |
www.theblankclub.com

Everyone from Agent Orange to Shonen Knife has rocked the stage
with the silver Mylar backdrop at this "seedy" club with an "industrial"
feel and a "killer" Downtown San Jose location; little wonder - Blank
expressionists point out that it's the "perfect-size place (small) for
seeing great punk bands" not to mention roots rock, country and Afro-
Cuban acts and a slew of DJs.

⊠ Blowfish Sushi To Die For

22 | 23 | 19 | $11

San Jose | 355 Santana Row (Stevens Creek Blvd.) | 408-345-3848 |
www.blowfishsushi.com

See review in City of San Francisco Directory.

Blue Chalk Cafe

18 | 16 | 16 | $9

Palo Alto | 630 Ramona St. (bet. Forest & Hamilton Aves.) | 650-326-1020 |
www.bluechalkcafe.com

"Open space, dancing, TV, great drinks, pool and snacks" – this two-
floor Palo Alto "bar has it all", whether you want to "meet with friends
or mingle with singles"; the vibe is "mellow" during the week drawing
"nice-looking" "Stanford kids", but it "can get crazy on weekends"
and "service can suffer", when it's "packed elbow to elbow" with "students and young professionals" "bumpin' and grinding" ("people, we
need our drinks!").

Britannia Arms

17 | 14 | 17 | $8

Monterey | 444 Alvarado St. (Bonifacio Pl.) | 831-656-9543
Cupertino | 1087 De Anza Blvd. (bet. Fallen Leaf Ln. & Rollingdell Dr.) | 408-252-7262
San Jose | 173 W. Santa Clara St. (bet. N. Almaden Ave. & N. San Pedro St.) | 408-278-1400
San Jose | 5027 Almaden Expwy. (Cherry Ave.) | 408-266-0550
www.britanniaarms.com

A "died-in-the-wool British pub crowd" congregates at these "mellow", individually owned "neighborhood hangouts" in Cupertino, San Jose and Monterey (there's a fifth in Aptos too) "popular" with the "young, fun regulars"; if a few blasé Anglophiles allude to a "utilitarian" ambiance and "standard" grub, supporters rejoin expect "no pretense, no frills" – just a "friendly" place to watch games, play darts, sing karaoke and listen to live music.

British Bankers Club

18 | 18 | 17 | $9

Menlo Park | 1090 El Camino Real (Santa Cruz Ave.) | 650-327-8769 | www.britishbankersclub.com

Set in a former bank building, this "stately" "Menlo Park meet market" puts a slightly "upscale" spin on what's "fundamentally a pub-grub place"; "interesting" DJ dance parties, live bands and "always a hoot" karaoke nights on Thursdays and Saturdays ensure that it's "populated by Stanford students", "software folk" and a "just-divorced" "older crowd" "looking to get back in the swing"; still, some withdraw interest, deeming it "dingy" and "depressing."

Cafe Rosso & Bianco

21 | 22 | 18 | $12

Palo Alto | 473 University Ave. (bet. Cowper & Kipling Sts.) | 650-752-0350 | www.cafeniebaum-coppola.com

See Cafe Zoetrope review in City of San Francisco Directory.

Cinebar

∇ 11 | 10 | 16 | $6

San Jose | 69 E. San Fernando St. (2nd St.) | 408-292-9562

It's "dark and cramped – in a good way" – at this quintessential "dive bar" populated by the "seedy underbelly of San Jose", including "dirty old men and punk rock types"; "cheap, strong" booze, a jukebox and a pool table ensure a "nice time is had by all" – or at least dedicated drinkers who want to "experience the barfly lifestyle."

Compadres Old Adobe

18 | 16 | 18 | $9

Palo Alto | 3877 El Camino Real (Page Mill Rd.) | 650-858-1141 | www.compadresrestaurants.com

"Only a stumble away from campus", this Palo Alto "local hangout for the Stanford set" (and its sister location in Oakland) "makes a mean margarita", which "comes very cheap during happy hour"; few amigos mind that it's basically just a "decent Mexican restaurant" and "not much in terms of nightlife", because just about "nothing beats working through a pitcher" of drinks with the "fun crowd."

Daru

- | - | - | M

Palo Alto | 632 Emerson St. (bet. Hamilton & Forest Aves.) | 650-322-3500 | www.mantrapaloalto.com

Attached to Palo Alto's Mantra, an upscale Cal-Indian destination, this sexy lounge with a backlit bar serves scaled-down versions of the restaurant's fusion fare, such as samosas and lamb kebabs; subcontinental pop music sets the scene for signature cocktails like the Jaipur Dream, and low sofas are suited for romantic interludes; happy-hour fans can double down twice daily for deals on drinks and appetizers from 4:30–6:30 and again from 9:30 until closing.

Dio Deka

`- | - | - | E`

Los Gatos | Hotel Los Gatos | 210 E. Main St. (Church St.) | 408-354-7700 | www.diodeka.com

All hands on Deka – Los Gatos' "fine new" Greek eatery with a "small" cocktail area and "professional" staff is a "must" and that's no myth according to admirers; order a selection from the bar menu, like *saganaki* (flaming cheese) or *octapodaki* (mesquite-grilled octopus), to accompany your "great martinis" or a bottle from the "top-notch wine bible" and soak up the "hip, casual setting", including an ample-sized courtyard.

E&O Trading Company

`20 | 21 | 19 | $10`

San Jose | 96 S. First St. (San Fernando St.) | 408-938-4100 | www.eotrading.com

See review in City of San Francisco Directory.

Elephant Bar & Restaurant

`16 | 18 | 16 | $10`

Burlingame | 1600 Old Bayshore Hwy. (bet. Broadway & Millbrae Ave.) | 650-259-9585
Campbell | 499 E. Hamilton Ave. (Hwy. 17) | 408-871-8401
Cupertino | 19780 Stevens Creek Blvd. (N. Portal Ave.) | 408-865-0701
www.elephantbar.com

Herds of bipeds "kick back with co-workers after a day at the office" at this "festive" chain of jungle-themed hangouts with "fun African-style decor"; big eaters appreciate the "affordable" grub that comes in "elephantine"-sized portions, but others are put off by this pachyderm, pouting that the "overly sweet drinks" and a "cookie-cutter feel" ("with clientele to match") make this watering hole seem like a "glorified Applebee's."

Empire Grill & Tap Room

`21 | 20 | 19 | $10`

Palo Alto | 651 Emerson St. (bet. Forest & Hamilton Aves.) | 650-321-3030

The "fabulous outdoor patio" of this Palo Alto pub is a "lovely place to have a glass of wine", a "mean martini" or one of many beers on tap; the "old-school" interior might be "austere", even "stuffy", but nevermind, the "long bar" is so "big" you don't "have to do contortions to get the bartender to pay attention"; P.S. "dress up to feel comfortable" among the "older" and "yuppielike" crowd.

☑ Evvia

`24 | 24 | 23 | $11`

Palo Alto | 420 Emerson St. (bet. Lytton & University Aves.) | 650-326-0983 | www.evvia.net

Wish the "cozy", "classy" bar area was "bigger, especially since it's so hard to get a table" opine "pre-dinner wine sippers" who squeeze into Palo Alto's "delightful", "romantic" Hellenic hot spot with a "professional" staff; choose a glass from the "perfect assortment" of vino before chowing down and enjoy the "lively" scene – much like its city sister, Kokkari Estiatorio, this "upscale" haunt "consistently delivers food, drink and ambiance fit for a Greek goddess."

	APPEAL	DECOR	SERVICE	COST

Faultline Brewing Company
17 | 17 | 16 | $9

Sunnyvale | 1235 Oakmead Pkwy. (Lawrence Expwy.) | 408-736-2739 | www.faultlinebrewing.com

Fans find no fault with this "lively oasis" in Sunnyvale on the "fringes of Silicon Valley", where you "can't go wrong for a business lunch or after-work drink"; natch, you'll find "many a table full of techie dorks" who "come early" to dine on "decent" food and toss back "interesting" house-brewed beers; however, a few nitpickers carp it has "all the charm of a big chain."

Fibbar Magees
19 | 13 | 16 | $7

Sunnyvale | 156 S. Murphy Ave. (bet. Evelyn & Washington Aves.) | 408-749-8373

Molly Magees
Mountain View | 241 Castro St. (bet. Dana & Villa Sts.) | 650-961-0108 www.fibbars.com

"You can't go wrong" with Fibbar Magees in Sunnyvale – it's a "fun place to drink with friends or dance" to live music – or Molly Magees, a local mainstay with a "nice beer selection" that may be the "only really good pub on the Peninsula"; but come Thursday through Saturday when DJs spin and it becomes a bit of a "meat market", the Mountain View sibling shows its "cool vibe" side.

☑ Gordon Biersch
18 | 16 | 18 | $9

Palo Alto | 640 Emerson St. (bet. Forest & Hamilton Aves.) | 650-323-7723
San Jose | 33 E. San Fernando St. (bet. 1st & 2nd Sts.) | 408-294-6785 www.gordonbiersch.com

See review in City of San Francisco Directory.

Hedley Club
▽ 24 | 23 | 19 | $9

San Jose | Hotel De Anza | 233 W. Santa Clara St. (Almaden Rd.) | 408-286-1000 | www.hoteldeanza.com

A "sophisticated crowd" settles into the "comfy banquettes" with a nightcap or two at this swish speakeasy in San Jose's Hotel De Anza, noting it's a "nice place to wind up after a good dinner out" (especially if you're "getting on in years"); lounge lizards "love the fireplace" that warms the art deco interior, and plan ahead to hear "cool" live jazz on Friday and Saturday nights.

☑ Highlands Inn
28 | 27 | 26 | $14

Carmel | Highlands Inn Park Hyatt Carmel | 120 Highlands Dr. (Hwy. 1) | 831-620-1234 | www.parkhyatt.com

It's "worth a trip from anywhere" for the "breathtaking, one-of-a-kind location" and "can't-be-beat" views of Monterey Bay confide those Inn the know who voted this Carmel destination in the Park Hyatt No. 1 in the SF Survey for Overall Appeal; yes, the two "old-school" lounges are "expensive", but it's "worth every penny" for a "sunset drink on a romantic evening", especially when jazz musicians play on Friday and Saturday nights.

Hog's Breath Inn
24 | 18 | 18 | $11

Carmel | San Carlos St. (bet. 5th & 6th Aves.) | 831-625-1044 | www.hogsbreathinn.net

"People are still looking" for former owner Clint Eastwood at this "comfy" Old West–themed saloon, the "only place to let your hair down in Carmel" according to gunslingers; true, the only evidence of Dirty Harry is the paintings of him on the walls, but no matter – "sitting on the patio on a nice summer day" or "snuggling with a loved one" by the fire pit is bound to make your day.

Improv, The
▽ 25 | 20 | 21 | $9

San Jose | Jose Theatre | 62 S. Second St. (bet. E. San Fernando & E. Santa Clara Sts.) | 408-280-7475 | www.improv.com

At this restored old theater "full of history" in San Jose, Harry Houdini once performed his magic tricks and now, years later, some of the "best" comedians take the stage, from Dana Carvey to Shawn Wayans, making for a "really entertaining" evening; sure, there's a drink minimum, but at least the "prices don't spoil the punch line."

Left at Albuquerque
15 | 14 | 14 | $8

Campbell | Pruneyard Shopping Ctr. | 1875 S. Bascom Ave. (bet. Campbell & Hamilton Aves.) | 408-558-1680 | www.leftatalb.com

See review in City of San Francisco Directory.

☑ Left Bank
20 | 21 | 18 | $11

Menlo Park | 635 Santa Cruz Ave. (Doyle St.) | 650-473-6543
San Jose | 377 Santana Row, Ste. 1100 (Olin Ave.) | 408-984-3500
San Mateo | 1100 Park Pl. (David St.) | 650-345-2250
www.leftbank.com

See review in East of San Francisco Directory.

Los Gatos Brewing Company
21 | 20 | 18 | $10

Los Gatos | 130 N. Santa Cruz Ave. (Grays Ln.) | 408-395-9929 | www.lgbrewingco.com

Though the "focus here is more on the restaurant than the bar", a "young professional crowd" still likes to tip back tasty beer brewed on-site and "hang out and meet new people" at this Los Gatos pub; the "large", "dimly lit" room can get "noisy", but "food that's much better than most" and "good crowd energy" explain why it's "still going strong" long after the dot-com implosion.

MacArthur Park
18 | 18 | 17 | $11

Palo Alto | 27 University Ave. (bet. Alma St. & El Camino Real) | 650-321-9990 | www.macpark.com

The old "perennial" Financial District mainstay may have gone to the big park in the sky but fans nostalgic for their "comfortable" rib house can pay a visit to the "stylish, proper" Palo Alto locale with a similar "clubby" feel; graze on half-price appetizers during the "amazing happy hour" and if the urge to sit outside hits, head to the tree-adorned patio with a "nice outside feel."

☑ Nectar Wine Lounge
23 | 22 | 21 | $12

Burlingame | 270 Lorton Ave. (bet. Burlingame & Howard Aves.) | 650-558-9200 | www.nectarwinelounge.com

See review in City of San Francisco Directory.

Nola
21 | 21 | 17 | $9

Palo Alto | 535 Ramona St. (bet. Hamilton & University Aves.) | 650-328-2722 | www.nolas.com

"Bringing the feel and funk of the Big Easy to Palo Alto", this "outlandish, colorful" New Orleans–style hangout with a "good mix of indoor and outdoor seating" "gets kicking post-dinner", when you might get "squeezed, stepped on and approached" as you reach for a "knockout drink"; it's "always packed" and "swinging" with "hottie Stanford co-eds" and "young investment bankers", but if "you're over 25", "you'll feel like a grandparent here."

Oasis

20 | 10 | 16 | $5

Menlo Park | 241 El Camino Real (bet. Cambridge & Partridge Aves.) | 650-326-8896 | www.theoasisbeergarden.com

Even "if you're wearing tennis shoes and having a bad hair day", you'll blend right in at the "beer and burger place of choice", perhaps the "most unpretentious joint in Menlo Park" for "Stanford students and alumni"; order at the counter, wade though the "peanut shells on the floor" and sit at a "wooden booth with a thousand names carved into it", then just "relax and watch the game."

Old Pro

17 | 12 | 15 | $7

Palo Alto | 541 Ramona St. (bet. Hamilton & University Aves.) | 650-326-1446 | www.oldpropa.com

Now that it's been renovated, the "bare-bones" standby with "simple charm" is no more – "the 'new' Old Pro looks like a sports bar on steroids" with "giant plasma screens" and a mechanical bull too; late hours, a Palo Alto rarity, mean it's "party stop"–central for "old-timers and gaggles of kids in collegiate gear" who "grab beers and burgers" while "cheering on favorite teams."

O'Neill's

- | - | - | M

San Mateo | 34 S. B St. (bet. Baldwin & 1st Aves.) | 650-347-1544 | www.tisoneills.com

This San Mateo spot with branches in SoMa and Fisherman's Wharf packs them in with pints and a popular pub quiz on Wednesdays; Irish expat Eoin O'Neill is behind this traditional watering hole where the whiskey, Guinness and scotch score high marks with the Hibernia-philes who also swing by Thursday–Sunday for DJs, live music or karaoke; N.B. the SF locations serve hearty Emerald Isle chow.

Pedro's Restaurant & Cantina

∇ 22 | 17 | 17 | $10

Los Gatos | 316 N. Santa Cruz Ave. (Hwy. 9) | 408-354-7570
Santa Clara | 3935 Freedom Circle (Mission College Blvd.) | 408-496-6777

"One of our favorite mainstream Mexican" cantinas, this duo in Los Gatos and Santa Clara "knocks you out" with its "excellent margaritas", "great chips and salsa and generous portions" ("always a good deal") agree amigos; the latter is a "classic Intel hangout after work", and both are staffed with "attentive" servers that ably "manage the large crowds."

Rose & Crown Pub, The

21 | 16 | 20 | $6

Palo Alto | 547 Emerson St. (bet. Hamilton & University Aves.) | 650-327-7673

The "closest thing in the South Bay to a real British pub", this "welcoming", "magnificently dingy dive" in Palo Alto staffed with "genuine U.K." servers attracts "Stanford students", an "older crowd" and a "minimal" number of "yuppie snobs"; the "jukebox and fun are what this bar is all about" believe bon-vivant–boosters who play darts, participate in Tuesday trivia nights and down brewskis, confiding there are "lots of good choices on draft."

	APPEAL	DECOR	SERVICE	COST

Roy's
24 | 23 | 23 | $14

Pebble Beach | Inn at Spanish Bay | 2700 17 Mile Dr. (Congress Rd.) | 831-647-7500 | www.roysrestaurant.com

See review in City of San Francisco Directory.

Rudy's Pub
▽ 19 | 11 | 16 | $8

Palo Alto | 117 University Ave. (bet. Alma & High Sts.) | 650-321-3319 | www.elbe-restaurant.com

"Packed with Stanford students", this bar attached to the German restaurant Elbe is "definitely not the right place for a romantic evening", but it fits the bill for a "loud, long night out" "with a group of friends" opine pub-crawlers; weekdays the vibe is "laid-back", but weekends, when the DJs spin, it turns into more of a "rowdy" "meat market" with a slightly "sketchy" clientele.

750ml
- | - | - | M

San Mateo | 227 S. San Mateo Dr. (bet. 2nd & 3rd Aves.) | 650-342-9463 | www.750ml-sanmateo.com

Try before you buy at this San Mateo wine destination, which allows oenophiles to explore new wines by the glass, half-glass or taste at the bar (both self-serve and full-serve choices), then step next door to the retail shop to take something home; a selection of cheeses, desserts and other snacks mean it's all about lingering, while the 1915 landmark building lends a stately feel to the experience.

Steelhead Brewing Co.
18 | 18 | 18 | $8

Burlingame | 333 California Dr. (Burlingame Ave.) | 650-344-6050 | www.steelheadbrewery.com

"If you want a great burger" and a "decent house brew" "while you watch the game" or feel like "just hanging out and shooting some pool", then put the pedal to the metal and head to this "lively", "spacious" brewpub in Burlingame, a branch of an Oregon-based mini-chain; but cynics snipe it's "chainlike and cavernous", quipping "so this is what young suburbanites do for a night out?"

St. Stephen's Green
▽ 16 | 13 | 17 | $6

Mountain View | 223 Castro St. (Villa St.) | 650-964-9151 | www.ststephensgreen.com

Like most watering holes with the "true Irish spirit", this "nothing fancy", "good ol' neighborhood pub" in Mountain View "encourages sitting around and talking" over a pint of Harp; but "World Cup" fans take a hiatus Thursday–Saturday, when it changes gears and is "converted into a dance club" with DJs, "drawing a good crowd"; still, a paucity of patrons protest that "'pubby' should not equal 'dank.'"

Swingin Door, The
- | - | - | M

San Mateo | 106 E. 25th Ave. (bet. El Camino Real & S. Delaware St.) | 650-522-9800 | www.theswingindoor.com

Now settled into the historic Fey building that housed the local favorite Prince of Wales Pub for 32 years, this two-floor San Mateo hangout nimbly fills its calendar with a host of events, from darts to comedy to karaoke; drop by for lively dueling piano shows Fridays and Saturdays, classic tinkling on Mondays or jazz on Tuesdays and stick around for the 18 beers on tap or the habañero burger, a throwback to its former tenant.

	APPEAL	DECOR	SERVICE	COST

☑ Tamarine
24 | 24 | 22 | $12

Palo Alto | 546 University Ave. (bet. Cowper & Webster Sts.) |
650-325-8500 | www.tamarinerestaurant.com

"Dress up" and "take someone you want to impress" to Palo Alto's
"subtle" yet "sexy" "hot spot" that's "set up for mingling" over cocktails and "absolutely fabulous" Vietnamese cuisine; the "compact" but
"awesome bar" is "packed during happy hour", when the "power business set" orders "delicious tropical drinks" ("the lychee martini is to
die for") and "interesting small dishes" "ideal for sharing and as conversation helpers", "plus the staff could not be friendlier."

Tarpy's Roadhouse
∇ 23 | 21 | 22 | $12

Monterey | 2999 Monterey-Salinas Hwy. (Canyon Del Rey Blvd.) |
831-647-1444 | www.tarpys.com

A "Monterey favorite" for margaritas and "good" American eats, this
"oasis", named for a local vigilante who was lynched on the grounds
back in 1873, sprawls over five acres, with a patio overlooking a colorful
garden; seven private rooms make this "noisier cousin of the Rio Grill in
Carmel" a "great place for weddings and parties", but even day-trippers
can't help but appreciate the ambiance of the 1917 stone roadhouse.

Tied House Cafe & Brewery
18 | 15 | 18 | $8

Mountain View | 954 Villa St. (bet. Bryant & Franklin Sts.) | 650-965-2739
San Jose | San Pedro Sq. | 65 N. San Pedro St. (Santa Clara St.) | 408-295-2739
www.tiedhouse.com

"Stick with the seasonal beer" and the "hard-to-screw-up foods" at this
pair of "casual" microbreweries in San Jose and Mountain View and
"you'll be ok" advise insiders; natch, the "reasonably priced" burgers
and garlic fries "go great" with the suds, nevertheless cynics cut loose,
muttering it's "nothing special" – and service can be "pitifully slow."

Trader Vic's
19 | 21 | 19 | $13

Palo Alto | Dinah's Garden Hotel | 4269 El Camino Real (bet. Charleston &
San Antonio Rds.) | 650-849-9800 | www.tradervicspaloalto.com
See review in East of San Francisco Directory.

Trials Pub
- | - | - | M

San Jose | 265 N. First St. (bet. Devine & Julian Sts.) | 408-947-0497 |
www.trialspub.com

"Always fun", this San Jose hangout set in a former brothel has the "potential" to be a spitting image of pubs across the Pond, what with the
"many U.K. beers fresh and on tap" and ghosts rumored to be in resi-
dence; little wonder it lures a "loyal following" of "twentysomethings"
who congregate for pints, darts, board games and trivia quizzes.

Zibibbo
23 | 23 | 21 | $12

Palo Alto | 430 Kipling St. (bet. Lytton & University Aves.) | 650-328-6722 |
www.zibibborestaurant.com

"Beautiful people abound" at Downtown Palo Alto's "glamorous" but
"relaxed" "place to be", a "huge" sibling of SF's Azie and Lulu that
"fires on all cylinders"; it feels like "there are big venture capital deals
going down" in the "nicely appointed" bar serving "killer" drinks while
the wine cafe "has a bit of magic" (and an "amazing" by-the-glass selection) making it date-"perfect"; P.S. there's also a "great open-air
section", where a fireplace flickers in cool weather.

INDEXES

Locations 136
Special Appeals 146

Locations

Includes venue names and Appeal ratings. ⊠ indicates places with the highest ratings, popularity and importance.

City of San Francisco

AT&T PARK/ SOUTH BEACH

Acme Chophouse	20
Jack Falstaff	20
MoMo's	20
330 Ritch	19
Tres Agaves	22
21st Amendment	20

BAYVIEW/ HUNTER'S POINT

Space 550	20

BERNAL HEIGHTS

Liberty Cafe	20
Stray Bar	-
Vino Rosso	-
Wild Side West	22

CASTRO

Amber	19
⊠ Badlands	17
Café	17
Café du Nord	23
Cafe Flore	21
440 Castro	18
Harvey's	18
⊠ Lime	21
NEW LookOut, The	-
Lucky 13	24
Mecca	22
Men's Room	16
Metro	17
Midnight Sun	17
Mint Karaoke	21
Mix	17
Moby Dick	19
Orbit Room Cafe	24
Pilsner Inn	19
2223 Restaurant	21
Twin Peaks	14

CHINA BASIN/ DOGPATCH

Cafe Cocomo	20
Dogpatch	20
Jelly's	16
Kelly's	19
Ramp	21
Retox Lounge	-
NEW Serpentine	-
Yield Wine Bar	25

CHINATOWN

Bow Bow Lounge	21
Buddha Bar	19
Li Po	22
Mr. Bing's	17
Rosewood	21

COW HOLLOW

⊠ Balboa Cafe	20
Bar None	14
⊠ Betelnut Pejiu Wu	24
Black Horse Pub	22
Blue Light	16
⊠ Brazen Head	25
Bus Stop	16
City Tavern	15
Comet Club	12
Eastside West	19
jovino	-
Left/Albuquerque	15
Liverpool Lil's	21
⊠ MatrixFillmore	21
Mauna Loa	17
Ottimista Enoteca	23
Perry's	19
Umami	-

DOWNTOWN

☑ Aqua	25
Azul Bar	–
Bacchus Kirk	17
NEW Bar Drake	–
B44	20
Biscuits & Blues	21
☑ BIX	26
☑ Bubble Lounge	22
Cafe Bastille	18
Café Claude	21
Campton Place	23
Cantina	–
Carnelian Room	24
Cellar	–
Cigar Bar	19
☑ Cityscape	24
Club EZ5	19
Cortez	22
E&O Trading Co.	20
Etiquette	–
☑ Farallon	24
Fifth Floor	–
First Crush	22
Ginger's Trois	–
Gold Dust Lounge	22
Grand Cafe	21
Grandviews	24
Harrington's B&G	17
Harry Denton Starlight	24
Hidden Vine	–
House of Shields	16
Irish Bank	19
Johnny Foley's	19
John's Grill	21
☑ Kokkari Estiatorio	25
Kuleto's	–
La Scene	16
Le Central Bistro	21
☑ Le Colonial	24
Lefty O'Doul's	17

London Wine	18
☑ Mandarin Lounge	27
☑ Michael Mina	24
☑ Millennium	26
Occidental Cigar	24
Otis	–
Perbacco	–
☑ Pied Piper Bar	26
Plouf	20
Ponzu	20
Postrio	22
Punchline Comedy	22
☑ Redwood Rm.	24
Rouge et Blanc	–
Royal Exchange	17
NEW Rrazz Room	–
Rubicon	21
Ruby Skye	20
Scala's Bistro	22
☑ Seasons Bar	26
Slide	22
Sugar Café	–
Tadich Grill	22
Tunnel Top	18
Vessel	–
Voda	19
Warfield	20

EMBARCADERO

☑ Americano	23
Beale St. B&G	18
☑ Boulevard	26
Butterfly	21
Chaya	23
NEW EPIC Roast	–
Ferry Plaza Wine	22
Fog City Diner	21
☑ Gordon Biersch	18
Grumpy's Pub	18
Hi-Dive	–
Houston's	20
MarketBar	18

LOCATIONS

NEW Mexico DF	–
One Market	21
Ozumo	23
Palomino	19
Pier 23 Cafe	21
Shanghai 1930	23
Z Slanted Door	24
13 Views	21
NEW Waterbar	–

FISHERMAN'S WHARF

Z Ana Mandara	25
Z Buena Vista	23
Dirty Martini	19
Fiddler's Green	19
Z Gary Danko	27
Hard Rock Cafe	14
Knuckles Sports	18
Lou's Pier 47	22
McCormick/Kuleto's	20
O'Neill's	–
Red Jack	18
Suede	17

FOREST HILLS/ WEST PORTAL

Dubliner, The	18

GLEN PARK

Glen Park Station	18

HAIGHT-ASHBURY/ COLE VALLEY

Alembic, The	24
Club Deluxe	21
Eos	22
Finnegans Wake	20
Gold Cane	13
Hobson's Choice	18
Kan Zaman	22
Kezar Bar	18
Kezar Pub	19
Magnolia Pub	23
Milk Bar	19

Murio's Trophy	12
Trax	19
Zam Zam	23

HAYES VALLEY/ CIVIC CENTER

Z Absinthe	23
Caffe Trieste	20
Cav Wine Bar	22
Hôtel Biron	24
Jade Bar	20
Z Jardinière	26
Marlena's	18
Martuni's	22
Place Pigalle	21
Rickshaw Stop	20
Sauce	20
Sugar Lounge	20
Suppenküche	22
Z Zuni Café	24

INNER RICHMOND

Bitter End	21
Blue Danube	21
Buckshot Bar	–
540 Club	24
Ireland's 32	22
Pig & Whistle	23
Plough & Stars	18
Rockit Room	19
RoHan	19
Would You Believe	11

INNER SUNSET

Blackthorn Tavern	16
Fireside Bar	23
Z Little Shamrock	25
Mucky Duck	16
NEW Wunder Brewing Co.	–
Yancy's	20

JAPANTOWN

NEW O Izakaya	–

LOCATIONS

12 Galaxies	21
Uptown	23
Velvet Cantina	-
Whisper	15
☑ Zeitgeist	23

NOB HILL

☑ Big 4	25
NEW Le Club	-
☑ Lobby/Ritz-Carlton	25
Tonga Room	22
☑ Top of the Mark	25

NOE VALLEY

Bliss Bar	19
Dubliner, The	18
Noe Valley Ministry	24

NORTH BEACH

NEW Apartment 24	-
Bamboo Hut	19
☑ Bimbo's 365 Club	24
Bocce Cafe	21
Café Prague	17
Cafe Zoetrope/Rosso	21
Caffè Greco	19
Caffe Puccini	20
Caffe Trieste	20
Capp's Corner	19
Centerfolds	24
Club 443	-
Cobb's Comedy	21
NEW Dell'Uva	-
Dragon Bar	-
NEW Enrico's	-
15 Romolo	23
Fuse	19
Gino & Carlo	18
NEW Horizon	-
Impala	20
Jazz at Pearl's	24
Kennedy's Irish	21
Larry Flynt's	15

NEW La Trappe	-
Lusty Lady	13
Mario's Bohemian	23
North Star Cafe	21
O'Reilly's Irish Pub	20
Peña Pachamama	-
Purple Onion	18
Rogue Ales	21
Rose Pistola	22
Saloon	21
San Fran. Brew.	21
Savoy Tivoli	19
Sip Bar & Lounge	17
☑ Specs Bar	25
Steps of Rome	20
Tony Nik's	23
Tosca Cafe	23
☑ Vesuvio	24
Woody Zips	-

OUTER RICHMOND

Abbey Tavern	15
Bazaar Café	20
Beach Chalet	21
Cliff House	23
Simple Pleasures	-
Tommy's Mexican	22
Trad'r Sam's	22

OUTER SUNSET

Rick's	19
Riptide	17

PACIFIC HEIGHTS

Fishbowl	17
g bar	17
Grove	21
Lion Pub	21

POLK GULCH

Bell Tower	16
Bigfoot Lodge	19
Blur	17

LOCATIONS

Z 111 Minna	22
O'Neill's	-
Oola	23
Paragon	21
Power Exchange	18
Powerhouse	21
Rest. LuLu	20
Roe Lounge	20
Roy's	24
Salt House	25
Shine	24
Slim's	20
Stud	19
supperclub	22
Sushi Groove So.	23
NEW Temple	-
Ten15 Folsom	16
NEW Terroir	-
Thirsty Bear Brew.	18
Town Hall	23
TWO	-
Varnish Fine Art	21
Z View Lounge	26
Wish	22
XYZ	20
Zebulon	21
Zeke's Sports B&G	-

TENDERLOIN

Ambassador, The	-
Aunt Charlie's	19
Bambuddha	21
Z Bourbon & Branch	26
Brick	-
Café Royale	21
Edinburgh Castle	22
NEW 800 Larkin	-
Great Amer. Music	24
Ha Ra	19
Mitchell Bros.	17
Olive Bar	19
Rye	23

suite one8one	18
Swig	19
222 Club	22
Whiskey Thieves	23

UPPER FILLMORE

Elite Cafe	21
Florio	23
Z Harry's	19

WESTERN ADDITION

Bar 821	20
Boom Boom Rm.	23
Cafe Abir	21
NEW Candybar	-
Z Fillmore	27
Fly	20
Frankie's Bohemian	17
Independent	22
Madrone Lounge	21
nopa	24
Poleng	22
Rasselas Jazz	23
Sheba	-
NEW Wine Jar	-
Z Yoshi's	24

East of San Francisco

ALBANY

Albany Bowl	17
Club Mallard	23
Schmidt's Tobacco	-

BERKELEY

Z Albatross Pub	25
Ashkenaz	18
Beckett's Irish Pub	22
Blakes/Telegraph	17
Café Rouge	21
Café Valparaiso	22
Caffe Trieste	20
Z César	25
downtown	21

RUTHERFORD

☑ Auberge du Soleil	28

SAN ANSELMO

Insalata's	22

SAUSALITO

Caffe Trieste	20
Cork Enoteca	21
No Name Bar	19
☑ Sushi Ran	25

ST. HELENA

Ana's Cantina	18
☑ Martini House	25
Silverado Brew.	18
☑ Tra Vigne	26

TIBURON

Guaymas	24
☑ Sam's Anchor Cafe	25

WEST MARIN/OLEMA

☑ Pelican Inn	27
Rancho Nicasio	23

YOUNTVILLE

☑ Bouchon	25
Mustards Grill	23

South of San Francisco

BURLINGAME

Elephant Bar	16
☑ Nectar Wine	23
Steelhead Brewing	18

CAMPBELL

Elephant Bar	16
Left/Albuquerque	15

CARMEL/ MONTEREY PENINSULA

Britannia Arms	17
☑ Highlands Inn	28
Hog's Breath Inn	24
Roy's	24
Tarpy's Roadhse.	23

CUPERTINO

Britannia Arms	17
Elephant Bar	16

LOS GATOS

Black Watch	21
Dio Deka	-
Los Gatos Brew.	21
Pedro's	22

MENLO PARK

British Bankers	18
☑ Left Bank	20
Oasis	20

MOUNTAIN VIEW

Fibbar/Molly Magees	19
St. Stephen's	16
Tied House Cafe	18

PALO ALTO

Antonio's Nut Hse.	16
Blue Chalk Cafe	18
Cafe Zoetrope/Rosso	21
Compadres	18
Daru	-
Empire Grill	21
☑ Evvia	24
☑ Gordon Biersch	18
MacArthur Park	18
Nola	21
Old Pro	17
Rose & Crown	21
Rudy's Pub	19
☑ Tamarine	24
Trader Vic's	19
Zibibbo	23

SAN JOSE

Agenda	15
Blank Club	14
☑ Blowfish Sushi	22
Britannia Arms	17
Cinebar	11
E&O Trading Co.	20
☑ Gordon Biersch	18

Hedley Club	24	750ml	-
Improv	25	Swingin Door	-
☑ Left Bank	20		

SANTA CLARA

| Tied House Cafe | 18 | Pedro's | 22 |
| Trials Pub | - | | |

SUNNYVALE

SAN MATEO

Faultline Brew.	17
☑ Left Bank	20	Fibbar/Molly Magees	19
O'Neill's	-		

Special Appeals

Listings cover the best in each category and include venue names, locations and Appeal ratings. Multi-location nightspots' features may vary by branch. ☑ indicates places with the highest ratings, popularity and importance.

ADDITIONS

Anchor & Hope | **SoMa**	⏚
Apartment 24 | **N Beach**	⏚
Bar Drake | **Downtown**	⏚
Bar 888 | **SoMa**	⏚
Bar Johnny | **Russian Hill**	⏚
Beretta | **Mission**	⏚
Bin 38 | **Marina**	⏚
Bollyhood Cafe | **Mission**	⏚
Bossa Nova | **SoMa**	⏚
Brick | **Tenderloin**	⏚
Buckshot Bar | **Inner Rich**	⏚
Candybar | **W Addition**	⏚
Cat Club | **SoMa**	⏚
Circa | **Marina**	⏚
Daru | **Palo Alto/S**	⏚
Dell'Uva | **N Beach**	⏚
800 Larkin | **Tenderloin**	⏚
83 Proof | **SoMa**	⏚
Enrico's | **N Beach**	⏚
EPIC Roast | **Embarcadero**	⏚
Franklin Sq. Wine | **Oakland/E**	⏚
Ginger's Trois | **Downtown**	⏚
Harlot | **SoMa**	⏚
Hi-Dive | **Embarcadero**	⏚
Horizon | **N Beach**	⏚
Koko Cocktails | **Polk Gulch**	⏚
La Trappe | **N Beach**	⏚
Lava Lounge | **SoMa**	⏚
Le Club | **Nob Hill**	⏚
Local Kitchen | **SoMa**	⏚
LookOut, The | **Castro**	⏚
Matador | **SoMa**	⏚
Mexico DF | **Embarcadero**	⏚
Monk's Kettle | **Mission**	⏚
Nickie's | **Lower Haight**	⏚
O Izakaya | **Japantown**	⏚
O'Neill's | **multi.**	⏚
Rrazz Room | **Downtown**	⏚
Serpentine | **Dogpatch**	⏚
Temple | **SoMa**	⏚
Terroir | **SoMa**	⏚
Uva Enoteca | **Lower Haight**	⏚
Va de Vi | **Walnut Creek/E**	⏚
Velvet Cantina | **Mission**	⏚
Waterbar | **Embarcadero**	⏚
Wine Bar | **Russian Hill**	⏚
Wine Jar | **W Addition**	⏚
Wunder Brewing Co. | **Inner Sunset**	⏚

AFTER WORK

Ace Wasabi's | **Marina**	20
☑ Americano | **Embarcadero**	23
☑ Aqua | **Downtown**	25
☑ Badlands | **Castro**	17
NEW Bar 888 | **SoMa**	⏚
Beale St. B&G | **Embarcadero**	18
Bell Tower | **Polk Gulch**	16
Blue Chalk Cafe | **Palo Alto/S**	18
British Bankers | **Menlo Pk/S**	18
Chaya | **Embarcadero**	23
Cosmopolitan, The | **SoMa**	18
DaDa | **SoMa**	⏚
Dave's | **SoMa**	13
E&O Trading Co. | **multi.**	20
Eddie Rickenbacker's | **SoMa**	15
NEW 83 Proof | **SoMa**	⏚
Empire Grill | **Palo Alto/S**	21
NEW EPIC Roast | **Embarcadero**	⏚
Faultline Brew. | **Sunnyvale/S**	17
Ferry Plaza Wine | **Embarcadero**	22

Finnegans Wake	**Cole Valley**	20
Gallery Lounge	**SoMa**	16
Ginger's Trois	**Downtown**	-
Gold Dust Lounge	**Downtown**	22
🇿 Gordon Biersch	**Embarcadero**	18
Grumpy's Pub	**Embarcadero**	18
Harrington's B&G	**Downtown**	17
🇿 Harry's	**Upper Fillmore**	19
Hi-Dive	**Embarcadero**	-
Houston's	**Embarcadero**	20
Irish Bank	**Downtown**	19
Jade Bar	**Hayes Valley**	20
Kate O'Brien's	**SoMa**	17
Kezar Pub	**Haight-Ashbury**	19
NEW Lava Lounge	**SoMa**	-
🇿 Lobby/St. Regis	**SoMa**	25
NEW Local Kitchen	**SoMa**	-
London Wine	**Downtown**	18
Marin Brewing	**Larkspur/N**	17
NEW Mexico DF	**Embarcadero**	-
Occidental Cigar	**Downtown**	24
🇿 111 Minna	**SoMa**	22
O'Neill's	**multi.**	-
One Market	**Embarcadero**	21
Oola	**SoMa**	23
Ozumo	**Embarcadero**	23
Pacific Coast	**Oakland/E**	19
🇿 Pied Piper Bar	**Downtown**	26
Pier 23 Cafe	**Embarcadero**	21
Plouf	**Downtown**	20
Pres a Vi	**Presidio**	-
Royal Exchange	**Downtown**	17
San Fran. Brew.	**N Beach**	21
🇿 Slanted Door	**Embarcadero**	24
🇿 Specs Bar	**N Beach**	25
St. Stephen's	**Mtn View/S**	16
Tadich Grill	**Downtown**	22
Thirsty Bear Brew.	**SoMa**	18
Tied House Cafe	**multi.**	18
Tunnel Top	**Downtown**	18

Varnish Fine Art	**SoMa**	21
NEW Waterbar	**Embarcadero**	-
XYZ	**SoMa**	20
Zebulon	**SoMa**	21
🇿 Zeitgeist	**Mission**	23

ART BARS

Brick	**Tenderloin**	-
Cafe Van Kleef	**Oakland/E**	24
DaDa	**SoMa**	-
Gallery Lounge	**SoMa**	16
Hôtel Biron	**Hayes Valley**	24
Madrone Lounge	**W Addition**	21
🇿 111 Minna	**SoMa**	22
Varnish Fine Art	**SoMa**	21

BEAUTIFUL PEOPLE

🇿 Absinthe	**Hayes Valley**	23
🇿 Ana Mandara	**Fish. Wharf**	25
NEW Apartment 24	**N Beach**	-
🇿 Aqua	**Downtown**	25
🇿 bacar	**SoMa**	24
🇿 Betelnut Pejiu Wu	**Cow Hollow**	24
NEW Bin 38	**Marina**	-
🇿 BIX	**Downtown**	26
🇿 Bubble Lounge	**Downtown**	22
🇿 César	**Berkeley/E**	25
Circa	**Marina**	-
Element Lounge	**Polk Gulch**	19
NEW Enrico's	**N Beach**	-
g bar	**Pacific Hts**	17
NEW Harlot	**SoMa**	-
Icon Lounge	**SoMa**	-
Jade Bar	**Hayes Valley**	20
Laszlo	**Mission**	20
NEW Le Club	**Nob Hill**	-
🇿 Le Colonial	**Downtown**	24
🇿 Lime	**Castro**	21
NEW Local Kitchen	**SoMa**	-
🇿 MatrixFillmore	**Cow Hollow**	21
Mecca	**Castro**	22

SPECIAL APPEALS

Z Michael Mina | **Downtown**	24
nopa | **W Addition**	24
Ozumo | **Embarcadero**	23
Postrio | **Downtown**	22
Z Redwood Rm. | **Downtown**	24
Rose Pistola | **N Beach**	22
Ruby Skye | **Downtown**	20
Shanghai 1930 | **Embarcadero**	23
Slide | **Downtown**	22
supperclub | **SoMa**	22
Sushi Groove So. | **SoMa**	23
Tonic | **Russian Hill**	17

BLUES

Ana's Cantina | **St. Helena/N**	18
Beach Chalet | **Outer Rich**	21
Beckett's Irish Pub | **Berkeley/E**	22
Biscuits & Blues | **Downtown**	21
Boom Boom Rm. | **W Addition**	23
Cafe Van Kleef | **Oakland/E**	24
Caffe Cicero | **Napa/N**	18
Calistoga Inn | **Calistoga/N**	22
Club Deluxe | **Haight-Ashbury**	21
Elbo Room | **Mission**	20
Freight & Salvage | **Berkeley/E**	21
Lou's Pier 47 | **Fish. Wharf**	22
Madrone Lounge | **W Addition**	21
19 Broadway | **Fairfax/N**	19
No Name Bar | **Sausalito/N**	19
O'Reilly's Holy Grail | **Polk Gulch**	22
Pier 23 Cafe | **Embarcadero**	21
Pig & Whistle | **Inner Rich**	23
Pyramid Brewery | **Walnut Creek/E**	19
Rancho Nicasio | **Nicasio/N**	23
Rasselas Jazz | **W Addition**	23
Riptide | **Outer Sunset**	17
Saloon | **N Beach**	21
Slim's | **SoMa**	20
Z Sweetwater Saloon | **Mill Valley/N**	28
Warfield | **Downtown**	20

BOTTLE SERVICE

(Bottle purchase sometimes
required to secure a table)

Agenda | **San Jose/S**	15
Z Americano | **Embarcadero**	23
NEW Apartment 24 | **N Beach**	-
Bambuddha | **Tenderloin**	21
NEW Bar 888 | **SoMa**	-
Cafe Cocomo | **Dogpatch**	20
Cellar | **Downtown**	-
Circolo | **Mission**	19
Comet Club | **Cow Hollow**	12
Daru | **Palo Alto/S**	-
Dragon Bar | **N Beach**	-
Element Lounge | **Polk Gulch**	19
Etiquette | **Downtown**	-
Fluid | **SoMa**	20
g bar | **Pacific Hts**	17
Glas Kat | **SoMa**	18
NEW Harlot | **SoMa**	-
NEW Horizon | **N Beach**	-
Impala | **N Beach**	20
John Colins | **SoMa**	22
NEW La Trappe | **N Beach**	-
NEW Lava Lounge | **SoMa**	-
NEW Le Club | **Nob Hill**	-
Z Medjool | **Mission**	23
Mezzanine | **SoMa**	21
Mr. Smith's | **SoMa**	22
Nihon | **Mission**	23
Pink | **Mission**	21
Red Devil | **Polk Gulch**	18
Roe Lounge | **SoMa**	20
Ruby Skye | **Downtown**	20
Shine | **SoMa**	24
Slide | **Downtown**	22
Suede | **Fish. Wharf**	17
Sugar Café | **Downtown**	-
suite one8one | **Tenderloin**	18
NEW Temple | **SoMa**	-
Ten15 Folsom | **SoMa**	16

Vessel | **Downtown** -|

Whisper | **Mission** 15|

CABARET

AsiaSF | **SoMa** 24|

Aunt Charlie's | **Tenderloin** 19|

Marlena's | **Hayes Valley** 18|

Mecca | **Castro** 22|

NEW Rrazz Room | **Downtown** -|

COFFEEHOUSES

Bazaar Café | **Outer Rich** 20|

Blue Danube | **Inner Rich** 21|

Cafe Abir | **W Addition** 21|

Cafe Flore | **Castro** 21|

Cafe Int'l | **Lower Haight** 21|

Café Prague | **N Beach** 17|

Café Royale | **Tenderloin** 21|

Caffè Greco | **N Beach** 19|

Caffe Puccini | **N Beach** 20|

Caffe Trieste | **multi.** 20|

Grove | **multi.** 21|

jovino | **Cow Hollow** -|

Mario's Bohemian | **N Beach** 23|

Simple Pleasures | **Outer Rich** -|

Steps of Rome | **N Beach** 20|

Sugar Café | **Downtown** -|

COMEDY CLUBS

(Call ahead to check nights, times, performers and covers)

Cobb's Comedy | **N Beach** 21|

Improv | **San Jose/S** 25|

Punchline Comedy | **Downtown** 22|

Purple Onion | **N Beach** 18|

DANCING

Agenda | **San Jose/S** 15|

Annie's Social Club | **SoMa** 20|

Anú | **SoMa** 18|

NEW Apartment 24 | **N Beach** -|

Ashkenaz | **Berkeley/E** 18|

AsiaSF | **SoMa** 24|

Azul Bar | **Downtown** -|

Z Badlands | **Castro** 17|

Bamboo Hut | **N Beach** 19|

Bissap/Little Baobab | **Mission** 23|

Blakes/Telegraph | **Berkeley/E** 17|

NEW Bollyhood Cafe | **Mission** -|

British Bankers | **Menlo Pk/S** 18|

Bruno's | **Mission** -|

Butter | **SoMa** 18|

Cafe Cocomo | **Dogpatch** 20|

Café du Nord | **Castro** 23|

Cat Club | **SoMa** -|

Cellar | **Downtown** -|

Circolo | **Mission** 19|

Club 443 | **N Beach** -|

Club Six | **SoMa** 18|

Comet Club | **Cow Hollow** 12|

Delirium Cocktails | **Mission** 16|

Dirty Martini | **Fish. Wharf** 19|

Divas | **Polk Gulch** -|

DNA Lounge | **SoMa** 16|

Double Dutch | **Mission** 23|

Dragon Bar | **N Beach** -|

eight | **SoMa** 21|

Elbo Room | **Mission** 20|

Element Lounge | **Polk Gulch** 19|

El Rio | **Mission** 23|

Endup | **SoMa** 20|

Esta Noche | **Mission** 10|

Etiquette | **Downtown** -|

Fiddler's Green | **Fish. Wharf** 19|

Glas Kat | **SoMa** 18|

Gravity | **Marina** 16|

NEW Harlot | **SoMa** -|

Harry Denton Starlight | **Downtown** 24|

HiFi | **Marina** 16|

Icon Lounge | **SoMa** -|

Jelly's | **China Basin** 16|

John Colins | **SoMa** 22|

Levende | **Mission** 22|

Madrone Lounge | **W Addition** 21|

Make-Out Room | **Mission** 22|

SPECIAL APPEALS

Z MatrixFillmore | **Cow Hollow** 21
Mezzanine | **SoMa** 21
Mighty | **Potrero Hill** 23
Milk Bar | **Haight-Ashbury** 19
Mr. Smith's | **SoMa** 22
NEW Nickie's | **Lower Haight** -
19 Broadway | **Fairfax/N** 19
Otis | **Downtown** -
Peña Pachamama | **N Beach** -
Pier 23 Cafe | **Embarcadero** 21
Pink | **Mission** 21
Poleng | **W Addition** 22
Ramp | **China Basin** 21
Red Devil | **Polk Gulch** 18
Rickshaw Stop | **Civic Ctr** 20
Roccapulco | **Mission** 20
Roe Lounge | **SoMa** 20
Rouge Nightclub | **Russian Hill** 13
Ruby Skye | **Downtown** 20
Rudy's Pub | **Palo Alto/S** 19
Saddle Rack | **Fremont/E** 21
Shattuck Down Low | **Berkeley/E** 16
Shine | **SoMa** 24
Sip Bar & Lounge | **N Beach** 17
Skylark | **Mission** 14
Slide | **Downtown** 22
Space 550 | **Bayview** 20
Stud | **SoMa** 19
Suede | **Fish. Wharf** 17
Sugar Café | **Downtown** -
suite one8one | **Tenderloin** 18
supperclub | **SoMa** 22
Swig | **Tenderloin** 19
Syn Lounge | **Mission** -
NEW Temple | **SoMa** -
Ten15 Folsom | **SoMa** 16
330 Ritch | **S Beach** 19
Z Top of the Mark | **Nob Hill** 25
Underground SF | **Lower Haight** 18
Vertigo | **Polk Gulch** -
Vessel | **Downtown** -
Whisper | **Mission** 15
White Horse Bar | **Oakland/E** 19

DIVES

Alley, The | **Oakland/E** 22
Annie's Social Club | **SoMa** 20
Aunt Charlie's | **Tenderloin** 19
Cinebar | **San Jose/S** 11
Club Mallard | **Albany/E** 23
Doc's Clock | **Mission** 18
Final Final | **Marina** 17
Finnegans Wake | **Cole Valley** 20
500 Club | **Mission** 22
Ginger's Trois | **Downtown** -
Glen Park Station | **Glen Pk** 18
Gold Cane | **Haight-Ashbury** 13
Grumpy's Pub | **Embarcadero** 18
Ha Ra | **Tenderloin** 19
Ireland's 32 | **Inner Rich** 22
Lefty O'Doul's | **Downtown** 17
Li Po | **Chinatown** 22
NEW Matador | **SoMa** -
Mauna Loa | **Cow Hollow** 17
Men's Room | **Castro** 16
Mr. Bing's | **Chinatown** 17
Murio's Trophy | **Haight-Ashbury** 12
Route 101 | **Polk Gulch** 13
Sadie's Elephant | **Potrero Hill** 22
Saloon | **N Beach** 21
Silver Peso | **Larkspur/N** 14
Stork Club | **Oakland/E** 19
Two AM Club | **Mill Valley/N** 15
Uptown | **Mission** 23
Would You Believe | **Inner Rich** 11

DJs

Agenda | **San Jose/S** 15
Amnesia | **Mission** 19
Ana's Cantina | **St. Helena/N** 18
Annie's Social Club | **SoMa** 20
NEW Apartment 24 | **N Beach** -

Name	Location	Rating
Ashkenaz	Berkeley/E	18
AsiaSF	SoMa	24
Attic Club	Mission	20
Aunt Charlie's	Tenderloin	19
Bacchus Wine	Russian Hill	23
Z Badlands	Castro	17
Bamboo Hut	N Beach	19
Bambuddha	Tenderloin	21
Beauty Bar	Mission	18
Bissap/Little Baobab	Mission	23
Blakes/Telegraph	Berkeley/E	17
Blank Club	San Jose/S	14
Bliss Bar	Noe Valley	19
Z Blowfish Sushi	San Jose/S	22
NEW Bollyhood Cafe	Mission	-
Boom Boom Rm.	W Addition	23
British Bankers	Menlo Pk/S	18
Bruno's	Mission	-
Butter	SoMa	18
Café	Castro	17
Cafe Cocomo	Dogpatch	20
Cafe Van Kleef	Oakland/E	24
Casanova	Mission	20
Cat Club	SoMa	-
Cellar	Downtown	-
Club EZ5	Downtown	19
Club 443	N Beach	-
Club Six	SoMa	18
Comet Club	Cow Hollow	12
Dalva	Mission	20
Dirty Martini	Fish. Wharf	19
Divas	Polk Gulch	-
DNA Lounge	SoMa	16
Dragon Bar	N Beach	-
eight	SoMa	21
Elbo Room	Mission	20
Element Lounge	Polk Gulch	19
El Rio	Mission	23
Endup	SoMa	20
Esta Noche	Mission	10
Etiquette	Downtown	-
Fiddler's Green	Fish. Wharf	19
440 Castro	Castro	18
Fuse	N Beach	19
g bar	Pacific Hts	17
Glas Kat	SoMa	18
Gravity	Marina	16
NEW Harlot	SoMa	-
Harry Denton Starlight	Downtown	24
Z Harry's	Upper Fillmore	19
Hemlock Tavern	Polk Gulch	20
HiFi	Marina	16
NEW Horizon	N Beach	-
House of Shields	Downtown	16
Jelly's	China Basin	16
Jillian's	SoMa	18
Kingman's	Oakland/E	21
Laszlo	Mission	20
Levende	multi.	22
Lingba Lounge	Potrero Hill	18
Luka's Taproom	Oakland/E	23
Madrone Lounge	W Addition	21
Make-Out Room	Mission	22
Mas Sake	Marina	19
Z MatrixFillmore	Cow Hollow	21
Mecca	Castro	22
Mezzanine	SoMa	21
Mighty	Potrero Hill	23
Milk Bar	Haight-Ashbury	19
Mr. Smith's	SoMa	22
19 Broadway	Fairfax/N	19
Z 111 Minna	SoMa	22
Orbit Room Cafe	Castro	24
Ozumo	Embarcadero	23
Pier 23 Cafe	Embarcadero	21
Pink	Mission	21
Ponzu	Downtown	20
Radio Bar	Oakland/E	23
Z Redwood Rm.	Downtown	24
Rickshaw Stop	Civic Ctr	20
Roccapulco	Mission	20

Roe Lounge | **SoMa**	20
RoHan | **Inner Rich**	19
Rosewood | **Chinatown**	21
Rouge Nightclub | **Russian Hill**	13
Ruby Room | **Oakland/E**	-
Ruby Skye | **Downtown**	20
Rudy's Pub | **Palo Alto/S**	19
Shattuck Down Low | **Berkeley/E**	16
Shine | **SoMa**	24
Skylark | **Mission**	14
Space 550 | **Bayview**	20
St. Stephen's | **Mtn View/S**	16
Stud | **SoMa**	19
Suede | **Fish. Wharf**	17
suite one8one | **Tenderloin**	18
Sushi Groove So. | **SoMa**	23
Syn Lounge | **Mission**	-
NEW Temple | **SoMa**	-
Ten15 Folsom | **SoMa**	16
330 Ritch | **S Beach**	19
Tonic | **Russian Hill**	17
Tunnel Top | **Downtown**	18
222 Club | **Tenderloin**	22
Underground SF | **Lower Haight**	18
Varnish Fine Art | **SoMa**	21
Vessel | **Downtown**	-
Voda | **Downtown**	19
Whisper | **Mission**	15
White Horse Bar | **Oakland/E**	19
Wish | **SoMa**	22

DRAG SHOWS

AsiaSF | **SoMa**	24
Aunt Charlie's | **Tenderloin**	19
Café | **Castro**	17
Esta Noche | **Mission**	10
Harvey's | **Castro**	18
Marlena's | **Hayes Valley**	18
Mecca | **Castro**	22
NEW Rrazz Room | **Downtown**	-
White Horse Bar | **Oakland/E**	19

DRINK SPECIALISTS

BEER
(* Microbrewery)

Z Albatross Pub | **Berkeley/E**	25
Amnesia | **Mission**	19
NEW Anchor & Hope | **SoMa**	-
Beach Chalet* | **Outer Rich**	21
Ben & Nick's | **Oakland/E**	18
Cato's Ale House | **Oakland/E**	19
Dalva | **Mission**	20
E&O Trading Co. | **Downtown**	20
Edinburgh Castle | **Tenderloin**	22
Elixir | **Mission**	19
Empire Grill | **Palo Alto/S**	21
Faultline Brew. | **Sunnyvale/S**	17
Gestalt Haus | **Mission**	-
Z Gordon Biersch | **multi.**	18
Jupiter | **Berkeley/E**	21
Kennedy's Irish | **N Beach**	21
NEW La Trappe | **N Beach**	-
Los Gatos Brew. | **Los Gatos/S**	21
Lucky 13 | **Castro**	24
Luka's Taproom | **Oakland/E**	23
Mad Dog in Fog | **Lower Haight**	18
Magnolia Pub* | **Haight-Ashbury**	23
Marin Brewing | **Larkspur/N**	17
NEW Monk's Kettle | **Mission**	-
O'Reilly's Holy Grail | **Polk Gulch**	22
O'Reilly's Irish Pub | **N Beach**	20
Pacific Coast | **Oakland/E**	19
Pig & Whistle | **Inner Rich**	23
Place Pigalle | **Hayes Valley**	21
Plough & Stars | **Inner Rich**	18
Pyramid Brewery* | **multi.**	19
Rogue Ales* | **N Beach**	21
Royal Exchange | **Downtown**	17
Rudy's Pub | **Palo Alto/S**	19
San Fran. Brew.* | **N Beach**	21
Schmidt's Tobacco | **Albany/E**	-
Silverado Brew.* | **St. Helena/N**	18

Steelhead Brewing* | **Burlingame/S**	18
Suppenküche | **Hayes Valley**	22
Swingin Door | **San Mateo/S**	-
Thirsty Bear Brew.* | **SoMa**	18
Tied House Cafe* | **multi.**	18
Tommy's Joynt | **Polk Gulch**	17
Z Toronado | **Lower Haight**	25
Trials Pub | **San Jose/S**	-
Triple Rock Brew.* | **Berkeley/E**	21
21st Amendment* | **S Beach**	20
NEW Wunder Brewing Co.* | **Inner Sunset**	-

CHAMPAGNE

Z Bubble Lounge | **Downtown**	22
District | **SoMa**	-
g bar | **Pacific Hts**	17
Z Nectar Wine | **Marina**	23

COCKTAILS

Z Absinthe | **Hayes Valley**	23
Alembic, The | **Haight-Ashbury**	24
Amber | **Castro**	19
Anú | **SoMa**	18
Z Aqua | **Downtown**	25
Z bacar | **SoMa**	24
NEW Bar 888 | **SoMa**	-
NEW Beretta | **Mission**	-
Z Betelnut Pejiu Wu | **Cow Hollow**	24
Bissap/Little Baobab | **Mission**	23
Z BIX | **Downtown**	26
Blondie's Bar | **Mission**	15
Z Boulevard | **Embarcadero**	26
Z Bourbon & Branch | **Tenderloin**	26
Brick | **Tenderloin**	-
Bruno's | **Mission**	-
Café Royale | **Tenderloin**	21
Campton Place | **Downtown**	23
Cantina | **Downtown**	-
Catalyst Cocktails | **SoMa**	-
Z César | **Berkeley/E**	25
Club Deluxe | **Haight-Ashbury**	21
Easy Lounge | **Oakland/E**	-
eight | **SoMa**	21
NEW 83 Proof | **SoMa**	-
Elite Cafe | **Upper Fillmore**	21
Empire Grill | **Palo Alto/S**	21
NEW EPIC Roast | **Embarcadero**	-
15 Romolo | **N Beach**	23
Fifth Floor | **Downtown**	-
Fuse | **N Beach**	19
Z Gary Danko | **Fish. Wharf**	27
g bar | **Pacific Hts**	17
Harris' | **Polk Gulch**	21
Hobson's Choice | **Haight-Ashbury**	18
Z Jardinière | **Hayes Valley**	26
John Colins | **SoMa**	22
Z Le Colonial | **Downtown**	24
Z Lime | **Castro**	21
Lingba Lounge | **Potrero Hill**	18
Z Lobby/St. Regis | **SoMa**	25
Luna Park | **Mission**	20
Lush Lounge | **Polk Gulch**	21
Martuni's | **Civic Ctr**	22
Mercury Appetizer | **Marina**	-
Z Michael Mina | **Downtown**	24
Z Millennium | **Downtown**	26
Nola | **Palo Alto/S**	21
nopa | **W Addition**	24
Olive Bar | **Tenderloin**	19
Z Oliveto Cafe | **Oakland/E**	25
Orbit Room Cafe | **Castro**	24
Ozumo | **Embarcadero**	23
Ponzu | **Downtown**	20
Rye | **Tenderloin**	23
Z Seasons Bar | **Downtown**	26
NEW Serpentine | **Dogpatch**	-
Shattuck Spats | **Berkeley/E**	15
Z Slanted Door | **Embarcadero**	24

Slide | **Downtown**	22
Sugar Lounge | **Hayes Valley**	20
Tommy's Mexican | **Outer Rich**	22
Tony Nik's | **N Beach**	23
🙎 Top of the Mark | **Nob Hill**	25
Tosca Cafe | **N Beach**	23
Tres Agaves | **S Beach**	22
Voda | **Downtown**	19
Zam Zam | **Haight-Ashbury**	23
🙎 Zuni Café | **Hayes Valley**	24

SAKE/SHOCHU/SOJU

Ace Wasabi's | **Marina**	20
Bacchus Wine | **Russian Hill**	23
🙎 Blowfish Sushi | **multi.**	22
Mas Sake | **Marina**	19
🆕 O Izakaya | **Japantown**	-
Ozumo | **Embarcadero**	23
RoHan | **Inner Rich**	19
Sushi Groove So. | **SoMa**	23
🙎 Sushi Ran | **Sausalito/N**	25
Tokyo Go Go | **Mission**	19

SCOTCH/SINGLE MALTS

Alembic, The | **Haight-Ashbury**	24
🙎 Bourbon & Branch | **Tenderloin**	26
Nihon | **Mission**	23

TEQUILA

Impala | **N Beach**	20
Maya | **SoMa**	20
🆕 Mexico DF | **Embarcadero**	-
Tommy's Mexican | **Outer Rich**	22
Tres Agaves | **S Beach**	22

WINE BARS

Amelie | **Russian Hill**	-
Bacchus Wine | **Russian Hill**	23
Bar Bambino | **Mission**	-
🆕 Bin 38 | **Marina**	-
🙎 Bubble Lounge | **Downtown**	22
Cafe Zoetrope/Rosso | **multi.**	21
Cav Wine Bar | **Hayes Valley**	22

COPIA | **Napa/N**	19
Cork Enoteca | **Sausalito/N**	21
🆕 Dell'Uva | **N Beach**	-
District | **SoMa**	-
Eos | **Cole Valley**	22
Ferry Plaza Wine | **Embarcadero**	22
First Crush | **Downtown**	22
🆕 Franklin Sq. Wine | **Oakland/E**	-
Hidden Vine | **Downtown**	-
Hôtel Biron | **Hayes Valley**	24
jovino | **Cow Hollow**	-
Liberty Cafe | **Bernal Hts**	20
🆕 Local Kitchen | **SoMa**	-
London Wine | **Downtown**	18
🙎 Nectar Wine | **multi.**	23
Ottimista Enoteca | **Cow Hollow**	23
Paréa | **Mission**	-
Pres a Vi | **Presidio**	-
Rouge et Blanc | **Downtown**	-
750ml | **San Mateo/S**	-
S.N.O.B. | **Polk Gulch**	17
🆕 Terroir | **SoMa**	-
🙎 Tra Vigne | **St. Helena/N**	26
🆕 Uva Enoteca | **Lower Haight**	-
Va de Vi | **Walnut Creek/E**	-
Varnish Fine Art | **SoMa**	21
Vino Rosso | **Bernal Hts**	-
🆕 Wine Bar | **Russian Hill**	-
🆕 Wine Jar | **W Addition**	-
Yield Wine Bar | **Dogpatch**	25

WINE BY THE GLASS

🙎 bacar | **SoMa**	24
🙎 Boulevard | **Embarcadero**	26
Cortez | **Downtown**	22
Cosmopolitan, The | **SoMa**	18
🙎 Farallon | **Downtown**	24
Fifth Floor | **Downtown**	-
🙎 Gary Danko | **Fish. Wharf**	27
g bar | **Pacific Hts**	17

Ⓩ Jardinière | **Hayes Valley**	26
Ⓩ Lark Creek Inn | **Larkspur/N**	26
Ⓩ Martini House | **St. Helena/N**	25
Ⓩ Michael Mina | **Downtown**	24
Ⓩ Millennium | **Downtown**	26
Rest. LuLu | **SoMa**	20
Rubicon | **Downtown**	21
Zibibbo | **Palo Alto/S**	23
Ⓩ Zuni Café | **Hayes Valley**	24

EXPENSE-ACCOUNTERS

Ⓩ Absinthe | **Hayes Valley**	23
Ⓩ Americano | **Embarcadero**	23
Ⓩ Ana Mandara | **Fish. Wharf**	25
Ⓩ Aqua | **Downtown**	25
Ⓩ bacar | **SoMa**	24
Ⓩ Betelnut Pejiu Wu | **Cow Hollow**	24
Ⓩ Big 4 | **Nob Hill**	25
Ⓩ BIX | **Downtown**	26
Boca | **Novato/N**	20
Ⓩ Boulevard | **Embarcadero**	26
Ⓩ Bubble Lounge | **Downtown**	22
Campton Place | **Downtown**	23
Carnelian Room | **Downtown**	24
Cliff House | **Outer Rich**	23
Elite Cafe | **Upper Fillmore**	21
NEW EPIC Roast | **Embarcadero**	-
Ⓩ Farallon | **Downtown**	24
Fifth Floor | **Downtown**	-
Ⓩ Gary Danko | **Fish. Wharf**	27
Grand Cafe | **Downtown**	21
Grandviews | **Downtown**	24
Harris' | **Polk Gulch**	21
Harry Denton Starlight | **Downtown**	24
Hedley Club | **San Jose/S**	24
Hime | **Marina**	-
Ⓩ Jardinière | **Hayes Valley**	26

Ⓩ Kokkari Estiatorio | **Downtown**	25
Ⓩ Lark Creek Inn | **Larkspur/N**	26
Le Central Bistro | **Downtown**	21
NEW Le Club | **Nob Hill**	-
Ⓩ Le Colonial | **Downtown**	24
Ⓩ Lobby/Ritz-Carlton | **Nob Hill**	25
Ⓩ Lobby/St. Regis | **SoMa**	25
Ⓩ Mandarin Lounge | **Downtown**	27
Ⓩ MatrixFillmore | **Cow Hollow**	21
Maya | **SoMa**	20
Ⓩ Michael Mina | **Downtown**	24
One Market | **Embarcadero**	21
Ozumo | **Embarcadero**	23
Perbacco | **Downtown**	-
Ⓩ Pied Piper Bar | **Downtown**	26
Postrio | **Downtown**	22
Pres a Vi | **Presidio**	-
Ⓩ Redwood Rm. | **Downtown**	24
Rose Pistola | **N Beach**	22
Roy's | **SoMa**	24
NEW Rrazz Room | **Downtown**	-
Rubicon | **Downtown**	21
Ⓩ Seasons Bar | **Downtown**	26
Shanghai 1930 | **Embarcadero**	23
Slide | **Downtown**	22
supperclub | **SoMa**	22
Ⓩ Top of the Mark | **Nob Hill**	25
Town Hall | **SoMa**	23
Umami | **Cow Hollow**	-
Va de Vi | **Walnut Creek/E**	-
NEW Waterbar | **Embarcadero**	-
XYZ | **SoMa**	20
Ⓩ Yoshi's | **W Addition**	24

EYE-OPENERS

(Serves alcohol before 8 AM on most days)

500 Club | **Mission**	22
Gino & Carlo | **N Beach**	18

FINE FOOD TOO

Z Absinthe | **Hayes Valley**	23
Acme Chophouse | **S Beach**	20
Alembic, The | **Haight-Ashbury**	24
Z Ana Mandara | **Fish. Wharf**	25
NEW Anchor & Hope | **SoMa**	–
Z Aqua | **Downtown**	25
Z Auberge du Soleil | **Rutherford/N**	28
Azie | **SoMa**	22
Z bacar | **SoMa**	24
Bacchus Kirk | **Downtown**	17
NEW Bar Johnny | **Russian Hill**	–
NEW Beretta | **Mission**	–
Z Betelnut Pejiu Wu | **Cow Hollow**	24
B44 | **Downtown**	20
Z Big 4 | **Nob Hill**	25
NEW Bin 38 | **Marina**	–
Bissap/Little Baobab | **Mission**	23
Z BIX | **Downtown**	26
Z Blowfish Sushi | **Mission**	22
Boca | **Novato/N**	20
NEW Bossa Nova | **SoMa**	–
Z Boulevard | **Embarcadero**	26
Brick | **Tenderloin**	–
Bruno's | **Mission**	–
Buckeye Roadhouse | **Mill Valley/N**	24
Cafe Bastille | **Downtown**	18
Café Claude | **Downtown**	21
Campton Place | **Downtown**	23
NEW Candybar | **W Addition**	–
Carnelian Room | **Downtown**	24
Z César | **Berkeley/E**	25
Cha Cha Cha | **Mission**	21
Circa | **Marina**	–
Circolo | **Mission**	19
Z Cityscape | **Downtown**	24
COPIA | **Napa/N**	19
Cork Enoteca | **Sausalito/N**	21
Cortez | **Downtown**	22
Cosmopolitan, The | **SoMa**	18
Dio Deka | **Los Gatos/S**	–
downtown | **Berkeley/E**	21
Eastside West | **Cow Hollow**	19
Elite Cafe | **Upper Fillmore**	21
NEW Enrico's | **N Beach**	–
Eos | **Cole Valley**	22
NEW EPIC Roast | **Embarcadero**	–
Z Farallon | **Downtown**	24
Fifth Floor | **Downtown**	–
Florio | **Upper Fillmore**	23
Fog City Diner | **Embarcadero**	21
Foreign Cinema | **Mission**	24
NEW Franklin Sq. Wine | **Oakland/E**	–
Z Gary Danko | **Fish. Wharf**	27
Grand Cafe | **Downtown**	21
Harris' | **Polk Gulch**	21
Z Highlands Inn | **Carmel/S**	28
Hime | **Marina**	–
NEW Horizon | **N Beach**	–
Z Jardinière | **Hayes Valley**	26
Z Kokkari Estiatorio | **Downtown**	25
Z Lark Creek Inn | **Larkspur/N**	26
La Scene | **Downtown**	16
NEW La Trappe | **N Beach**	–
Le Central Bistro | **Downtown**	21
NEW Le Club | **Nob Hill**	–
Z Le Colonial | **Downtown**	24
Liberty Cafe | **Bernal Hts**	20
Z Lime | **Castro**	21
NEW Local Kitchen | **SoMa**	–
Luella | **Russian Hill**	23
Luna Park | **Mission**	20
Maya | **SoMa**	20
Mercury Appetizer | **Marina**	–
NEW Mexico DF | **Embarcadero**	–
Z Michael Mina | **Downtown**	24
Z Millennium | **Downtown**	26

subscribe to ZAGAT.com

NEW Nickie's | **Lower Haight**	–
Nihon | **Mission**	23
nopa | **W Addition**	24
NEW O Izakaya | **Japantown**	–
Z Oliveto Cafe | **Oakland/E**	25
One Market | **Embarcadero**	21
Oola | **SoMa**	23
O'Reilly's Holy Grail | **Polk Gulch**	22
Paréa | **Mission**	–
Perbacco | **Downtown**	–
Plouf | **Downtown**	20
Poleng | **W Addition**	22
Ponzu | **Downtown**	20
Postrio | **Downtown**	22
Pres a Vi | **Presidio**	–
Presidio Social Club | **Presidio**	–
Ramblas | **Mission**	19
Rancho Nicasio | **Nicasio/N**	23
Rasselas Jazz | **W Addition**	23
Rest. LuLu | **SoMa**	20
Rose Pistola | **N Beach**	22
Roy's | **SoMa**	24
Rubicon | **Downtown**	21
Salt House | **SoMa**	25
Sauce | **Hayes Valley**	20
Scala's Bistro | **Downtown**	22
NEW Serpentine | **Dogpatch**	–
Shanghai 1930 | **Embarcadero**	23
Sheba | **W Addition**	–
Z Slanted Door | **Embarcadero**	24
Slow Club | **Mission**	21
Suppenküche | **Hayes Valley**	22
supperclub | **SoMa**	22
Z Tamarine | **Palo Alto/S**	24
Town Hall | **SoMa**	23
Townhouse B&G | **Emeryville/E**	20
Tres Agaves | **S Beach**	22
21st Amendment | **S Beach**	20
2223 Restaurant | **Castro**	21

Umami | **Cow Hollow**	–
NEW Uva Enoteca | **Lower Haight**	–
Va de Vi | **Walnut Creek/E**	–
NEW Waterbar | **Embarcadero**	–
XYZ | **SoMa**	20
Z Yoshi's | **multi.**	24
Zibibbo | **Palo Alto/S**	23
Z Zuni Café | **Hayes Valley**	24

FIREPLACES

Z Albatross Pub | **Berkeley/E**	25
Z Auberge du Soleil | **Rutherford/N**	28
Bacchus Kirk | **Downtown**	17
Bambuddha | **Tenderloin**	21
Beckett's Irish Pub | **Berkeley/E**	22
Z Big 4 | **Nob Hill**	25
Bitter End | **Inner Rich**	21
Blue Chalk Cafe | **Palo Alto/S**	18
Boca | **Novato/N**	20
Buckeye Roadhouse | **Mill Valley/N**	24
Cliff House | **Outer Rich**	23
Club Mallard | **Albany/E**	23
Compadres | **Palo Alto/S**	18
Divas | **Polk Gulch**	–
Endup | **SoMa**	20
Z Evvia | **Palo Alto/S**	24
Fibbar/Molly Magees | **Sunnyvale/S**	19
Fiddler's Green | **Fish. Wharf**	19
500 Club | **Mission**	22
Foreign Cinema | **Mission**	24
g bar | **Pacific Hts**	17
Ginger's Trois | **Downtown**	–
Glen Park Station | **Glen Pk**	18
Guaymas | **Tiburon/N**	24
NEW Harlot | **SoMa**	–
Harrington's B&G | **Downtown**	17
Harris' | **Polk Gulch**	21
Hedley Club | **San Jose/S**	24

☑ Highlands Inn | **Carmel/S**	28	
Hog's Breath Inn | **Carmel/S**	24	
Homestead | **Mission**	20	
Houston's | **Embarcadero**	20	
Ireland's 32 | **Inner Rich**	22	
Johnny Foley's | **Downtown**	19	
Kezar Pub | **Haight-Ashbury**	19	
☑ Kokkari Estiatorio | **Downtown**	25	
☑ Lark Creek Inn | **Larkspur/N**	26	
NEW Lava Lounge | **SoMa**	-	
☑ Left Bank | **Larkspur/N**	20	
Lion Pub | **Pacific Hts**	21	
☑ Little Shamrock | **Inner Sunset**	25	
☑ Lobby/Ritz-Carlton | **Nob Hill**	25	
☑ Martini House | **St. Helena/N**	25	
☑ MatrixFillmore | **Cow Hollow**	21	
Mauna Loa | **Cow Hollow**	17	
Men's Room | **Castro**	16	
Nola | **Palo Alto/S**	21	
O'Neill's | **multi.**	-	
O'Reilly's Holy Grail | **Polk Gulch**	22	
Piazza D'Angelo | **Mill Valley/N**	22	
Plouf | **Downtown**	20	
Poleng | **W Addition**	22	
Rancho Nicasio | **Nicasio/N**	23	
Rasselas Jazz | **W Addition**	23	
Riptide | **Outer Sunset**	17	
Schmidt's Tobacco | **Albany/E**	-	
☑ Seasons Bar | **Downtown**	26	
Shanghai 1930 | **Embarcadero**	23	
Sheba | **W Addition**	-	
Silverado Resort | **Napa/N**	24	
Skates on Bay | **Berkeley/E**	21	
S.N.O.B. | **Polk Gulch**	17	
Sugar Café | **Downtown**	-	
Swig | **Tenderloin**	19	
Tarpy's Roadhse. | **Monterey/S**	23	

Townhouse B&G | **Emeryville/E**	20	
Trials Pub | **San Jose/S**	-	
222 Club | **Tenderloin**	22	
White Horse Bar | **Oakland/E**	19	
Wild Side West | **Bernal Hts**	22	
Yield Wine Bar | **Dogpatch**	25	
Zibibbo | **Palo Alto/S**	23	

FIRST DATE

☑ Albatross Pub | **Berkeley/E**	25	
☑ Ana Mandara | **Fish. Wharf**	25	
Beach Chalet | **Outer Rich**	21	
NEW Bin 38 | **Marina**	-	
Bocce Cafe | **N Beach**	21	
Brick | **Tenderloin**	-	
Bruno's | **Mission**	-	
Cafe Flore | **Castro**	21	
Caffe Puccini | **N Beach**	20	
Caffe Trieste | **N Beach**	20	
Cliff House | **Outer Rich**	23	
Daru | **Palo Alto/S**	-	
Elite Cafe | **Upper Fillmore**	21	
Eos | **Cole Valley**	22	
Hedley Club | **San Jose/S**	24	
☑ Kokkari Estiatorio | **Downtown**	25	
NEW Le Club | **Nob Hill**	-	
Liberty Cafe | **Bernal Hts**	20	
London Wine | **Downtown**	18	
Lone Palm | **Mission**	22	
☑ Pied Piper Bar | **Downtown**	26	
Sheba | **W Addition**	-	
13 Views | **Embarcadero**	21	
Tonga Room | **Nob Hill**	22	
Tony Nik's | **N Beach**	23	
Tosca Cafe | **N Beach**	23	

FRAT HOUSE

Abbey Tavern | **Outer Rich**	15	
Bar None | **Cow Hollow**	14	
Blue Chalk Cafe | **Palo Alto/S**	18	
Blue Light | **Cow Hollow**	16	
Bus Stop | **Cow Hollow**	16	

subscribe to ZAGAT.com

Cigar Bar	**Downtown**	19	No Name Bar	**Sausalito/N**	19
Circa	**Marina**	–	Rancho Nicasio	**Nicasio/N**	23
City Tavern	**Cow Hollow**	15	Starry Plough	**Berkeley/E**	20
Comet Club	**Cow Hollow**	12	Stray Bar	**Bernal Hts**	–
Dirty Martini	**Fish. Wharf**	19	Trials Pub	**San Jose/S**	–
Fiddler's Green	**Fish. Wharf**	19	Triple Rock Brew.	**Berkeley/E**	21
Final Final	**Marina**	17	Uptown	**Mission**	23
Fuse	**N Beach**	19	Yancy's	**Inner Sunset**	20

BOWLING

Albany Bowl	**Albany/E**	17

DARTS

Abbey Tavern	**Outer Rich**	15
Albany Bowl	**Albany/E**	17
☑ Albatross Pub	**Berkeley/E**	25
Ana's Cantina	**St. Helena/N**	18
Antonio's Nut Hse.	**Palo Alto/S**	16
Bar None	**Cow Hollow**	14
Bitter End	**Inner Rich**	21
Black Horse Pub	**Cow Hollow**	22
Blackthorn Tavern	**Inner Sunset**	16
Black Watch	**Los Gatos/S**	21
Blue Chalk Cafe	**Palo Alto/S**	18
Britannia Arms	**multi.**	17
Buckshot Bar	**Inner Rich**	–
Calistoga Inn	**Calistoga/N**	22
Conn. Yankee	**Potrero Hill**	17
Eagle Tavern	**SoMa**	21
Edinburgh Castle	**Tenderloin**	22
Elixir	**Mission**	19
Fibbar/Molly Magees	**Sunnyvale/S**	19
Final Final	**Marina**	17
Finnegans Wake	**Cole Valley**	20
540 Club	**Inner Rich**	24
Glen Park Station	**Glen Pk**	18
Harrington's B&G	**Downtown**	17
Ireland's 32	**Inner Rich**	22
Kelley's Tavern	**Marina**	18
Kennedy's Irish	**N Beach**	21

Other listings (left column continued):

☑ Gordon Biersch	**multi.**	18
Greens Sports	**Russian Hill**	18
Horseshoe	**Marina**	18
Impala	**N Beach**	20
Ireland's 32	**Inner Rich**	22
Irish Bank	**Downtown**	19
Jupiter	**Berkeley/E**	21
Kate O'Brien's	**SoMa**	17
Kelley's Tavern	**Marina**	18
Marin Brewing	**Larkspur/N**	17
Mars Bar	**SoMa**	17
North Star Cafe	**N Beach**	21
Perry's	**Cow Hollow**	19
Raleigh's	**Berkeley/E**	24
Royal Oak	**Russian Hill**	19
Ruby Skye	**Downtown**	20
☑ Sam's Anchor Cafe	**Tiburon/N**	25
Savoy Tivoli	**N Beach**	19
Shanghai Kelly's	**Polk Gulch**	17
Shattuck Down Low	**Berkeley/E**	16
Zeke's Sports B&G	**SoMa**	–

GAMES

BOARD GAMES

☑ Albatross Pub	**Berkeley/E**	25
Blakes/Telegraph	**Berkeley/E**	17
Buckshot Bar	**Inner Rich**	–
Cafe Abir	**W Addition**	21
NEW Candybar	**W Addition**	–
NEW La Trappe	**N Beach**	–
Lone Star	**SoMa**	20
Madrone Lounge	**W Addition**	21

Kilowatt | **Mission**	22
☑ Little Shamrock | **Inner Sunset**	25
London Wine | **Downtown**	18
Lone Star | **SoMa**	20
Mad Dog in Fog | **Lower Haight**	18
Marin Brewing | **Larkspur/N**	17
Mucky Duck | **Inner Sunset**	16
Pacific Coast | **Oakland/E**	19
☑ Pelican Inn | **Muir Bch/N**	27
Phoenix | **Mission**	19
Pig & Whistle | **Inner Rich**	23
Pilsner Inn | **Castro**	19
Plough & Stars | **Inner Rich**	18
Red Jack | **Fish. Wharf**	18
Rose & Crown | **Palo Alto/S**	21
Saddle Rack | **Fremont/E**	21
San Fran. Brew. | **N Beach**	21
Silverado Brew. | **St. Helena/N**	18
Starry Plough | **Berkeley/E**	20
Stork Club | **Oakland/E**	19
Stray Bar | **Bernal Hts**	-
☑ Sweetwater Saloon | **Mill Valley/N**	28
Swingin Door | **San Mateo/S**	-
Thirsty Bear Brew. | **SoMa**	18
Trials Pub | **San Jose/S**	-
21st Amendment | **S Beach**	20
Yancy's | **Inner Sunset**	20
Zeke's Sports B&G | **SoMa**	-

FOOSBALL

Antonio's Nut Hse. | **Palo Alto/S**	16
Britannia Arms | **San Jose/S**	17
Edinburgh Castle | **Tenderloin**	22
Marin Brewing | **Larkspur/N**	17
Mauna Loa | **Cow Hollow**	17
Place Pigalle | **Hayes Valley**	21
Rickshaw Stop | **Civic Ctr**	20
Rockit Room | **Inner Rich**	19
Rudy's Pub | **Palo Alto/S**	19
330 Ritch | **S Beach**	19

PINBALL

Albany Bowl | **Albany/E**	17
Antonio's Nut Hse. | **Palo Alto/S**	16
Black Watch | **Los Gatos/S**	21
Blakes/Telegraph | **Berkeley/E**	17
Bottom of Hill | **Potrero Hill**	22
Brainwash | **SoMa**	18
Café | **Castro**	17
Club Mallard | **Albany/E**	23
Eagle Tavern | **SoMa**	21
Elbo Room | **Mission**	20
Endup | **SoMa**	20
Finnegans Wake | **Cole Valley**	20
500 Club | **Mission**	22
440 Castro | **Castro**	18
Greens Sports | **Russian Hill**	18
HiFi | **Marina**	16
Hole in the Wall | **SoMa**	13
Kennedy's Irish | **N Beach**	21
Kilowatt | **Mission**	22
Knockout, The | **Mission**	23
Lone Star | **SoMa**	20
Lucky 13 | **Castro**	24
Luka's Taproom | **Oakland/E**	23
Mauna Loa | **Cow Hollow**	17
Moby Dick | **Castro**	19
Molotov | **Lower Haight**	17
Murio's Trophy | **Haight-Ashbury**	12
Oasis | **Menlo Pk/S**	20
Old Pro | **Palo Alto/S**	17
Pig & Whistle | **Inner Rich**	23
Pilsner Inn | **Castro**	19
Powerhouse | **SoMa**	21
Red Jack | **Fish. Wharf**	18
Route 101 | **Polk Gulch**	13
Sadie's Elephant | **Potrero Hill**	22
Stork Club | **Oakland/E**	19
Stray Bar | **Bernal Hts**	-
Stud | **SoMa**	19
Thee Parkside | **Potrero Hill**	17

Truck | **Mission**	⌐
Two AM Club | **Mill Valley/N**	15
Uptown | **Mission**	23
White Horse Bar | **Oakland/E**	19
Wild Side West | **Bernal Hts**	22
☒ Zeitgeist | **Mission**	23

POOL TABLES

Abbey Tavern | **Outer Rich**	15
Albany Bowl | **Albany/E**	17
☒ Albatross Pub | **Berkeley/E**	25
Ana's Cantina | **St. Helena/N**	18
Annie's Social Club | **SoMa**	20
Antonio's Nut Hse. | **Palo Alto/S**	16
Argus Lounge | **Mission**	19
Bacchus Kirk | **Downtown**	17
Bar None | **Cow Hollow**	14
Bitter End | **Inner Rich**	21
Blackthorn Tavern | **Inner Sunset**	16
Blue Chalk Cafe | **Palo Alto/S**	18
Blue Light | **Cow Hollow**	16
Bottom of Hill | **Potrero Hill**	22
Britannia Arms | **Cupertino/S**	17
British Bankers | **Menlo Pk/S**	18
☒ Bubble Lounge | **Downtown**	22
Buckshot Bar | **Inner Rich**	⌐
Bus Stop | **Cow Hollow**	16
Café | **Castro**	17
Café du Nord | **Castro**	23
Café Royale | **Tenderloin**	21
Cigar Bar | **Downtown**	19
Cinebar | **San Jose/S**	11
Club Mallard | **Albany/E**	23
Delirium Cocktails | **Mission**	16
Dirty Martini | **Fish. Wharf**	19
Divas | **Polk Gulch**	⌐
Dogpatch | **Dogpatch**	20
Dubliner, The | **W Portal**	18
Eagle Tavern | **SoMa**	21
Edinburgh Castle | **Tenderloin**	22
☒☒☒ 800 Larkin | **Tenderloin**	⌐

Elbo Room | **Mission**	20
Esta Noche | **Mission**	10
Fibbar/Molly Magees | **Mtn View/S**	19
Final Final | **Marina**	17
Finnegans Wake | **Cole Valley**	20
540 Club | **Inner Rich**	24
Fly | **W Addition**	20
Gestalt Haus | **Mission**	⌐
Gino & Carlo | **N Beach**	18
Gold Cane | **Haight-Ashbury**	13
Greens Sports | **Russian Hill**	18
Ha Ra | **Tenderloin**	19
Hemlock Tavern | **Polk Gulch**	20
Hole in the Wall | **SoMa**	13
Horseshoe | **Marina**	18
Ireland's 32 | **Inner Rich**	22
Kelley's Tavern | **Marina**	18
Kennedy's Irish | **N Beach**	21
Kezar Pub | **Haight-Ashbury**	19
Kilowatt | **Mission**	22
Knockout, The | **Mission**	23
Knuckles Sports | **Fish. Wharf**	18
Latin Amer. Club | **Mission**	22
☒☒☒ Le Club | **Nob Hill**	⌐
Lexington Club | **Mission**	19
Lone Star | **SoMa**	20
Lucky 13 | **Castro**	24
Luka's Taproom | **Oakland/E**	23
Mad Dog in Fog | **Lower Haight**	18
Marlena's | **Hayes Valley**	18
Mars Bar | **SoMa**	17
Mauna Loa | **Cow Hollow**	17
Mix | **Castro**	17
Moby Dick | **Castro**	19
Molotov | **Lower Haight**	17
Mucky Duck | **Inner Sunset**	16
Murio's Trophy | **Haight-Ashbury**	12
North Star Cafe | **N Beach**	21
Old Pro | **Palo Alto/S**	17

SPECIAL APPEALS

Phone Booth | **Mission**	20
Pig & Whistle | **Inner Rich**	23
Pilsner Inn | **Castro**	19
Place Pigalle | **Hayes Valley**	21
Plough & Stars | **Inner Rich**	18
Power Exchange | **SoMa**	18
Powerhouse | **SoMa**	21
Raleigh's | **Berkeley/E**	24
Rockit Room | **Inner Rich**	19
Route 101 | **Polk Gulch**	13
Ruby Room | **Oakland/E**	-
Ruby Skye | **Downtown**	20
Rye | **Tenderloin**	23
Saddle Rack | **Fremont/E**	21
Sadie's Elephant | **Potrero Hill**	22
Savoy Tivoli | **N Beach**	19
Shattuck Down Low | **Berkeley/E**	16
Silver Peso | **Larkspur/N**	14
Steelhead Brewing | **Burlingame/S**	18
Stork Club | **Oakland/E**	19
Stud | **SoMa**	19
Thirsty Bear Brew. | **SoMa**	18
330 Ritch | **S Beach**	19
Trax | **Haight-Ashbury**	19
Truck | **Mission**	-
12 Galaxies | **Mission**	21
Two AM Club | **Mill Valley/N**	15
Uptown | **Mission**	23
Whiskey Thieves | **Tenderloin**	23
White Horse Bar | **Oakland/E**	19
Wild Side West | **Bernal Hts**	22
Would You Believe | **Inner Rich**	11
☒ Zeitgeist | **Mission**	23
Zeke's Sports B&G | **SoMa**	-

SKEE-BALL

Buckshot Bar | **Inner Rich**	-

TRIVIA NIGHTS

☒ Albatross Pub | **Berkeley/E**	25
Bacchus Kirk | **Downtown**	17

Beale St. B&G | **Embarcadero**	18
Beckett's Irish Pub | **Berkeley/E**	22
Bitter End | **Inner Rich**	21
Blur | **Polk Gulch**	17
Britannia Arms | **multi.**	17
Chieftain Irish Pub | **SoMa**	21
Edinburgh Castle | **Tenderloin**	22
540 Club | **Inner Rich**	24
Harvey's | **Castro**	18
Lone Star | **SoMa**	20
Mad Dog in Fog | **Lower Haight**	18
Molotov | **Lower Haight**	17
O'Neill's | **multi.**	-
☒ Parkway Theater | **Oakland/E**	26
Pig & Whistle | **Inner Rich**	23
Riptide | **Outer Sunset**	17
Rose & Crown | **Palo Alto/S**	21
Tonic | **Russian Hill**	17
Trials Pub | **San Jose/S**	-

VIDEO GAMES

Abbey Tavern | **Outer Rich**	15
Albany Bowl | **Albany/E**	17
Aunt Charlie's | **Tenderloin**	19
Bar None | **Cow Hollow**	14
Black Watch | **Los Gatos/S**	21
Britannia Arms | **multi.**	17
Buckshot Bar | **Inner Rich**	-
Café | **Castro**	17
Centerfolds | **N Beach**	24
Club Mallard | **Albany/E**	23
Delaney's | **Marina**	14
Eagle Tavern | **SoMa**	21
Elbo Room | **Mission**	20
Final Final | **Marina**	17
Finnegans Wake | **Cole Valley**	20
500 Club | **Mission**	22
440 Castro | **Castro**	18
g bar | **Pacific Hts**	17
Glen Park Station | **Glen Pk**	18
Greens Sports | **Russian Hill**	18

Ha Ra | **Tenderloin**	19
Horseshoe | **Marina**	18
Kennedy's Irish | **N Beach**	21
Kezar Pub | **Haight-Ashbury**	19
Kilowatt | **Mission**	22
Knuckles Sports | **Fish. Wharf**	18
Lucky 13 | **Castro**	24
Luka's Taproom | **Oakland/E**	23
Mauna Loa | **Cow Hollow**	17
Men's Room | **Castro**	16
Murio's Trophy | **Haight-Ashbury**	12
North Star Cafe | **N Beach**	21
Oasis | **Menlo Pk/S**	20
Old Pro | **Palo Alto/S**	17
Radio Bar | **Oakland/E**	23
Red Jack | **Fish. Wharf**	18
Riptide | **Outer Sunset**	17
Route 101 | **Polk Gulch**	13
Rudy's Pub | **Palo Alto/S**	19
Silver Peso | **Larkspur/N**	14
Stork Club | **Oakland/E**	19
Stray Bar | **Bernal Hts**	-
Stud | **SoMa**	19
Swingin Door | **San Mateo/S**	-
Trad'r Sam's | **Outer Rich**	22
Trax | **Haight-Ashbury**	19
12 Galaxies | **Mission**	21
Two AM Club | **Mill Valley/N**	15
Uptown | **Mission**	23
Whiskey Thieves | **Tenderloin**	23
White Horse Bar | **Oakland/E**	19
Wild Side West | **Bernal Hts**	22
Would You Believe | **Inner Rich**	11
Yancy's | **Inner Sunset**	20
Z Zeitgeist | **Mission**	23

GAY

(See also Lesbian;
* certain nights only)

Aunt Charlie's | **Tenderloin**	19
Z Badlands | **Castro**	17
Café | **Castro**	17
Cafe Flore* | **Castro**	21
Divas | **Polk Gulch**	-
Eagle Tavern | **SoMa**	21
eight | **SoMa**	21
Endup | **SoMa**	20
Esta Noche | **Mission**	10
440 Castro | **Castro**	18
Ginger's Trois | **Downtown**	-
Harvey's | **Castro**	18
Hole in the Wall | **SoMa**	13
Lone Star | **SoMa**	20
NEW LookOut, The | **Castro**	-
Lush Lounge | **Polk Gulch**	21
Marlena's | **Hayes Valley**	18
Mecca | **Castro**	22
Men's Room | **Castro**	16
Metro | **Castro**	17
Midnight Sun | **Castro**	17
Mix | **Castro**	17
Moby Dick | **Castro**	19
Olive Bar* | **Tenderloin**	19
Pilsner Inn | **Castro**	19
Pink* | **Mission**	21
Powerhouse | **SoMa**	21
Stud | **SoMa**	19
Trax | **Haight-Ashbury**	19
Twin Peaks | **Castro**	14
White Horse Bar | **Oakland/E**	19

HAPPY HOUR

Beale St. B&G | **Embarcadero**	18
Ben & Nick's | **Oakland/E**	18
Blue Chalk Cafe | **Palo Alto/S**	18
Brainwash | **SoMa**	18
Butter | **SoMa**	18
Café Prague | **N Beach**	17
Casanova | **Mission**	20
Chaya | **Embarcadero**	23
Cigar Bar | **Downtown**	19
Club Deluxe | **Haight-Ashbury**	21
Club EZ5 | **Downtown**	19
Comet Club | **Cow Hollow**	12

Cosmopolitan, The | **SoMa**	18	One Market | **Embarcadero**	21
Dalva | **Mission**	20	O'Reilly's Irish Pub | **N Beach**	20
Delirium Cocktails | **Mission**	16	Pedro's | **Los Gatos/S**	22
Doc's Clock | **Mission**	18	Pier 23 Cafe | **Embarcadero**	21
Eastside West | **Cow Hollow**	19	Plough & Stars | **Inner Rich**	18
Edinburgh Castle | **Tenderloin**	22	Ponzu | **Downtown**	20
Esta Noche | **Mission**	10	Pyramid Brewery |	19
Fishbowl | **Pacific Hts**	17	**Walnut Creek/E**	
540 Club | **Inner Rich**	24	Red Jack | **Fish. Wharf**	18
Fly | **W Addition**	20	Revolution Café | **Mission**	22
440 Castro | **Castro**	18	Rite Spot Cafe | **Mission**	22
g bar | **Pacific Hts**	17	Rogue Ales | **N Beach**	21
Gold Dust Lounge | **Downtown**	22	RoHan | **Inner Rich**	19
Greens Sports | **Russian Hill**	18	Route 101 | **Polk Gulch**	13
☒ Harry's | **Upper Fillmore**	19	Sadie's Elephant | **Potrero Hill**	22
Hedley Club | **San Jose/S**	24	San Fran. Brew. | **N Beach**	21
Hemlock Tavern | **Polk Gulch**	20	Thee Parkside | **Potrero Hill**	17
Hotel Utah | **SoMa**	20	Thirsty Bear Brew. | **SoMa**	18
House of Shields | **Downtown**	16	Tied House Cafe | **multi.**	18
Il Pirata | **Potrero Hill**	15	Tonga Room | **Nob Hill**	22
Ireland's 32 | **Inner Rich**	22	Tonic | **Russian Hill**	17
Jade Bar | **Hayes Valley**	20	Tony Nik's | **N Beach**	23
John Colins | **SoMa**	22	☒ Toronado | **Lower Haight**	25
Kennedy's Irish | **N Beach**	21	Trax | **Haight-Ashbury**	19
Kilowatt | **Mission**	22	Tunnel Top | **Downtown**	18
Kingman's | **Oakland/E**	21	12 Galaxies | **Mission**	21
Latin Amer. Club | **Mission**	22	21st Amendment | **S Beach**	20
Los Gatos Brew. | **Los Gatos/S**	21	Varnish Fine Art | **SoMa**	21
Lou's Pier 47 | **Fish. Wharf**	22	☒ Zeitgeist | **Mission**	23
Lucky 13 | **Castro**	24		
Mad Dog in Fog | **Lower Haight**	18	**HOTEL BARS**	
Magnolia Pub |	23	Auberge du Soleil	
Haight-Ashbury		☒ Auberge du Soleil |	28
Mauna Loa | **Cow Hollow**	17	**Rutherford/N**	
Mecca | **Castro**	22	Basque Hotel	
Metro | **Castro**	17	15 Romolo | **N Beach**	23
Midnight Sun | **Castro**	17	Calistoga Inn	
Mix | **Castro**	17	Calistoga Inn | **Calistoga/N**	22
Murio's Trophy |	12	Campton Place Hotel	
Haight-Ashbury		Campton Place | **Downtown**	23
☒ 111 Minna | **SoMa**	22	Claremont Resort & Spa	
		Paragon | **Berkeley/E**	21

Clift Hotel
  ☑ Redwood Rm. | **Downtown**   24

Dinah's Garden Hotel
  Trader Vic's | **Palo Alto/S**   19

Fairmont Hotel
  Tonga Room | **Nob Hill**   22

Fitzgerald Hotel
  Hidden Vine | **Downtown**   ⌐

Four Seasons Hotel
  ☑ Seasons Bar | **Downtown**   26

Grand Hyatt Hotel
  Grandviews | **Downtown**   24

Highlands Inn
  ☑ Highlands Inn | **Carmel/S**   28

Hilton San Francisco
  ☑ Cityscape | **Downtown**   24

Hotel Adagio
  Cortez | **Downtown**   22

Hotel California
  ☑ Millennium | **Downtown**   26

Hotel De Anza
  Hedley Club | **San Jose/S**   24

Hotel Kabuki
  NEW O Izakaya | **Japantown**   ⌐

Hotel Los Gatos
  Dio Deka | **Los Gatos/S**   ⌐

Hotel Monaco
  Grand Cafe | **Downtown**   21

Hotel Nikko
  NEW Rrazz Room | **Downtown**   ⌐

Hotel Palomar
  Fifth Floor | **Downtown**   ⌐

Hotel Vitale
  ☑ Americano | **Embarcadero**   23

Huntington Hotel
  ☑ Big 4 | **Nob Hill**   25

Hyatt at Fisherman's Wharf
  Knuckles Sports | **Fish. Wharf**   18

Hyatt Regency Hotel
  13 Views | **Embarcadero**   21

Inn at Spanish Bay
  Roy's | **Pebble Bch/S**   24

InterContinental San Francisco
  NEW Bar 888 | **SoMa**   ⌐

Laurel Inn
  g bar | **Pacific Hts**   17

Mandarin Oriental Hotel
  ☑ Mandarin Lounge | **Downtown**   27

Mark Hopkins InterContinental
  ☑ Top of the Mark | **Nob Hill**   25

Marriott Hotel
  ☑ View Lounge | **SoMa**   26

Palace Hotel
  ☑ Pied Piper Bar | **Downtown**   26

Pelican Inn
  ☑ Pelican Inn | **Muir Bch/N**   27

Phoenix Hotel
  Bambuddha | **Tenderloin**   21

Prescott Hotel
  Postrio | **Downtown**   22

Renoir Hotel
  Etiquette | **Downtown**   ⌐

Ritz-Carlton
  ☑ Lobby/Ritz-Carlton | **Nob Hill**   25

Serrano Hotel
  Ponzu | **Downtown**   20

Silverado Resort
  Silverado Resort | **Napa/N**   24

Sir Francis Drake Hotel
  NEW Bar Drake | **Downtown**   ⌐
  Harry Denton Starlight | **Downtown**   24
  Scala's Bistro | **Downtown**   22

St. Regis Hotel
  ☑ Lobby/St. Regis | **SoMa**   25

Villa Florence Hotel
  Kuleto's | **Downtown**   ⌐

Warwick Regis Hotel

La Scene | **Downtown** | 16

Westin St. Francis

Z Michael Mina | **Downtown** | 24

W Hotel

XYZ | **SoMa** | 20

IRISH

Abbey Tavern	**Outer Rich**	15
Beckett's Irish Pub	**Berkeley/E**	22
Chieftain Irish Pub	**SoMa**	21
Delaney's	**Marina**	14
Dubliner, The	**multi.**	18
Fibbar/Molly Magees	**Mtn View/S**	19
Fiddler's Green	**Fish. Wharf**	19
Finnegans Wake	**Cole Valley**	20
Ireland's 32	**Inner Rich**	22
Irish Bank	**Downtown**	19
Johnny Foley's	**Downtown**	19
Kate O'Brien's	**SoMa**	17
Kelley's Tavern	**Marina**	18
Kennedy's Irish	**N Beach**	21
Liberties	**Mission**	17
Z Little Shamrock	**Inner Sunset**	25
O'Neill's	**multi.**	–
O'Reilly's Holy Grail	**Polk Gulch**	22
O'Reilly's Irish Pub	**N Beach**	20
Phoenix	**Mission**	19
Plough & Stars	**Inner Rich**	18
St. Stephen's	**Mtn View/S**	16

JAZZ CLUBS

Z BIX	**Downtown**	26
Café Claude	**Downtown**	21
NEW Enrico's	**N Beach**	–
Jazz at Pearl's	**N Beach**	24
Rasselas Jazz	**W Addition**	23
Savanna Jazz	**Mission**	21
Shanghai 1930	**Embarcadero**	23
Z Yoshi's	**multi.**	24

KARAOKE BARS

(Call to check nights, times and prices)

Ana's Cantina	**St. Helena/N**	18
Annie's Social Club	**SoMa**	20
Bow Bow Lounge	**Chinatown**	21
Britannia Arms	**multi.**	17
British Bankers	**Menlo Pk/S**	18
Lingba Lounge	**Potrero Hill**	18
Mint Karaoke	**Castro**	21
Shattuck Down Low	**Berkeley/E**	16
Silver Clouds	**Marina**	–

LATIN

Ana's Cantina	**St. Helena/N**	18
Boca	**Novato/N**	20
NEW Bossa Nova	**SoMa**	–
Cafe Cocomo	**Dogpatch**	20
Café Valparaiso	**Berkeley/E**	22
Compadres	**Palo Alto/S**	18
Esta Noche	**Mission**	10
Guaymas	**Tiburon/N**	24
Impala	**N Beach**	20
Maya	**SoMa**	20
NEW Mexico DF	**Embarcadero**	–
Pedro's	**multi.**	22
Peña Pachamama	**N Beach**	–
Puerto Alegre	**Mission**	21
Roccapulco	**Mission**	20
Tommy's Mexican	**Outer Rich**	22
Tres Agaves	**S Beach**	22
Velvet Cantina	**Mission**	–

LESBIAN

(* Certain nights only; call ahead)

Aunt Charlie's	**Tenderloin**	19
Café	**Castro**	17
Cafe Flore*	**Castro**	21
El Rio	**Mission**	23
Harvey's*	**Castro**	18
Lexington Club	**Mission**	19
Pink*	**Mission**	21
Stray Bar*	**Bernal Hts**	–

White Horse Bar | **Oakland/E** _19_

Wild Side West | **Bernal Hts** _22_

LIVE ENTERTAINMENT

(See also Blues, Cabaret, Comedy Clubs, Drag Shows, Jazz Club Karaoke Bars, Music Clubs, Piano Bars, Spoken Word, Strip Clubs)

Abbey Tavern | Irish | **Outer Rich** _15_

Agenda | varies | **San Jose/S** _15_

Amnesia | varies | **Mission** _19_

Z Ana Mandara | jazz | **Fish. Wharf** _25_

Z bacar | jazz | **SoMa** _24_

Bazaar Café | guitar/vocals | **Outer Rich** _20_

Beale St. B&G | lingerie nights | **Embarcadero** _18_

Black Magic | open mike | **Marina** _18_

Blackthorn Tavern | varies | **Inner Sunset** _16_

Blakes/Telegraph | varies | **Berkeley/E** _17_

Bocce Cafe | jazz/piano | **N Beach** _21_

Z Bubble Lounge | jazz | **Downtown** _22_

Butterfly | jazz | **Embarcadero** _21_

Cafe Bastille | jazz | **Downtown** _18_

Cafe Cocomo | salsa | **Dogpatch** _20_

Café Prague | jazz | **N Beach** _17_

Caffe Trieste | opera | **multi.** _20_

Cat Club | varies | **SoMa** _–_

Chaya | jazz | **Embarcadero** _23_

Club Six | varies | **SoMa** _18_

Divas | transgender shows | **Polk Gulch** _–_

Dogpatch | jazz | **Dogpatch** _20_

downtown | jazz | **Berkeley/E** _21_

Eagle Tavern | varies | **SoMa** _21_

Endup | varies | **SoMa** _20_

Fibbar/Molly Magees | Irish | **Sunnyvale/S** _19_

Fiddler's Green | varies | **Fish. Wharf** _19_

Foreign Cinema | films | **Mission** _24_

440 Castro | DJs | **Castro** _18_

Glas Kat | R&B/soul | **SoMa** _18_

Gold Dust Lounge | bands | **Downtown** _22_

Hard Rock Cafe | rock | **Fish. Wharf** _14_

Harris' | jazz | **Polk Gulch** _21_

Harry Denton Starlight | varies | **Downtown** _24_

Hedley Club | jazz | **San Jose/S** _24_

Hemlock Tavern | DJs | **Polk Gulch** _20_

Hotel Utah | varies | **SoMa** _20_

House of Shields | jazz | **Downtown** _16_

Houston's | jazz | **Embarcadero** _20_

Ireland's 32 | Irish | **Inner Rich** _22_

Jelly's | salsa | **China Basin** _16_

Johnny Foley's | comedy/jazz | **Downtown** _19_

Jupiter | varies | **Berkeley/E** _21_

Kan Zaman | belly dancing | **Haight-Ashbury** _22_

Z Le Colonial | jazz | **Downtown** _24_

Z Left Bank | jazz | **multi.** _20_

Mad Dog in Fog | varies | **Lower Haight** _18_

Marin Brewing | varies | **Larkspur/N** _17_

Noe Valley Ministry | varies | **Noe Valley** _24_

Z 111 Minna | DJs | **SoMa** _22_

Paragon | jazz | **Berkeley/E** _21_

Z Pelican Inn | varies | **Muir Bch/N** _27_

Plough & Stars | bluegrass/Irish | **Inner Rich** _18_

Puerto Alegre | mariachi | **Mission** _21_

Ramp | salsa/world | **China Basin** _21_

Rick's | Hawaiian | **Outer Sunset** _19_

Rite Spot Cafe | varies | **Mission** 22

Roccapulco | salsa | **Mission** 20

Rose & Crown | comedy/jazz |
Palo Alto/S 21

Rose Pistola | jazz | **N Beach** 22

San Fran. Brew. | varies |
N Beach 21

Simple Pleasures | varies |
Outer Rich –

St. Stephen's | varies |
Mtn View/S 16

330 Ritch | hip-hop/rock |
S Beach 19

Tonga Room | varies | **Nob Hill** 22

🇿 Top of the Mark | varies |
Nob Hill 25

Town Hall | guitar | **SoMa** 23

Townhouse B&G | jazz |
Emeryville/E 20

🇿 View Lounge | jazz | **SoMa** 26

🇿 Zuni Café | piano |
Hayes Valley 24

LOUNGES

Agenda | **San Jose/S** 15

Ambassador, The | **Tenderloin** –

Amber | **Castro** 19

🇿 Americano | **Embarcadero** 23

🇿 Ana Mandara | **Fish. Wharf** 25

Anú | **SoMa** 18

NEW Apartment 24 | **N Beach** –

Aunt Charlie's | **Tenderloin** 19

Azul Bar | **Downtown** –

Bambuddha | **Tenderloin** 21

NEW Bin 38 | **Marina** –

Bliss Bar | **Noe Valley** 19

Blur | **Polk Gulch** 17

🇿 Bourbon & Branch |
Tenderloin 26

Bow Bow Lounge | **Chinatown** 21

Bruno's | **Mission** –

🇿 Bubble Lounge | **Downtown** 22

NEW Candybar | **W Addition** –

Catalyst Cocktails | **SoMa** –

Circolo | **Mission** 19

Club EZ5 | **Downtown** 19

DaDa | **SoMa** –

Daru | **Palo Alto/S** –

District | **SoMa** –

Double Dutch | **Mission** 23

Easy Lounge | **Oakland/E** –

Element Lounge | **Polk Gulch** 19

Etiquette | **Downtown** –

Fluid | **SoMa** 20

Gallery Lounge | **SoMa** 16

g bar | **Pacific Hts** 17

Gold Dust Lounge | **Downtown** 22

Grandviews | **Downtown** 24

NEW Harlot | **SoMa** –

Harris' | **Polk Gulch** 21

Harry Denton Starlight |
Downtown 24

NEW Horizon | **N Beach** –

Icon Lounge | **SoMa** –

Impala | **N Beach** 20

John Colins | **SoMa** 22

Kingman's | **Oakland/E** 21

NEW Koko Cocktails |
Polk Gulch –

Laszlo | **Mission** 20

NEW La Trappe | **N Beach** –

NEW Lava Lounge | **SoMa** –

NEW Le Club | **Nob Hill** –

🇿 Le Colonial | **Downtown** 24

Levende | **multi.** 22

🇿 Lime | **Castro** 21

Lingba Lounge | **Potrero Hill** 18

Lion Pub | **Pacific Hts** 21

🇿 Lobby/Ritz-Carlton |
Nob Hill 25

🇿 Lobby/St. Regis | **SoMa** 25

Lone Palm | **Mission** 22

Lush Lounge | **Polk Gulch** 21

Madrone Lounge | **W Addition** 21

Ⓩ Mandarin Lounge | **Downtown**	27
Ⓩ MatrixFillmore | **Cow Hollow**	21
Milk Bar | **Haight-Ashbury**	19
Mr. Smith's | **SoMa**	22
🆕 O Izakaya | **Japantown**	-
Otis | **Downtown**	-
Poleng | **W Addition**	22
Ponzu | **Downtown**	20
Pres a Vi | **Presidio**	-
Red Devil | **Polk Gulch**	18
Retox Lounge | **Dogpatch**	-
Rockit Room | **Inner Rich**	19
Roe Lounge | **SoMa**	20
RoHan | **Inner Rich**	19
🆕 Rrazz Room | **Downtown**	-
Ruby Room | **Oakland/E**	-
Rye | **Tenderloin**	23
Ⓩ Seasons Bar | **Downtown**	26
Shanghai 1930 | **Embarcadero**	23
Shattuck Down Low |	16
Berkeley/E	
Sheba | **W Addition**	-
Shine | **SoMa**	24
Silverado Resort | **Napa/N**	24
Sip Bar & Lounge | **N Beach**	17
Skylark | **Mission**	14
Slide | **Downtown**	22
Sugar Café | **Downtown**	-
Sugar Lounge | **Hayes Valley**	20
suite one8one | **Tenderloin**	18
Syn Lounge | **Mission**	-
Tonic | **Russian Hill**	17
222 Club | **Tenderloin**	22
Vessel | **Downtown**	-
Ⓩ View Lounge | **SoMa**	26
Voda | **Downtown**	19
🆕 Wine Jar | **W Addition**	-
Wish | **SoMa**	22

MATURE CROWDS

Ⓩ Absinthe | **Hayes Valley**	23
Ⓩ Ana Mandara | **Fish. Wharf**	25

Ⓩ Aqua | **Downtown**	25
Ashkenaz | **Berkeley/E**	18
Ⓩ Auberge du Soleil |	28
Rutherford/N	
Ⓩ bacar | **SoMa**	24
🆕 Bar Drake | **Downtown**	-
🆕 Bar 888 | **SoMa**	-
Ⓩ Big 4 | **Nob Hill**	25
Boca | **Novato/N**	20
Ⓩ Boulevard | **Embarcadero**	26
Ⓩ Brazen Head | **Cow Hollow**	25
Buckeye Roadhouse |	24
Mill Valley/N	
Cafe Zoetrope/Rosso | **multi.**	21
Caffe Puccini | **N Beach**	20
Campton Place | **Downtown**	23
Ⓩ Cityscape | **Downtown**	24
Cliff House | **Outer Rich**	23
downtown | **Berkeley/E**	21
Elite Cafe | **Upper Fillmore**	21
Empire Grill | **Palo Alto/S**	21
Eos | **Cole Valley**	22
🆕 EPIC Roast |	-
Embarcadero	
Ⓩ Farallon | **Downtown**	24
Fifth Floor | **Downtown**	-
First Crush | **Downtown**	22
Ⓩ Gary Danko | **Fish. Wharf**	27
Ginger's Trois | **Downtown**	-
Grand Cafe | **Downtown**	21
Grandviews | **Downtown**	24
Harris' | **Polk Gulch**	21
Hedley Club | **San Jose/S**	24
Hidden Vine | **Downtown**	-
Ⓩ Highlands Inn | **Carmel/S**	28
Ⓩ Jardinière | **Hayes Valley**	26
Jazz at Pearl's | **N Beach**	24
John's Grill | **Downtown**	21
Ⓩ Kokkari Estiatorio | **Downtown**	25
La Scene | **Downtown**	16
Lefty O'Doul's | **Downtown**	17

🇿 Lobby/Ritz-Carlton | **Nob Hill**	25
🇿 Lobby/St. Regis | **SoMa**	25
London Wine | **Downtown**	18
🇿 Mandarin Lounge | **Downtown**	27
🇿 Michael Mina | **Downtown**	24
🇿 Millennium | **Downtown**	26
NEW O Izakaya | **Japantown**	-
One Market | **Embarcadero**	21
🇿 Pied Piper Bar | **Downtown**	26
Postrio | **Downtown**	22
Pres a Vi | **Presidio**	-
Presidio Social Club | **Presidio**	-
NEW Rrazz Room | **Downtown**	-
Rubicon | **Downtown**	21
🇿 Seasons Bar | **Downtown**	26
Shanghai 1930 | **Embarcadero**	23
Swingin Door | **San Mateo/S**	-
🇿 Top of the Mark | **Nob Hill**	25
Tosca Cafe | **N Beach**	23
Twin Peaks | **Castro**	14
Va de Vi | **Walnut Creek/E**	-
NEW Waterbar | **Embarcadero**	-
🇿 Yoshi's | **multi.**	24
🇿 Zuni Café | **Hayes Valley**	24

MEAT MARKETS

🇿 Badlands | **Castro**	17
🇿 Balboa Cafe | **Cow Hollow**	20
Bar None | **Cow Hollow**	14
🇿 Betelnut Pejiu Wu | **Cow Hollow**	24
Blue Light | **Cow Hollow**	16
Bus Stop | **Cow Hollow**	16
Café | **Castro**	17
Cat Club | **SoMa**	-
Circa | **Marina**	-
City Tavern | **Cow Hollow**	15
Comet Club | **Cow Hollow**	12
Cosmopolitan, The | **SoMa**	18
Dragon Bar | **N Beach**	-

Eastside West | **Cow Hollow**	19
Fiddler's Green | **Fish. Wharf**	19
Final Final | **Marina**	17
440 Castro | **Castro**	18
🇿 Gordon Biersch | **multi.**	18
Harry Denton Starlight | **Downtown**	24
🇿 Harry's | **Upper Fillmore**	19
Harvey's | **Castro**	18
Horseshoe | **Marina**	18
Icon Lounge | **SoMa**	-
Impala | **N Beach**	20
Ireland's 32 | **Inner Rich**	22
Jillian's | **SoMa**	18
Kelley's Tavern | **Marina**	18
Left/Albuquerque | **multi.**	15
Lexington Club | **Mission**	19
NEW LookOut, The | **Castro**	-
Mars Bar | **SoMa**	17
🇿 MatrixFillmore | **Cow Hollow**	21
🇿 Medjool | **Mission**	23
Metro | **Castro**	17
MoMo's | **S Beach**	20
Perry's | **Cow Hollow**	19
Powerhouse | **SoMa**	21
Red Devil | **Polk Gulch**	18
🇿 Redwood Rm. | **Downtown**	24
Rouge Nightclub | **Russian Hill**	13
Sip Bar & Lounge | **N Beach**	17
Steps of Rome | **N Beach**	20
Stud | **SoMa**	19
Suede | **Fish. Wharf**	17
Swig | **Tenderloin**	19
Thirsty Bear Brew. | **SoMa**	18

MUSIC CLUBS

(See also Blues & Jazz Clubs)

🇿 Bimbo's 365 Club | **N Beach**	24
Blank Club | **San Jose/S**	14
Bottom of Hill | **Potrero Hill**	22
Brainwash | **SoMa**	18
Café Amsterdam | **Fairfax/N**	21

Café du Nord | **Castro**	23
☑ Fillmore | **W Addition**	27
Great Amer. Music | **Tenderloin**	24
Independent | **W Addition**	22
Mezzanine | **SoMa**	21
Mighty | **Potrero Hill**	23
Mystic Theatre | **Petaluma/N**	22
924 Gilman | **Berkeley/E**	26
☑ Paramount Theater | **Oakland/E**	26
Saddle Rack | **Fremont/E**	21
Space 550 | **Bayview**	20
Stork Club | **Oakland/E**	19
Swig | **Tenderloin**	19
NEW Temple | **SoMa**	-
Thee Parkside | **Potrero Hill**	17
☑ Yoshi's | **multi.**	24

OUTDOOR SPACES

GARDEN
Bar Bambino | **Mission**	-
Bocce Cafe | **N Beach**	21
Empire Grill | **Palo Alto/S**	21
Frantoio | **Mill Valley/N**	25
Jupiter | **Berkeley/E**	21
Pacific Coast | **Oakland/E**	19
Pilsner Inn | **Castro**	19
Pyramid Brewery | **Walnut Creek/E**	19
Raleigh's | **Berkeley/E**	24
Rosewood | **Chinatown**	21
Tied House Cafe | **Mtn View/S**	18
Wild Side West | **Bernal Hts**	22
☑ Zeitgeist | **Mission**	23

PATIO/TERRACE
Acme Chophouse | **S Beach**	20
Agenda | **San Jose/S**	15
☑ Americano | **Embarcadero**	23
☑ Ana Mandara | **Fish. Wharf**	25
☑ Auberge du Soleil | **Rutherford/N**	28
Bambuddha | **Tenderloin**	21

Bar None | **Cow Hollow**	14
Bazaar Café | **Outer Rich**	20
Beale St. B&G | **Embarcadero**	18
NEW Bin 38 | **Marina**	-
Bissap/Little Baobab | **Mission**	23
Blackthorn Tavern | **Inner Sunset**	16
Blondie's Bar | **Mission**	15
Blue Chalk Cafe | **Palo Alto/S**	18
Blue Danube | **Inner Rich**	21
Boca | **Novato/N**	20
Bottom of Hill | **Potrero Hill**	22
Britannia Arms | **multi.**	17
British Bankers | **Menlo Pk/S**	18
Buckeye Roadhouse | **Mill Valley/N**	24
Café | **Castro**	17
Café Amsterdam | **Fairfax/N**	21
Cafe Cocomo | **Dogpatch**	20
Cafe Flore | **Castro**	21
Cafe Int'l | **Lower Haight**	21
Café Rouge | **Berkeley/E**	21
Cafe Van Kleef | **Oakland/E**	24
Cafe Zoetrope/Rosso | **Palo Alto/S**	21
Calistoga Inn | **Calistoga/N**	22
Cato's Ale House | **Oakland/E**	19
☑ César | **Oakland/E**	25
Cigar Bar | **Downtown**	19
Club Mallard | **Albany/E**	23
Cole's Chop Hse. | **Napa/N**	24
Compadres | **multi.**	18
COPIA | **Napa/N**	19
Cork Enoteca | **Sausalito/N**	21
Cosmopolitan, The | **SoMa**	18
Dio Deka | **Los Gatos/S**	-
Double Dutch | **Mission**	23
Dragon Bar | **N Beach**	-
Eagle Tavern | **SoMa**	21
E&O Trading Co. | **multi.**	20
Easy Lounge | **Oakland/E**	-

eight | **SoMa**	21
NEW 83 Proof | **SoMa**	-
Elephant Bar | **multi.**	16
El Rio | **Mission**	23
Endup | **SoMa**	20
NEW Enrico's | **N Beach**	-
NEW EPIC Roast | **Embarcadero**	-
Faultline Brew. | **Sunnyvale/S**	17
Fibbar/Molly Magees | **multi.**	19
Finnegans Wake | **Cole Valley**	20
540 Club | **Inner Rich**	24
Foreign Cinema | **Mission**	24
Gallery Lounge | **SoMa**	16
g bar | **Pacific Hts**	17
Glen Park Station | **Glen Pk**	18
Gold Cane | **Haight-Ashbury**	13
Z Gordon Biersch | **multi.**	18
Greens Sports | **Russian Hill**	18
Guaymas | **Tiburon/N**	24
Harrington's B&G | **Downtown**	17
Heinold's Saloon | **Oakland/E**	23
Hemlock Tavern | **Polk Gulch**	20
Z Highlands Inn | **Carmel/S**	28
Hog's Breath Inn | **Carmel/S**	24
Houston's | **Embarcadero**	20
Il Pirata | **Potrero Hill**	15
Jack Falstaff | **S Beach**	20
Jelly's | **China Basin**	16
Jillian's | **SoMa**	18
Jupiter | **Berkeley/E**	21
Kate O'Brien's | **SoMa**	17
Kelly's | **China Basin**	19
Kennedy's Irish | **N Beach**	21
Kezar Pub | **Haight-Ashbury**	19
Z Lark Creek Inn | **Larkspur/N**	26
Z Le Colonial | **Downtown**	24
Left/Albuquerque | **Campbell/S**	15
Z Left Bank | **multi.**	20
Liberty Cafe | **Bernal Hts**	20
Liverpool Lil's | **Cow Hollow**	21
Lone Star | **SoMa**	20
NEW LookOut, The | **Castro**	-
Lucky 13 | **Castro**	24
MacArthur Park | **Palo Alto/S**	18
Mad Dog in Fog | **Lower Haight**	18
Marin Brewing | **Larkspur/N**	17
MarketBar | **Embarcadero**	18
Marlena's | **Hayes Valley**	18
Mars Bar | **SoMa**	17
Z Martini House | **St. Helena/N**	25
Maya | **SoMa**	20
Z Medjool | **Mission**	23
Metro | **Castro**	17
Mix | **Castro**	17
MoMo's | **S Beach**	20
19 Broadway | **Fairfax/N**	19
No Name Bar | **Sausalito/N**	19
Oasis | **Menlo Pk/S**	20
Old Pro | **Palo Alto/S**	17
O'Neill's | **Fish. Wharf**	-
O'Reilly's Irish Pub | **N Beach**	20
Ottimista Enoteca | **Cow Hollow**	23
Palomino | **Embarcadero**	19
Paragon | **multi.**	21
Pedro's | **Santa Clara/S**	22
Piazza D'Angelo | **Mill Valley/N**	22
Pier 23 Cafe | **Embarcadero**	21
Pilsner Inn | **Castro**	19
Powerhouse | **SoMa**	21
Pres a Vi | **Presidio**	-
Presidio Social Club | **Presidio**	-
Pyramid Brewery | **multi.**	19
Ramp | **China Basin**	21
Rancho Nicasio | **Nicasio/N**	23
Red Jack | **Fish. Wharf**	18
Revolution Café | **Mission**	22
Rose & Crown | **Palo Alto/S**	21
Roy's | **Pebble Bch/S**	24
Saddle Rack | **Fremont/E**	21
Savoy Tivoli | **N Beach**	19

Schmidt's Tobacco | **Albany/E**	−
Silverado Brew. | **St. Helena/N**	18
Silverado Resort | **Napa/N**	24
Silver Clouds | **Marina**	−
Space 550 | **Bayview**	20
Steelhead Brewing | **Burlingame/S**	18
suite one8one | **Tenderloin**	18
Z Sushi Ran | **Sausalito/N**	25
Swingin Door | **San Mateo/S**	−
Tarpy's Roadhse. | **Monterey/S**	23
Thee Parkside | **Potrero Hill**	17
330 Ritch | **S Beach**	19
Tied House Cafe | **multi.**	18
Town Hall | **SoMa**	23
Townhouse B&G | **Emeryville/E**	20
Trader Vic's | **Palo Alto/S**	19
Z Tra Vigne | **St. Helena/N**	26
21st Amendment | **S Beach**	20
Va de Vi | **Walnut Creek/E**	−
Vertigo | **Polk Gulch**	−
NEW Waterbar | **Embarcadero**	−
Whisper | **Mission**	15
Zibibbo | **Palo Alto/S**	23

ROOFTOP

Z Medjool | **Mission**	23
Triple Rock Brew. | **Berkeley/E**	21

SIDEWALK

Z Absinthe | **Hayes Valley**	23
Bacchus Wine | **Russian Hill**	23
Z Balboa Cafe | **Cow Hollow**	20
Bell Tower | **Polk Gulch**	16
NEW Beretta | **Mission**	−
Z Betelnut Pejiu Wu | **Cow Hollow**	24
B44 | **Downtown**	20
Z BIX | **Downtown**	26
Z Blowfish Sushi | **Mission**	22
Blue Danube | **Inner Rich**	21
Z Bouchon | **Yountville/N**	25
Brainwash | **SoMa**	18

Cafe Abir | **W Addition**	21
Cafe Bastille | **Downtown**	18
Café Claude | **Downtown**	21
Cafe Flore | **Castro**	21
Cafe Van Kleef | **Oakland/E**	24
Cafe Zoetrope/Rosso | **N Beach**	21
Caffe Cicero | **Napa/N**	18
Caffè Greco | **N Beach**	19
Caffe Puccini | **N Beach**	20
Caffe Trieste | **multi.**	20
Z César | **Berkeley/E**	25
Chaya | **Embarcadero**	23
City Tavern | **Cow Hollow**	15
Daru | **Palo Alto/S**	−
NEW Dell'Uva | **N Beach**	−
Eastside West | **Cow Hollow**	19
Eddie Rickenbacker's | **SoMa**	15
Elite Cafe | **Upper Fillmore**	21
Fat Lady | **Oakland/E**	19
Fog City Diner | **Embarcadero**	21
Grove | **multi.**	21
Grumpy's Pub | **Embarcadero**	18
Z Harry's | **Upper Fillmore**	19
Irish Bank | **Downtown**	19
jovino | **Cow Hollow**	−
Left/Albuquerque | **Cow Hollow**	15
Z Left Bank | **Menlo Pk/S**	20
Liberties | **Mission**	17
Lou's Pier 47 | **Fish. Wharf**	22
Mario's Bohemian | **N Beach**	23
Martuni's | **Civic Ctr**	22
NEW Monk's Kettle | **Mission**	−
Z Nectar Wine | **multi.**	23
Z Oliveto Cafe | **Oakland/E**	25
Orbit Room Cafe | **Castro**	24
Perry's | **Cow Hollow**	19
Place Pigalle | **Hayes Valley**	21
Plouf | **Downtown**	20
Poleng | **W Addition**	22
Purple Onion | **N Beach**	18
Riptide | **Outer Sunset**	17

Rogue Ales | **N Beach**	21
Rose Pistola | **N Beach**	22
San Fran. Brew. | **N Beach**	21
Sheba | **W Addition**	–
Simple Pleasures | **Outer Rich**	–
Slow Club | **Mission**	21
Steps of Rome | **N Beach**	20
Sugar Café | **Downtown**	–
Trials Pub | **San Jose/S**	–
Ⓩ Zuni Café | **Hayes Valley**	24

WATERSIDE

Ⓩ Americano | **Embarcadero**	23
Ⓩ Ana Mandara | **Fish. Wharf**	25
Beach Chalet | **Outer Rich**	21
NEW EPIC Roast | **Embarcadero**	–
Ⓩ Gordon Biersch | **Embarcadero**	18
Guaymas | **Tiburon/N**	24
Heinold's Saloon | **Oakland/E**	23
Hi-Dive | **Embarcadero**	–
Jelly's | **China Basin**	16
Kelly's | **China Basin**	19
McCormick/Kuleto's | **Fish. Wharf**	20
Pier 23 Cafe | **Embarcadero**	21
Ramp | **China Basin**	21
Ⓩ Sam's Anchor Cafe | **Tiburon/N**	25
Skates on Bay | **Berkeley/E**	21
Ⓩ Slanted Door | **Embarcadero**	24
NEW Waterbar | **Embarcadero**	–

PEOPLE-WATCHING

Ace Wasabi's | **Marina**	20
Ⓩ Americano | **Embarcadero**	23
Ⓩ Betelnut Pejiu Wu | **Cow Hollow**	24
Blondie's Bar | **Mission**	15
Ⓩ Bubble Lounge | **Downtown**	22
Café | **Castro**	17
Cafe Bastille | **Downtown**	18

Café Claude | **Downtown**	21
Cafe Flore | **Castro**	21
Caffè Greco | **N Beach**	19
Caffe Puccini | **N Beach**	20
Caffe Trieste | **N Beach**	20
Cat Club | **SoMa**	–
El Rio | **Mission**	23
Endup | **SoMa**	20
NEW Enrico's | **N Beach**	–
Grove | **Marina**	21
Harvey's | **Castro**	18
Hemlock Tavern | **Polk Gulch**	20
Hobson's Choice | **Haight-Ashbury**	18
Ⓩ Jardinière | **Hayes Valley**	26
Jupiter | **Berkeley/E**	21
Kelly's | **China Basin**	19
Ⓩ Le Colonial | **Downtown**	24
NEW LookOut, The | **Castro**	–
Ⓩ MatrixFillmore | **Cow Hollow**	21
Metro | **Castro**	17
Ⓩ Michael Mina | **Downtown**	24
Ⓩ Oliveto Cafe | **Oakland/E**	25
Ⓩ 111 Minna | **SoMa**	22
Pilsner Inn | **Castro**	19
Ramp | **China Basin**	21
Red Devil | **Polk Gulch**	18
Ⓩ Redwood Rm. | **Downtown**	24
Revolution Café | **Mission**	22
Ruby Skye | **Downtown**	20
San Fran. Brew. | **N Beach**	21
Savoy Tivoli | **N Beach**	19
Steps of Rome | **N Beach**	20
Tommy's Joynt | **Polk Gulch**	17
Twin Peaks | **Castro**	14
Ⓩ Yoshi's | **W Addition**	24
Ⓩ Zuni Café | **Hayes Valley**	24

PHOTO BOOTHS

Agenda | **San Jose/S**	15
Annie's Social Club | **SoMa**	20
Buckshot Bar | **Inner Rich**	–

Club Six | **SoMa**	18
Knockout, The | **Mission**	23
Shine | **SoMa**	24

PIANO BARS

Alley, The | **Oakland/E**	22
Ⓩ Big 4 | **Nob Hill**	25
Cosmopolitan, The | **SoMa**	18
Ⓩ Jardinière | **Hayes Valley**	26
Lefty O'Doul's | **Downtown**	17
Ⓩ Lobby/Ritz-Carlton | **Nob Hill**	25
Ⓩ Mandarin Lounge | **Downtown**	27
Martuni's | **Civic Ctr**	22
Ⓩ Seasons Bar | **Downtown**	26
Sheba | **W Addition**	-
Swingin Door | **San Mateo/S**	-

PUB GRUB

Ⓩ Albatross Pub | **Berkeley/E**	25
Beckett's Irish Pub | **Berkeley/E**	22
Bitter End | **Inner Rich**	21
Britannia Arms | **multi.**	17
British Bankers | **Menlo Pk/S**	18
Chieftain Irish Pub | **SoMa**	21
Edinburgh Castle | **Tenderloin**	22
Fibbar/Molly Magees | **multi.**	19
Fiddler's Green | **Fish. Wharf**	19
Ireland's 32 | **Inner Rich**	22
Irish Bank | **Downtown**	19
Johnny Foley's | **Downtown**	19
Kate O'Brien's | **SoMa**	17
Kennedy's Irish | **N Beach**	21
Kezar Pub | **Haight-Ashbury**	19
Ⓩ Little Shamrock | **Inner Sunset**	25
Liverpool Lil's | **Cow Hollow**	21
Mad Dog in Fog | **Lower Haight**	18
Magnolia Pub | **Haight-Ashbury**	23
Marin Brewing | **Larkspur/N**	17
Old Pro | **Palo Alto/S**	17
O'Neill's | **multi.**	-

O'Reilly's Holy Grail | **Polk Gulch**	22
O'Reilly's Irish Pub | **N Beach**	20
Pacific Coast | **Oakland/E**	19
Ⓩ Pelican Inn | **Muir Bch/N**	27
Pyramid Brewery | **multi.**	19
Rose & Crown | **Palo Alto/S**	21
Schmidt's Tobacco | **Albany/E**	-
Starry Plough | **Berkeley/E**	20
St. Stephen's | **Mtn View/S**	16
Trials Pub | **San Jose/S**	-
NEW Wunder Brewing Co. | **Inner Sunset**	-

PUNK BARS

Annie's Social Club | **SoMa**	20
Bottom of Hill | **Potrero Hill**	22
Casanova | **Mission**	20
Doc's Clock | **Mission**	18
Hemlock Tavern | **Polk Gulch**	20
Homestead | **Mission**	20
Kilowatt | **Mission**	22
Knockout, The | **Mission**	23
Lucky 13 | **Castro**	24
Molotov | **Lower Haight**	17
924 Gilman | **Berkeley/E**	26
Sadie's Elephant | **Potrero Hill**	22
Stork Club | **Oakland/E**	19
Thee Parkside | **Potrero Hill**	17
Ⓩ Toronado | **Lower Haight**	25
Ⓩ Zeitgeist | **Mission**	23

QUIET CONVERSATION

Amelie | **Russian Hill**	-
NEW Bar Drake | **Downtown**	-
NEW Bar 888 | **SoMa**	-
Ⓩ Big 4 | **Nob Hill**	25
Cafe Flore | **Castro**	21
Café Prague | **N Beach**	17
Caffe Puccini | **N Beach**	20
Caffe Trieste | **multi.**	20
NEW Candybar | **W Addition**	-
Cav Wine Bar | **Hayes Valley**	22

☑ Cityscape | **Downtown**	24
Cliff House | **Outer Rich**	23
15 Romolo | **N Beach**	23
Fifth Floor | **Downtown**	-
Frantoio | **Mill Valley/N**	25
Ginger's Trois | **Downtown**	-
Grandviews | **Downtown**	24
Grove | **Pacific Hts**	21
Hidden Vine | **Downtown**	-
☑ Highlands Inn | **Carmel/S**	28
Hôtel Biron | **Hayes Valley**	24
jovino | **Cow Hollow**	-
NEW La Trappe | **N Beach**	-
NEW Le Club | **Nob Hill**	-
Liberty Cafe | **Bernal Hts**	20
☑ Lobby/Ritz-Carlton | **Nob Hill**	25
☑ Mandarin Lounge | **Downtown**	27
McCormick/Kuleto's | **Fish. Wharf**	20
Paréa | **Mission**	-
Postrio | **Downtown**	22
Presidio Social Club | **Presidio**	-
Rubicon | **Downtown**	21
☑ Seasons Bar | **Downtown**	26
Shattuck Spats | **Berkeley/E**	15
Simple Pleasures | **Outer Rich**	-
Swingin Door | **San Mateo/S**	-
☑ Tamarine | **Palo Alto/S**	24
NEW Terroir | **SoMa**	-
Tosca Cafe | **N Beach**	23
Twin Peaks | **Castro**	14
Wild Side West | **Bernal Hts**	22
NEW Wine Bar | **Russian Hill**	-
NEW Wine Jar | **W Addition**	-

ROADHOUSES

Eagle Tavern | **SoMa**	21
Fat Lady | **Oakland/E**	19
Rancho Nicasio | **Nicasio/N**	23

☑ Sweetwater Saloon | **Mill Valley/N**	28
Thee Parkside | **Potrero Hill**	17
☑ Toronado | **Lower Haight**	25
Townhouse B&G | **Emeryville/E**	20
Two AM Club | **Mill Valley/N**	15
☑ Zeitgeist | **Mission**	23

ROMANTIC

☑ Ana Mandara | **Fish. Wharf**	25
☑ Auberge du Soleil | **Rutherford/N**	28
Beach Chalet | **Outer Rich**	21
☑ Big 4 | **Nob Hill**	25
☑ BIX | **Downtown**	26
☑ Boulevard | **Embarcadero**	26
☑ Bourbon & Branch | **Tenderloin**	26
Bruno's | **Mission**	-
☑ Bubble Lounge | **Downtown**	22
Café du Nord | **Castro**	23
Caffe Trieste | **N Beach**	20
Campton Place | **Downtown**	23
Daru | **Palo Alto/S**	-
NEW EPIC Roast | **Embarcadero**	-
☑ Farallon | **Downtown**	24
15 Romolo | **N Beach**	23
Fifth Floor | **Downtown**	-
Hedley Club | **San Jose/S**	24
☑ Highlands Inn | **Carmel/S**	28
Hog's Breath Inn | **Carmel/S**	24
Hôtel Biron | **Hayes Valley**	24
☑ Kokkari Estiatorio | **Downtown**	25
☑ Lark Creek Inn | **Larkspur/N**	26
NEW La Trappe | **N Beach**	-
NEW Le Club | **Nob Hill**	-
☑ Le Colonial | **Downtown**	24
☑ Lobby/Ritz-Carlton | **Nob Hill**	25
☑ Michael Mina | **Downtown**	24

subscribe to ZAGAT.com

☑ Pelican Inn | **Muir Bch/N**	27
☑ Pied Piper Bar | **Downtown**	26
Pres a Vi | **Presidio**	–
☑ Seasons Bar | **Downtown**	26
Sheba | **W Addition**	–
13 Views | **Embarcadero**	21
☑ Top of the Mark | **Nob Hill**	25
Tosca Cafe | **N Beach**	23
☑ Vesuvio | **N Beach**	24
NEW Waterbar | **Embarcadero**	–

SLEEPERS

(Good to excellent ratings,
but little known)

Black Horse Pub | **Cow Hollow**	22
Bow Bow Lounge | **Chinatown**	21
Cafe Abir | **W Addition**	21
Cafe Int'l | **Lower Haight**	21
Caffe Puccini | **N Beach**	20
Cole's Chop Hse. | **Napa/N**	24
Cork Enoteca | **Sausalito/N**	21
Frantoio | **Mill Valley/N**	25
Grandviews | **Downtown**	24
Hedley Club | **San Jose/S**	24
Heinold's Saloon | **Oakland/E**	23
Homestead | **Mission**	20
Improv | **San Jose/S**	25
Kingman's | **Oakland/E**	21
Luella | **Russian Hill**	23
Mint Karaoke | **Castro**	21
Occidental Cigar | **Downtown**	24
Pedro's | **multi.**	22
Phone Booth | **Mission**	20
Poleng | **W Addition**	22
Powerhouse | **SoMa**	21
Radio Bar | **Oakland/E**	23
Rasselas Jazz | **W Addition**	23
Rite Spot Cafe | **Mission**	22
Roccapulco | **Mission**	20
Silverado Resort | **Napa/N**	24
Tarpy's Roadhse. | **Monterey/S**	23
13 Views | **Embarcadero**	21

222 Club | **Tenderloin**	22
Yield Wine Bar | **Dogpatch**	25

SPOKEN WORD

Bissap/Little Baobab | **Mission**	23
Blue Danube | **Inner Rich**	21
Cafe Int'l | **Lower Haight**	21
Café Royale | **Tenderloin**	21
Café Valparaíso | **Berkeley/E**	22
Edinburgh Castle | **Tenderloin**	22
☑ Fillmore | **W Addition**	27
Freight & Salvage | **Berkeley/E**	21
Madrone Lounge | **W Addition**	21
Peña Pachamama | **N Beach**	–

SPORTS BARS

Abbey Tavern | **Outer Rich**	15
Bar None | **Cow Hollow**	14
Britannia Arms | **multi.**	17
Bus Stop | **Cow Hollow**	16
Chieftain Irish Pub | **SoMa**	21
City Tavern | **Cow Hollow**	15
Conn. Yankee | **Potrero Hill**	17
Dubliner, The | **multi.**	18
Final Final | **Marina**	17
Gino & Carlo | **N Beach**	18
Gold Cane | **Haight-Ashbury**	13
☑ Gordon Biersch | **multi.**	18
Greens Sports | **Russian Hill**	18
Horseshoe | **Marina**	18
Houston's | **Embarcadero**	20
Jillian's | **SoMa**	18
Kezar Pub | **Haight-Ashbury**	19
Knuckles Sports | **Fish. Wharf**	18
Mix | **Castro**	17
Molotov | **Lower Haight**	17
Mucky Duck | **Inner Sunset**	16
Murio's Trophy | **Haight-Ashbury**	12
Old Pro | **Palo Alto/S**	17
Silver Peso | **Larkspur/N**	14
Woody Zips | **N Beach**	–
Zeke's Sports B&G | **SoMa**	–

STRIP CLUBS

Centerfolds | **N Beach**	24
Gold Club | **SoMa**	17
Larry Flynt's | **N Beach**	15
Lusty Lady | **N Beach**	13
Mitchell Bros. | **Tenderloin**	17

SWANKY

Z Absinthe | **Hayes Valley**	23
Ambassador, The | **Tenderloin**	-
Z Americano | **Embarcadero**	23
Z Ana Mandara | **Fish. Wharf**	25
Z Aqua | **Downtown**	25
Z bacar | **SoMa**	24
NEW Bar 888 | **SoMa**	-
Z Betelnut Pejiu Wu | **Cow Hollow**	24
B44 | **Downtown**	20
Z Big 4 | **Nob Hill**	25
Z Bimbo's 365 Club | **N Beach**	24
Z BIX | **Downtown**	26
Bliss Bar | **Noe Valley**	19
Z Boulevard | **Embarcadero**	26
Z Bourbon & Branch | **Tenderloin**	26
Bruno's | **Mission**	-
Z Bubble Lounge | **Downtown**	22
Butterfly | **Embarcadero**	21
Campton Place | **Downtown**	23
Carnelian Room | **Downtown**	24
Chaya | **Embarcadero**	23
Circa | **Marina**	-
Club Deluxe | **Haight-Ashbury**	21
Cortez | **Downtown**	22
Cosmopolitan, The | **SoMa**	18
Daru | **Palo Alto/S**	-
District | **SoMa**	-
Elite Cafe | **Upper Fillmore**	21
NEW Enrico's | **N Beach**	-
NEW EPIC Roast | **Embarcadero**	-
Z Evvia | **Palo Alto/S**	24

Z Farallon | **Downtown**	24
Fifth Floor | **Downtown**	-
Fluid | **SoMa**	20
Foreign Cinema | **Mission**	24
Z Gary Danko | **Fish. Wharf**	27
g bar | **Pacific Hts**	17
Grand Cafe | **Downtown**	21
Grandviews | **Downtown**	24
Harris' | **Polk Gulch**	21
Harry Denton Starlight | **Downtown**	24
Hedley Club | **San Jose/S**	24
Hime | **Marina**	-
Z Jardinière | **Hayes Valley**	26
Z Kokkari Estiatorio | **Downtown**	25
Z Lark Creek Inn | **Larkspur/N**	26
La Scene | **Downtown**	16
NEW Le Club | **Nob Hill**	-
Z Le Colonial | **Downtown**	24
Z Lobby/Ritz-Carlton | **Nob Hill**	25
Z Lobby/St. Regis | **SoMa**	25
Z Mandarin Lounge | **Downtown**	27
Mecca | **Castro**	22
Z Michael Mina | **Downtown**	24
Z Millennium | **Downtown**	26
Nihon | **Mission**	23
Z Oliveto Cafe | **Oakland/E**	25
One Market | **Embarcadero**	21
O'Reilly's Holy Grail | **Polk Gulch**	22
Ozumo | **Embarcadero**	23
Z Pied Piper Bar | **Downtown**	26
Postrio | **Downtown**	22
Pres a Vi | **Presidio**	-
Z Redwood Rm. | **Downtown**	24
Rose Pistola | **N Beach**	22
Rouge et Blanc | **Downtown**	-
Roy's | **SoMa**	24
Rubicon | **Downtown**	21

Rye | **Tenderloin** 23
Scala's Bistro | **Downtown** 22
Z Seasons Bar | **Downtown** 26
Shanghai 1930 | **Embarcadero** 23
Z Slanted Door | **Embarcadero** 24
Slide | **Downtown** 22
Suede | **Fish. Wharf** 17
supperclub | **SoMa** 22
Z Sushi Ran | **Sausalito/N** 25
13 Views | **Embarcadero** 21
Tony Nik's | **N Beach** 23
Z Top of the Mark | **Nob Hill** 25
Umami | **Cow Hollow** -
Z View Lounge | **SoMa** 26
NEW Waterbar | **Embarcadero** -
Wish | **SoMa** 22
XYZ | **SoMa** 20

THEME BARS

Bamboo Hut | **N Beach** 19
Beauty Bar | **Mission** 18
Bigfoot Lodge | **Polk Gulch** 19
Bissap/Little Baobab | **Mission** 23
Black Magic | **Marina** 18
NEW Bollyhood Cafe | **Mission** -
Butter | **SoMa** 18
Conga Lounge | **Oakland/E** 23
E&O Trading Co. | **multi.** 20
Z Farallon | **Downtown** 24
Nola | **Palo Alto/S** 21
Z Pied Piper Bar | **Downtown** 26
Rick's | **Outer Sunset** 19
Ruby Room | **Oakland/E** -
Shanghai 1930 | **Embarcadero** 23
supperclub | **SoMa** 22
Tonga Room | **Nob Hill** 22
Trader Vic's | **multi.** 19
Trad'r Sam's | **Outer Rich** 22
Tres Agaves | **S Beach** 22
Voda | **Downtown** 19

TRENDY

Ace Wasabi's | **Marina** 20
Ambassador, The | **Tenderloin** -
Z bacar | **SoMa** 24
Beauty Bar | **Mission** 18
NEW Beretta | **Mission** -
Z Betelnut Pejiu Wu | **Cow Hollow** 24
Z BIX | **Downtown** 26
Bliss Bar | **Noe Valley** 19
NEW Bossa Nova | **SoMa** -
Z Bourbon & Branch | **Tenderloin** 26
Z Bubble Lounge | **Downtown** 22
Butter | **SoMa** 18
Club Six | **SoMa** 18
Dalva | **Mission** 20
DNA Lounge | **SoMa** 16
Double Dutch | **Mission** 23
eight | **SoMa** 21
NEW 83 Proof | **SoMa** -
15 Romolo | **N Beach** 23
Foreign Cinema | **Mission** 24
Fuse | **N Beach** 19
NEW Harlot | **SoMa** -
Icon Lounge | **SoMa** -
Jade Bar | **Hayes Valley** 20
NEW Local Kitchen | **SoMa** -
Madrone Lounge | **W Addition** 21
Z MatrixFillmore | **Cow Hollow** 21
Z Medjool | **Mission** 23
Mezzanine | **SoMa** 21
Mighty | **Potrero Hill** 23
Nihon | **Mission** 23
nopa | **W Addition** 24
NEW O Izakaya | **Japantown** -
Z 111 Minna | **SoMa** 22
Perbacco | **Downtown** -
Poleng | **W Addition** 22
Pres a Vi | **Presidio** -
Radio Bar | **Oakland/E** 23

SPECIAL APPEALS

Red Devil	**Polk Gulch**	18
🅉 Redwood Rm.	**Downtown**	24
Rosewood	**Chinatown**	21
Ruby Skye	**Downtown**	20
Rye	**Tenderloin**	23
🆕 Serpentine	**Dogpatch**	-
Skylark	**Mission**	14
Slide	**Downtown**	22
Suede	**Fish. Wharf**	17
Sugar Lounge	**Hayes Valley**	20
supperclub	**SoMa**	22
Sushi Groove So.	**SoMa**	23
Swig	**Tenderloin**	19
Tres Agaves	**S Beach**	22
Truck	**Mission**	-
Tunnel Top	**Downtown**	18
Umami	**Cow Hollow**	-

VELVET ROPE

Ambassador, The	**Tenderloin**	-
AsiaSF	**SoMa**	24
Bambuddha	**Tenderloin**	21
🅉 Bubble Lounge	**Downtown**	22
Circa	**Marina**	-
Dragon Bar	**N Beach**	-
Fluid	**SoMa**	20
g bar	**Pacific Hts**	17
🆕 Harlot	**SoMa**	-
HiFi	**Marina**	16
Icon Lounge	**SoMa**	-
Impala	**N Beach**	20
Pink	**Mission**	21
🅉 Redwood Rm.	**Downtown**	24
Roccapulco	**Mission**	20
Ruby Skye	**Downtown**	20
Slide	**Downtown**	22
Suede	**Fish. Wharf**	17
Swig	**Tenderloin**	19
Ten15 Folsom	**SoMa**	16
Vessel	**Downtown**	-
Whisper	**Mission**	15

VIEWS

🅉 Americano	**Embarcadero**	23
🅉 Ana Mandara	**Fish. Wharf**	25
🅉 Auberge du Soleil	**Rutherford/N**	28
Beach Chalet	**Outer Rich**	21
Butterfly	**Embarcadero**	21
Calistoga Inn	**Calistoga/N**	22
Carnelian Room	**Downtown**	24
Chaya	**Embarcadero**	23
🅉 Cityscape	**Downtown**	24
Cliff House	**Outer Rich**	23
🆕 EPIC Roast	**Embarcadero**	-
Grandviews	**Downtown**	24
Harry Denton Starlight	**Downtown**	24
🅉 Highlands Inn	**Carmel/S**	28
Insalata's	**San Anselmo/N**	22
Kelly's	**China Basin**	19
McCormick/Kuleto's	**Fish. Wharf**	20
🅉 Medjool	**Mission**	23
Metro	**Castro**	17
Palomino	**Embarcadero**	19
Paragon	**Berkeley/E**	21
Pier 23 Cafe	**Embarcadero**	21
Pres a Vi	**Presidio**	-
Presidio Social Club	**Presidio**	-
🅉 Sam's Anchor Cafe	**Tiburon/N**	25
Silverado Resort	**Napa/N**	24
Skates on Bay	**Berkeley/E**	21
🅉 Slanted Door	**Embarcadero**	24
Tarpy's Roadhse.	**Monterey/S**	23
13 Views	**Embarcadero**	21
🅉 Top of the Mark	**Nob Hill**	25
Triple Rock Brew.	**Berkeley/E**	21
🅉 View Lounge	**SoMa**	26
🆕 Waterbar	**Embarcadero**	-

ALPHABETICAL
PAGE INDEX

All nightspots are in San Francisco unless otherwise noted (East of San
Francisco=E; North of San Francisco=N; South of San Francisco=S).

vote at ZAGAT.com   181

Z indicates places with the highest ratings, popularity and importance.

ALPHA INDEX

Wine Vintage Chart

This chart, based on our 0 to 30 scale, is designed to help you select wine. The ratings (by **Howard Stravitz,** a law professor at the University of South Carolina) reflect the vintage quality and the wine's readiness to drink. We exclude the 1991–1993 vintages because they are not that good. A dash indicates the wine is either past its peak or too young to rate. Loire ratings are for dry white wines.

Whites

	88	89	90	94	95	96	97	98	99	00	01	02	03	04	05	06
French:																
Alsace	-	25	25	24	23	23	22	25	23	25	27	25	22	24	25	-
Burgundy	-	23	22	-	28	27	24	22	26	25	24	27	23	27	26	24
Loire Valley	-	-	-	-	-	-	-	-	-	24	25	26	23	24	27	24
Champagne	24	26	29	-	26	27	24	23	24	24	22	26	-	-	-	-
Sauternes	29	25	28	-	21	23	25	23	24	24	28	25	26	21	26	23
California:																
Chardonnay	-	-	-	-	-	-	-	-	24	23	26	26	25	27	29	25
Sauvignon Blanc	-	-	-	-	-	-	-	-	-	-	27	28	26	27	26	27
Austrian:																
Grüner Velt./Riesling	-	-	-	-	25	21	26	26	25	22	23	25	26	25	26	-
German:	25	26	27	24	23	26	25	26	23	21	29	27	24	26	28	-

Reds

	88	89	90	94	95	96	97	98	99	00	01	02	03	04	05	06
French:																
Bordeaux	23	25	29	22	26	25	23	25	24	29	26	24	25	24	27	25
Burgundy	-	24	26	-	26	27	25	22	27	22	24	27	25	25	27	25
Rhône	26	28	28	24	26	22	25	27	26	27	26	-	25	24	25	-
Beaujolais	-	-	-	-	-	-	-	-	-	24	-	23	25	22	28	26
California:																
Cab./Merlot	-	-	28	29	27	25	28	23	26	22	27	26	25	24	24	23
Pinot Noir	-	-	-	-	-	-	24	23	24	23	27	28	26	25	24	-
Zinfandel	-	-	-	-	-	-	-	-	-	-	25	23	27	24	23	-
Oregon:																
Pinot Noir	-	-	-	-	-	-	-	-	-	-	-	27	25	26	27	-
Italian:																
Tuscany	-	-	25	22	24	20	29	24	27	24	27	20	25	25	22	24
Piedmont	-	27	27	-	23	26	27	26	25	28	27	20	24	25	26	-
Spanish:																
Rioja	-	-	-	26	26	24	25	22	25	24	27	20	24	25	26	24
Ribera del Duero/Priorat	-	-	-	26	26	27	25	24	25	24	27	20	24	26	26	24
Australian:																
Shiraz/Cab.	-	-	-	24	26	23	26	28	24	24	27	27	25	26	24	-
Chilean:	-	-	-	-	-	-	24	-	25	23	26	24	25	24	26	-

ON THE GO.
IN THE KNOW.

ZAGAT TO GO℠

Unlimited access
to Zagat dining &
travel content
in hundreds of
major cities.

Search by name,
location, ratings,
cuisine, special
features & Top Lists.

For BlackBerry,® Palm,®
Windows Mobile®
and mobile phones.

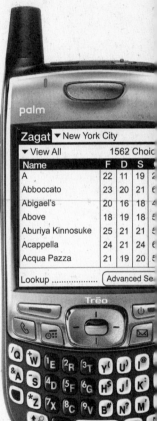

Get it now at **mobile.zagat.com**
or text* **ZAGAT** to **78247**